BUFFY AND THE ART OF STORY SEASON TWO PART 2

EPISODES 12-22: HOW TO WRITE ABOUT LOVE, PYRRHIC VICTORY, AND BETRAYAL

L. M. LILLY

INTRODUCTION

As I say at the start of the podcast version of *Buffy and the Art of Story*, if you love *Buffy the Vampire Slayer* and you love creating stories – or just taking them apart to see how they work – you're in the right place. I started watching *Buffy* when it began on network TV. I loved every episode (okay, almost every episode), especially the dialogue. But it was only after the DVDs came out and I watched full seasons within a shorter timeframe that I saw how well constructed it is. The plots, the themes, the characters, the pace....

That was the start of rewatching the entire series in order, which I've now done more times than I can count. So when I started longing to start my own podcast, combining my love of fiction writing and *Buffy* seemed natural. I learned so much from the show over the years. Why not delve into it in a more deliberate way?

Is This Book For You?

If you, too, love *Buffy* and find the nuts and bolts of storytelling fascinating, you'll enjoy revisiting the second half of Season Two in these pages. (This book breaks down episodes 13-22 of Season Two. You can find previous episodes in my earlier *Buffy* books at LisaLilly.com/BuffyBooks.)

Reading will likely help your own fiction skills, too. I focus the most on plot, looking for major plot points and turns. But I also examine each episode to see how skillfully the writers weave in exposition through conflict, create strong characters, deal with intriguing themes without tons of monologuing or philosophizing, and excel at pretty much every aspect of storytelling.

While you may want to watch each episode before reading the chapter about it, it's not necessary. I take you through the entire storyline.

If you prefer, you can save money and listen to the *Buffy and the Art of Story* podcast for free. As of this writing, I'm nearly done with Season 4. My author website even includes a rough (sometimes very rough) transcript of each Season One and Two episode.

But in this book the episodes are edited for better flow and organization. Plus I've also included topics at the start of each highlighting the key fiction writing aspects the episode illustrates. At the end of each chapter, you'll find questions to think about for your own fiction.

Story Structure

The major plot points and turns I look for in each episode are drawn from all I've learned over the decades about fiction and screenwriting. I use them to plot my own fiction. And I find every good story I read, watch, or listen to includes them, in order, with few exceptions:

- **Opening conflict** (draws the viewer in fast)
- **Story Spark** or Inciting Incident (sets the main plot rolling)
- **One-Quarter Twist** or the first major plot turn (occurs one-quarter or one-third through any story and spins the plot in a new direction)

- **The Midpoint** (when the protagonist commits fully to the quest, suffers a major reversal, or both)
- **Three-Quarter Turn** or last major plot turn (arises from the protagonist's actions at the Midpoint and turns the plot yet again)
- **Climax** (self-explanatory I hope)
- **Falling Action** (subplots and open questions resolve)

If you find this story structure helpful, you can download a free story structure template to use with your own writing at WritingAsASecondCareer.com/Story.

Who Am I?

If you haven't read my other books, you might wonder who I am and why I'm sharing storytelling advice. So here it is:

As Lisa M. Lilly, I'm the author of the bestselling four-book Awakening supernatural thriller series. Books in the series have been downloaded over 90,000 times in over 35 countries. The second book in my current series, the Q.C. Davis Mysteries, *The Charming Man*, was a 2019 Finalist in The Wishing Shelf Book Awards. Windy City Reviews called the fourth book, *The Troubled Man*, one of the best Chicago mysteries, favorably comparing it to the work of Louise Penny (one of my idols) and Jo Nesbo. As I write this introduction, the fifth Q.C. Davis Mystery, *The Hidden Man*, just released.

I also write non-fiction books for writers under L. M. Lilly, and work as an attorney and adjunct professor of law. I founded WritingAsASecondCareer.com to share information with people juggling writing novels with working at other jobs or careers. Not that I know anything about that...

A Quick Note On Spoilers

Each chapter focuses on a single episode with no spoilers until the end. There, after a section break, I talk about how the episode foreshadows later events in *Buffy* and occasionally *Angel* or other television shows. If you haven't watched all of *Buffy* or aren't familiar with the whole of the Buffyverse, proceed with caution.

Ready? Let's dive into the Hellmouth.

CHAPTER 1
SURPRISE (S2 E13)

This chapter talks about Surprise, Season Two Episode Thirteen, where Buffy nearly loses Angel on her birthday. Written by Marti Noxon and directed by Michael Lange.

In particular, we'll look at:

- Strong hooks that keep the audience coming back
- Dialogue that conveys backstory through conflict
- Wit and humor that makes danger and drama more intense by contrast
- Pacing, story, and dream sequences
- Single episode plot points and two-story arc plot turns that keep the episode moving and engaging

Okay, let's dive into the Hellmouth.

Because Surprise is the first part of the two-part story that ends in Innocence, this chapter only takes us to the Midpoint of that two-part plot. We'll pick up there in the next chapter with Innocence.

Opening Conflict In Surprise

Our opening conflict: Buffy's in bed, but she wakes up during the night, restless, and drinks water. Then she walks into the hall. Drusilla appears behind her, but Buffy doesn't notice.

The scene seems real until Buffy opens the door and steps into the Bronze, still wearing a pair of shiny silk pajamas. The music is mellow. Willow sits at a high top table. She gives Buffy a cheery wave and speaks in French. A monkey sits in front of her.

(The monkey makes me think of Oz's joke about the monkey being the only one of the animal crackers who wears pants, but my French isn't good enough for me to know if what Willow says relates to that.)

Buffy sees her mother, Joyce, who's holding a very large cup and saucer.

Joyce: Do you really think you're ready, Buffy?

Buffy: What?

Joyce drops the saucer. It breaks on the floor. Buffy seems a little disturbed, but then sees Angel and smiles. They walk towards each other. But Drusilla stakes him from behind.

Angel reaches toward Buffy. His hand almost touches her. Two rings fall off of his finger as he turns to dust. Buffy says, "Angel!"

Drusilla: Happy birthday, Buffy.

Buffy wakes up.

Dreams In Fiction

I mentioned in previous Buffy and the Art of Story books the old saying, "Tell a dream, lose a reader." Readers often don't appreciate being drawn into something that turns out to be a dream and perhaps doesn't move the story forward.

In *Buffy*, however, the writers often use dreams to advance the plot. As we'll see, this episode's dream is key to much of what happens in the early part of the story. Also, it creates conflict and tension.

Because we've established in past episodes that Buffy has prophetic dreams, the fact that she sees Drusilla kill Angel in a dream is deeply disturbing to the audience. It also lets us know that on some level Buffy might be aware that Drusilla is alive, despite that, as we'll see in a later scene, Buffy and the others hope both Spike and Dru died in the church in an earlier episode.

We're at 2 minutes 22 seconds at the end of the dream, and we go to credits.

Exposition As Angel Reassures Buffy

The next day Buffy knocks on Angel's door, making sure he's all right. She tells him about her dream and says that in it, Drusilla was alive "and she killed you right in front of me."

Angel reassures her that it's not real. But she says her dream about the Master came true. This is the first instance of getting in a little exposition through conflict for any audience members who have missed this. Or missed that Buffy's dreams are sometimes prophetic.

There's a reason for Buffy to talk about the dream that came true because she's worried. And Angel, while reassuring her, also somewhat contradicts her. He says not every dream she has comes true (more exposition). Then he asks what else she dreamed last night. This question helps calm Buffy. She hesitates and says she dreamed that she and Giles opened an office supply warehouse in Vegas.

(I just love that because as a writer, I have always been so fond of office supply stores. I love seeing the notebooks, pens, and, going way back, the typewriter supplies.)

10% Into The Episode

Normally we would see our Story Spark or Inciting Incident here. It's what usually comes about 10% into any story, and it sets the main plot in motion.

Because this is a two-part episode, though, we don't see the spark for the overall two-episode story arc here. All the same, Buffy makes a key comment at 4 minutes 20 seconds.

Buffy: But what if Drusilla is alive? We never saw her body.

This is right about 10% into the episode. And it raises the central conflict here that Drusilla is in fact alive and is actively working on a plot that will endanger not just Buffy and all of Sunnydale, but the world.

Angel reassures Buffy on two levels. He says Drusilla's not alive, but if she is, they'll deal with it.

This scene includes dramatic irony, which we often see in *Buffy*. That's where the audience knows something that the characters do not. We know from a few episodes ago that a ritual Spike performed restored Drusilla to her former strength. She is very powerful. The audience also knows, though Buffy does not, that Spike was injured, but Dru got him out of the church.

Buffy And Angel Together

Buffy starts saying "what if" again, but Angel kisses her. The Buffy and Angel theme music plays when they kiss. Then he says, "What if what?"

Buffy: I'm sorry, were we talking?

She says she has to go to school. He says he knows, but instead they start kissing again. She goes to the door as if to leave but shuts it and stays inside with Angel. He says she still hasn't told him what she wants for her birthday.

Buffy: Surprise me.

Angel: Okay I will.

I never noticed this before, but in light of the end of this episode, this is heartbreaking. And such a good use of the episode title.

Moving Toward The Story Spark

We are moving toward the Story Spark for the two-episode arc. Buffy is having trouble leaving and breaking away from

Angel. She says she likes seeing him first thing in the morning. He says it's bedtime for him.

Buffy: Then I like seeing you at bedtime. (She gives a little laugh.) You know what I mean.

Angel (smiles): I think so. What do you mean?

Buffy: I like seeing you. And the part at the end of the night where we say goodbye, it's getting harder.

We switch to Willow at school. They're sitting on a bench outside. She is a little in awe that Buffy said "I like seeing you at bedtime."

That leads to them talking about sex. Buffy says she doesn't know what to do. Willow asks what she wants. And Buffy says to act on want can be wrong. But what if she never feels this way again?

These lines encapsulate the dilemma at the heart of this episode and the Buffy/Angel relationship.

Willow: Carpe diem. You told me that once.

Buffy: Fish of the day?

Willow: Not carp, carpe. It means seize the day.

Story Spark In Surprise/Innocence

Now we get our Story Spark. Buffy says she thinks she and Angel are going to. That once you get to a certain point seizing is sort of inevitable.

Willow says "Wow" twice. Props to Alyson Hannigan for how she is able to say the same word, and she'll say it again after the commercial break, with a slightly different inflection each time.

After Buffy says seizing is inevitable, we go to a commercial break.

This was about 8 minutes in, and the two-episode arc would be about 88 minutes total, so we're right about 10% through the story.

Placing Hooks In Your Story

Also, another great hook. As the scene ends, we learn Buffy

is thinking seriously about making love for the first time with Angel.

While a strong hook can be used to end a scene (or chapter), after which you switch to a new scene, it can also be used to break a scene in the middle. Here, on returning from the commercial break, Willow says "Wow" again. So we are right where we left.

If you're writing a novel, you can do this by ending a chapter mid-scene. It will make it hard for readers to put down the book at that chapter break, which is otherwise a natural place to stop reading.

Also, if it's a long scene – or like this one a scene that is just two people talking, which sometimes can lack momentum – you can increase the pace by breaking it at a strategic point.

Shifting Gears

Buffy now says, "Speaking of wow, what about Oz? Any wow potential there?"

Willow: I like his hands.

Buffy: A fixation on insignificant detail is a definite crush sign.

Which is for some reason a line I just really enjoy. Willow says she doesn't know, Oz is a senior. Buffy, in one of the first really funny lines in the episode, says –

Buffy: You think he's too old because he's a senior? Please, my boyfriend had a bicentennial.

Willow is still waffling.

Buffy: You can't spend the rest of your life waiting for Xander to wake up and smell the hottie. Make a move. Do the talking thing.

But Willow is worried.

Willow: What if the talking thing becomes the awkward silence thing?

Buffy tells her she won't know unless she tries.

Oz And Exposition

Oz is sitting under a tree strumming an electric guitar. (Not plugged in of course because they're outside.)

Willow asks if his band has a gig. He says no, practice, and then says, "See our band's kind of moving toward this new sound where we suck. So, practice." She thinks they sound good. They talk for a while, and then there is one of those awkward silences she was worried about.

Oz tells her he is going to ask her to go out with him tomorrow night and he's kind of nervous about it.

Willow: Well, if it helps at all, I'm gonna say yes.

Oz: Yeah, it helps, it creates a comfort zone. Do you want to go out with me tomorrow night?

Willow (puts her hand to her head): Oh I can't.

Oz: Well, see, I like that you're unpredictable.

Willow explains it's Buffy's birthday and that they're throwing her a surprise party. But with a shy smile she says he could come as her date. He agrees and she walks away. Both of them are smiling.

This short scene moves the Willow-Oz season arc along. It also gets out exposition – that Buffy's friends are planning a surprise party for her – through humor and conflict.

Cordelia And More Conflict-Based Exposition

Xander and Cordelia are at Cordelia's locker, talking about the party. Xander says they're both going, and maybe they should go together. Cordelia asks why, and Xander says maybe they should admit they're dating.

So again, we get some conflict here that fills in the audience in case they have not been watching every episode.

Cordelia: Groping in a broom closet isn't dating. It's not dating until the guy spends money.

Xander says, "Fine, I'll spend, we'll grope, whatever," but he thinks it's ridiculous that they are hiding from their friends. Being very Cordelia-like she says of course he wants to tell everyone. He has nothing to be ashamed of.

Humor Before The Darkness

All of these scenes – the Willow and Oz banter, the Cordelia and Xander sparring, Buffy talking about seizing the day – all these things could make us think that we are in one of the lighter episodes. It's fun so far. That makes the turn, which will happen shortly, to the end of the world aspects so much more striking and visceral.

Xander has had enough of Cordelia's comments. He walks away and runs into Giles and Buffy. Jenny Calendar joins them at one of the ever-present tables where people gather in Sunnydale High.

Giles comments that Buffy looks a little tired. She tells him about her dream that Drusilla killed Angel and that it really freaked her out. He asks if she thinks it's a portent. She's not sure. So he tells her they should be careful but not to worry unduly.

A Turn Toward End-Of-The-World Sparks A Story

We switch to the factory warehouse where Spike and Drusilla are living. This is the Inciting Incident or Story Spark in the Drusilla side of the story. It could also serve as an episode One-Quarter Twist. It's about 12.5 minutes in, and our episodes are usually about 44 minutes long.

We see a vampire with glasses, Dalton. He's the one we previously saw stealing the cross from the tomb and struggling to translate the manuscript that ultimately led to Drusilla's cure. Now he says he has Drusilla's package.

Spike, who is in a wheelchair, his face scarred, seems rather down. He asks if Drusilla's sure she wants to have a party. Maybe they should do it in Vienna. He doesn't like this place. Sunnydale is cursed.

But she says her gatherings are always perfect, she has good games for everyone. A moment later, though, she loses it because the flowers are all wrong. She starts shredding them, and almost shrieking.

Spike (very calm): Let's try something different with the flowers then.

She calms down and switches to her presents, asking if she can open them. And says, "Can I? Can I?"

Spike says, "just a peek" When she looks in an oblong box, he asks if she likes it.

Drusilla: It reeks of death....It will be the best party ever. Because it will be the last.

And commercial break. So again, a nice hook. We don't know what's in the box, but we now know Drusilla is having a party, and it's her birthday as well as Buffy's. And they're planning something that has dire consequences.

A Moment With Joyce And Another Hook

When we come back from the commercial break, Buffy is talking to her mom, Joyce, about taking a trip to the mall for Buffy's birthday. Joyce asks Buffy if seventeen feels any different than sixteen.

So we know that today is Buffy's official birthday. Buffy says now that her mom mentions it, she does feel more responsible. She wants to talk about getting her driver's license and reminds Joyce of her promise that they could talk about it again when Buffy turned seventeen.

Joyce is skeptical. She's holding a plate. And she says, "Do you really think you're ready, Buffy?" and drops the plate. It breaks just like in Buffy's dream.

We then switch to Jenny Calendar in her classroom. There was no commercial break there, but notice that we have a nice end-of-scene hook with this repetition from Buffy's dream, making us think Angel is in danger. Specifically, from Drusilla.

And instead of immediately picking up with Dru, or with Buffy going to Giles or to Angel, we switch to Jenny. So the desire to know how that plays out keeps us engaged through this next scene, which otherwise might not seem that compelling.

Jenny Calendar's Secrets Revealed

A man in old-fashioned clothes enters Jenny's classroom, startling her. She eventually calls him Uncle.

He says the elder woman has been watching the signs. Jenny says the curse still holds, nothing's wrong. But the uncle tells her the elder woman says "his pain is lessening, she can feel it." And Jenny hesitantly says, "There is a girl." He asks Jenny with great intensity how she could let this happen.

Jenny promises that Angel still suffers, and he even makes amends. He saved her life.

Her uncle yells at her and says how can she forget that Angel killed the most beloved member of their tribe? Vengeance demands that his pain is eternal, as theirs is.

Uncle: If this girl gives him one minute of happiness it's one minute too much.

And he berates her, saying, "You think you are Jenny Calendar now?" He reminds her she is Jana of the Calderash people. And says the time for watching is past, it must end now. Jenny should do what she must to "take her from him." She says she will see to it.

Another Hook Keeps Us Engaged

Note that in that last scene, again you have a wonderful hook at the end. This great revelation about Jenny being from the tribe of the young woman that Angel killed, which resulted in the curse that gave him back his soul. And now she's saying she will separate Angel and Buffy.

We then switch to a less dramatic scene (at 17 minutes 42 seconds in), where Buffy and Giles talk about Buffy's dreams and what they should do about it. Not quite as exciting. But we are tense and there's all this conflict going. So it keeps us engaged, along with some great dialogue.

Buffy Worries, Giles Reassures

Xander and Willow come into the library, excited, saying, "Happy Birthday, Buffy!" Buffy is not enthused. Giles tries to reassure her. He says dreams aren't prophecies, she can still protect Angel. And he reminds her that she subverted the dream she had that the Master rose.

Xander: You ground his bones to make your bread.

Buffy says that's true, except for the bread part. But she wants to stay a step ahead. And Giles says absolutely. He'll read up on Drusilla. Buffy should go to class and come back and meet Giles at the library that evening.

After she leaves Willow and Xander are sad. Willow says so much for the surprise party, and she bought little hats and everything. But Giles says they are having a party tonight.

Xander: Looks like Mr. Caution Man, but the sound he makes is funny.

Giles explains that the party should go ahead, though he won't be wearing a little hat. Buffy and Angel might be in danger, but they have been before and they will be again.

Giles: One thing I've learned in my tenure here on the Hellmouth is that there is no good time to relax. Buffy's turning seventeen just this once and she deserves a party.

I feel like these words from Giles are such good advice for life and for dealing with stress. This is part of what I love about the show. While most of us are not dealing with life or death stakes day in and day out, there are significant stresses and sometimes terrible things do happen. And it's a reminder to still take those moments and still celebrate parts of life. Not try to put everything good and fun aside.

Willow says Angel is coming to the party anyway, so Buffy can protect him and have cake.

Down A Dark Corridor

We next see Buffy walking in a dark hall at school. (Like the locker rooms, the halls in Sunnydale are pretty dark in the evening.)

Jenny surprises her and says there's a change of plans. Giles had to go home and get a book, so Buffy won't find him in the library. They're meeting somewhere else. Giles gave Jenny directions.

Buffy comments on the oddity of Giles needing to get a book. Apparently there aren't enough of them in the library? But she doesn't seem suspicious. As they go down a dark alley, Buffy sees vampires and a truck. She tells Jenny to stop. Jenny seems worried and says maybe don't get out.

Buffy: Sorry, sacred duty, yada yada yada.

She approaches the vampires. And we see Dalton again, the vamp with the glasses. Buffy says every time she sees him, he's stealing something. He runs. Other vampires get out and attack Buffy. All of this is a nice use of misdirection. We're thinking Jenny is putting her plan in place to separate Buffy and Angel. But she actually was just getting Buffy to the Bronze for the party.

Now we see that as Buffy fights, the others are inside the Bronze. A few of them are wearing hats. There are balloons, and they're hiding around the pool table so Buffy won't see them when she comes in.

Angel asks where Buffy is, and Willow says, "I think I hear her coming." We're hearing the sounds of Buffy fighting. Eventually the last vampire and Buffy end up on the stage at the Bronze and she dusts him.

Surprise Near The Midpoint Of The Episode

We're reaching the Midpoint of the episode, which is the One-Quarter Twist in the two-episode arc. At 21 minutes 43 seconds in, just after Buffy has dusted the vampire, Cordelia pops out from behind the pool table and despite that everyone else is visible (so Buffy is not really surprised) yells, "Surprise!"

I love that the episode title comes in right here almost at the Midpoint of the episode.

Buffy is very happy that they all planned this party for her. Willow asks Oz if he's okay.

Oz: Hey, did everybody see that guy just turn to dust?

Xander: Vampires are real, a lot of them live in Sunnydale, Willow will fill you in.

Willow: I know it's hard to accept at first.

Oz: Actually, it explains a lot.

I love that Oz is the one person who doesn't even temporarily deny what he saw or reframe it. It's not so much that he doesn't do it here – because everyone else is saying yes, we saw that. But clearly along the way he hasn't made up reasons for what happened the way we saw Cordelia early on, saying, oh, they were a gang. Oz also hasn't forgotten. He clearly filed away unusual happenings in his brain as things that he couldn't yet explain. And now he has an explanation. So he feels better.

Jenny comes in, carrying an oblong box, and says the vampires left it behind.

A Hook And How The One-Quarter Twist Turns The Story

This is the One-Quarter Twist in the two-episode arc. The One-Quarter Twist usually comes in a quarter way through any story, sometimes a little bit later in television. And it spins the story in a new direction, but comes from outside of the protagonist. And we definitely have that here when Buffy opens this box. Inside is a long arm clad in dark armor or cloth and a black glove.

It bursts out and grabs Buffy by the throat and chokes her. She cannot get it off her neck. That is 23 minutes, 6 seconds in of a roughly 87, 88 minute story. And we go to a commercial break.

Another amazing hook. Because unlike other times when Buffy is attacked, she genuinely looks here as if she is not able to fight back or get that hand off her neck. When we come back from the commercial, we pick up right where we left off. So another example of a break in the middle of the scene.

Angel grabs the arm, helps Buffy get it off her, and slams it back in the box, which he closes.

Xander: Clearly the Hellmouth's answer to what you get the Slayer that has everything.

Angel: It can't be. She wouldn't.

Xander: What, vamp version of snakes in a can or do you care to share?

Angel explains that this arm is part of The Judge.

The Legend Of The Judge

Giles and Angel talk about the story of The Judge. It's an old legend, before Angel's time. He's a demon meant to rid the world from the plague of humanity. He separates the righteous and wicked and burns the righteous. Giles says the story is that The Judge couldn't be killed. An army was sent against him and most of them died. But they finally dismembered The Judge. Which couldn't kill him, but his body parts were scattered and buried all over the world.

Angel says Drusilla is just crazy enough to reassemble The Judge and bring forth Armageddon. At which point Cordelia asks if anyone is going to have cake.

This mixing of humor with drama and great danger is done so well here. It gives the audience a tiny break from the intensity so that we don't have just that one note of danger, danger, danger. And the break, by doing that, highlights how serious this is.

Jenny says Angel's the only one who can do it. He has to take the arm to the most remote region possible, and he agrees. Buffy says she can do it. But Jenny says Buffy can't disappear from school for months. Buffy is appalled at the idea of Angel being gone months and says why will it take so long? Angel says he'll have to get a cargo ship. He can't fly because he can't guard against daylight, and there's no other choice. This threat is so serious. He has to go right now. Tonight.

And Buffy is saying "but it's my birthday." Jenny gets between them and says she'll drive Angel to the docks.

Dalton In Trouble

We switch to Drusilla, who is angry at Dalton. She stamps on his glasses. Then she tells him to make a wish and puts her two fingers out to jab his eyes, saying she's going to blow out the candles because he has lost this box.

Spike says maybe give Dalton a chance to get it back.

Spike: He's the only one I have with half a brain.

Dalton is sweating. He says he swears he'll get the box. Dru jabs her fingers toward his eyes but stops at the last second and says okay.

She's all fun and games again. She pats his head, puts his broken glasses back on him, and tells him to hurry back.

Symbolic Rings

At the docks, Angel is carrying the box. He and Buffy stop to say goodbye. He says he'll be back, and she asks when? It could be six months. It could be a year. They don't know if he'll come back.

Buffy: If you haven't noticed, someone pretty much always wants us dead.

Angel: We can't know, Buffy, nobody can. That's just the deal.

This, too, is part of the show's overall philosophy. And probably a philosophy that weaves through all of Whedon's shows. That you never know what's coming next, and you just have to do your best with what you're facing.

Angel gives Buffy a Claddagh ring from his finger. He says he was going to give it to her for her birthday. And says that his people, before he was changed, exchanged it as a sign of devotion. If you turn the heart toward you, it means you belong to someone. And he says, "like this," showing the one he is still wearing. They kiss after he tells her to put her ring on.

Romeo And Juliet Raise The Stakes

This so reminds me of Romeo and Juliet. We'll see Joss Whedon use Shakespeare quite a bit, calling back to Shakespeare plots. Romeo and Juliet had that secret wedding.

My sophomore English teacher made a big point about a faux wedding when we watched West Side Story to see how it compared to Romeo and Juliet. She noted how Tony and Maria have a pretend wedding where she dresses up in a wedding dress, and they pretend to say the vows. My teacher's point was to say see how serious this is. And that the book doesn't suggest you should just have sex with the first person you think you've fallen for.

I find it really interesting here that Buffy uses this as well. This wedding sort of symbolism -- exchanging the rings, belonging to one another. I see it here not so much as my high school English teacher jumping in and saying, oh, you need to have this big commitment before sex. But to again raise the stakes and show how important this relationship is to the two of them. That makes it more devastating when we get to the consequences.

Actions Show Emotion And Commitment

Just as Angel starts to say, "I love you," vampires interrupt. This is 30 minutes in. Buffy yells at Angel, "The box!" because he set it down. One of the vampires grabs it as Angel wrestles Dalton. Other vampires fight Buffy. One of them throws Buffy into the water.

I think this is supposed to be the ocean. Angel abandons Dalton to dive in after Buffy. His action shows how committed Angel is to Buffy.

Later I always wondered, though, does he think she can't swim? She's the Slayer. Is he really worried she will drown? On the other hand, the one time Buffy died (for just a minute, as she says) was when she drowned. So perhaps that's part of it too.

But I think it also is meant to show that in the moment,

Angel chooses Buffy even at the risk of putting the whole world in peril. And even though a second ago he was ready to leave to protect the world.

An Episode Three-Quarter Turn?

In a way that moment serves as a Three-Quarter Turn for the episode. We're not even at the Midpoint of our two-episode arc, but our single episode here keeps moving in part because it includes its own major plot turns. Here, we shifted from Buffy's fears about Drusilla and the progress of Buffy's and Angel's relationship to how to stop assembly of The Judge. That shift happens because now Spike and Dru have another piece of the judge that they need.

In the library, Xander, Willow, and Giles are researching and waiting for Angel and Buffy to get back.

Giles worries that Buffy should have returned by now. Willow says maybe Buffy needed a moment, and she feels terrible for Buffy. But Xander goes into this, I guess you would call it a daydream. He says it wouldn't work out between Buffy and Angel anyway. Think about a future where they settle down and Angel's sitting with a big blood belly in front of the TV. Dreaming of the time when Buffy thought the whole creature of the night thing was cool. Then Xander will arrive and take her out for prime rib dinner.

Willow tries to stop him and he says something like, "Wait, did I tell you about the part where she cries?"

Late Night Research

Buffy has returned, which is why Willow tries to halt Xander's flow of words. But she doesn't really notice. She says they (the vampires) got the box.

Giles is extremely concerned. He says The Judge's touch can burn humanity out of a person, that only a true creature of evil can survive. No one else can. Also, no weapon forged can kill him. So Buffy says they need to keep him from being assembled.

Everyone does what they call a Round Robin. Which is each of our friends calling their parents and saying they're staying at one of the other's houses.

We get a glimpse of Xander's home life. He calls home, and says "Mom," but then has to add, "It's me. Xander." Xander doesn't have any siblings. So the fact that his mom didn't know it was him gives us a just this hint, through humor, of Xander's back story.

During the night as they look through different books, Willow pauses to say how amazing and cool Oz was about everything. Xander says he's over it, a little tired of hearing about Oz. And she says he's just jealous because he didn't have a date for the party. And he says, "No, I sure didn't."

Buffy falls asleep over some books in Giles' office. Angel says she hasn't been sleeping well. She's been tossing and turning. Giles gives him a look and Angel says, "She told me. Because of her dreams."

Buffy Dreams The Judge Is Assembled

Buffy is in fact dreaming at the moment. The word "dreams" serves as a nice transition from the scene in the library to Buffy's dream. We see Drusilla's party at the factory. There are candles and flowers. Buffy is walking in a long white dress, so we have more wedding imagery. Buffy sees the box. As she is going toward it, Drusilla appears and says, "Now now. Hands off my presents."

She is holding Angel, and she slashes his throat. Buffy screams. She's back in the library. Angel says, "I'm right here," and holds her. It's unclear whether she's slipping into another dream or whether Angel holding her is part of the dream. Because we switch back to Drusilla's party and it looks exactly the same as in Buffy's dream. But we'll find out as it goes on that this is a real scene.

A Hook At Drusilla's Party

Dalton is at the punch bowl. Drusilla is dancing. Spike

brings her the last box of The Judge. There are tons of vampires around. They place the last piece, which is The Judge's head. Lights flash all around. The pieced-together boxes form into one, which opens and The Judge emerges. He's giant. And he's blue. Which sounds funny, but he is ominous looking.

Drusilla: He's perfect, my darling. Just what I wanted.

And we go to a commercial break. So again, that hook. The Judge has emerged.

Also, once again that break was in the middle of a scene. We come back and The Judge looks at Spike and Drusilla kind of scornfully.

The Judge: You two stink of humanity. You share affection and jealousy.

Spike asks what of it and reminds The Judge that they're the ones who brought him here.

Drusilla asks if he wants a party favor. The Judge gestures toward poor Dalton and says, "Bring him to me."

Spike questions him, saying what's all this bringing stuff? He thought The Judge could just zap people. But The Judge explains he needs to gather his full strength to return. He basically needs to be fed. They bring him Dalton, who he burns up. Dru says, "Do it again! Do it again!"

So we've established through conflict why The Judge can't immediately go out and just burn all of humanity.

Buffy And Angel See The Judge

Back in the library, Buffy says she knows where Spike and Drusilla are – at the factory. She and Angel will go there and do recon. The others should check the docks, airports, and anywhere else The Judge could be coming in, or pieces of The Judge could be coming in, to stop it.

This is how we know that Buffy did not see the last scene in her dream. She doesn't know The Judge is now fully assembled.

Buffy and Angel go to the factory. They are in an area above the main room, almost like a catwalk, and they look down. They see the candles and the punch bowl. And Buffy says, "I saw this."

Then they see The Judge walking around. Their eyes widen. The Judge senses them, then looks up and sees them.

Forgiveness For Plot Problems?

I always wonder, did they think no one would notice them? That as long as they just stayed up on the cat walk they would be invisible? They don't seem to make any attempt to hide, so it doesn't seem like a great plan. But I doubt I thought that the first time I saw it.

This is an example of how when there is great emotional weight to a story, when you are so invested in it, as an audience member you're willing to just kind of whistle past things in the plot that don't hold together. Because we want this scene with Buffy and Angel and The Judge. We want to see what happens. And the rest of the story is so fantastic.

I don't recommend leaving plot holes in your story, then finding a way so that the reader won't notice. Because there always will be some who do see them, and regardless, too many plot holes undercut the audience experience. You don't want your reader to think "that makes no sense" right at a crucial part of the story.

But sometimes it works. Here, I saw the problem when I stepped back to watch specifically from a story perspective. But I'm sure it worked for me the first time. And it doesn't really diminish anything for me anytime I rewatch.

The Confrontation

Buffy and Angel try to run. Vampires overtake them and bring them down to The Judge. Drusilla says, "I only dreamed you'd come," looking at Buffy.

So we know that just as Buffy dreams of Drusilla, Drusilla dreams of Buffy. They share this prophetic dreaming.

Angel: Leave her alone.

Now we get some great Spike.
Spike: Yeah, that'll work. Now say pretty please.
The Judge wants Buffy.
Drusilla: It's chilling, isn't it. She's so full of good intentions.
Angel: Take me instead.
Spike: You're not clear on the concept. There's no instead. Just first and second.

Drusilla wants Buffy to be first so Angel can watch her die. But as The Judge approaches, Buffy kicks him. He staggers back a bit and Angel, who during this dialogue has been scanning the ceiling, grabs this chain. It seems to be part of a pulley system. He pulls it and all these TVs and light fixtures drop down on The Judge.

On The Run

Angel and Buffy run. The vampires chase. Buffy and Angel go down into those tunnels under Sunnydale. Eventually they climb up a ladder and out through a manhole cover into a park somewhere. It's pouring rain. They're getting drenched, and they go to Angel's apartment, which is underground.

So I guess we assume Drusilla and Spike don't know where Angel lives. I find that interesting. Darla found it easy enough to figure out where he lived in Season One. But we have established that Spike doesn't know. He needed Willy to get Angel to him in an earlier episode.

Anyway, this is another example of a minor plot question I didn't ask when I initially watched. Or any time I watched until I broke it down in the Buffy and the Art of Story podcast.

The Midpoint Commitment Of Surprise And Innocence

Angel gives Buffy dry clothes. He turns his back while she starts to change. But he hears her kind of gasp in pain. She got cut. He sits down behind her on the bed and looks at her shoulder. He says it's already closed up, she's fine. She has taken her sweater off. She's wearing a tank top or camisole under it.

As he's touching her shoulder, there is so much tension and

chemistry between them. She leans back into him and says she almost lost him today. And she feels like if she lost him – and she doesn't finish. Instead, she says, "We can't be sure of anything."

So we are moving to the Midpoint Commitment where our protagonist throws caution to the wind and commits to the quest. And, remember, we also could see the protagonist suffer a major reversal. We are going to see both here.

Angel and Buffy are committing to this relationship.

Angel: I love you. I try not to but I can't stop.

Buffy: Me too. I can't either.

They kiss. As it becomes more intense, we hear the Buffy and Angel theme music.

Angel: Buffy, maybe we shouldn't.

Buffy: Don't. Just kiss me.

The camera pans away as they sink onto his bed. That is at 43 minutes, and it is our Midpoint Commitment. And part of the climax of this episode.

Almost immediately we get a reversal.

The Midpoint Reversal Of The Two-Episode Story

We could see also this next moment as the Falling Action of the episode. Because first we have this really nice second of them sleeping curled together, covered by blankets.

Then Angel sits. He gasps in terrible pain and staggers outside into the alley. we have jarring music and lightning, and Angel screams "Buffy."

Inside, though, she is sleeping. She doesn't hear him. And he shouts her name out in the alley again.

And it's To Be Continued.

This instant is our reversal for Buffy and Angel. It is also a game changer.

The Game Changes

In that last scene, we first wrapped up the episode main plot, which was what will happen with Buffy's and Angel's relationship? It reached the point where they do make love, and they are closer than ever.

And then we get the Game Changer. It isn't a cliffhanger, though it does leave us hanging for the next episode. But it changes everything. We finished out the main plot. Now everything changes going forward. It will be a new world.

What an amazing way to end the episode.

When I looked it up on Wikipedia, it said that the two episodes aired back-to-back, Surprise one night and Innocence the next. I don't remember that.

What I do remember is after Innocence there was a very, very long break. Maybe some kind of a winter hiatus that the shows often did. And it was awful. Waiting during that time for the next episode.

Whedon Interview On Surprise

The DVD edition includes an interview with Joss Whedon. He talks about Buffy and Angel being the classic star-crossed romance. Vampire Slayer, Vampire. And that he knew from the start it wouldn't be easy and "that would be where all the fun was."

He also noted something that I wondered about in earlier episodes and mention in Buffy and the Art of Story Season 2 Part 1. Based on hints early on that Jenny perhaps could not be trusted, I wondered if it was always the plan that she was part of this clan that lost their favorite when Angel killed her. But in the interview Whedon said that wasn't originally the plan for Jenny. They didn't know that she would turn out to be from the clan. He said he tries to leave things open for characters so they can do what they need to. Do what seems most intriguing when they get there.

World Building

This way of leaving some aspects of a character open relates to how some writers approach world building. Particularly in fantasy, but really in any story, you're building a world. The question is, do you try to figure out all the elements of the world, build the world in advance, and then tell each installment of a story within those limits?

Or do you create just as much of the world as you need and then create more parts of it as you go on with your story (or your next novel or novella or movie)? The latter is sometimes called Just-In-Time world building.

While I tend to plot each novel in advance in the sense that I plan my major plot turns, I vary that when it comes to world building. Both when I wrote the Awakening supernatural thriller series (which also falls within the fantasy genre) and with my Q.C. Davis Mystery series, I tend to do it more like what Joss Whedon is saying here. I build what I need, leaving some parts open so I can go various places in future books. I find that more fun. I feel like it gives me more freedom. But it is really about finding what works best for you.

Spoilers and Foreshadowing

THE RINGS

In the dream when Drusilla dusts Angel and he reaches for Buffy, we see two rings fall off Angel's finger. That's a subtle foreshadowing of the later scene where Angel gives her one ring and keeps the other on his finger.

In Season 3, Buffy will place her ring on the floor of Angel's mansion as a way of letting go. (And, of course, he will then be returned to earth.)

We'll see another Claddagh ring before that when Buffy meets Scott Hope in Season Three. He brings her a Claddagh ring, not knowing her history. The reaction Buffy has to it, which triggers some emotional growth for her, tells Giles how disturbed she still is over killing Angel.

Surprise Me

Buffy says, "Surprise me." And Angel says, "Okay, I will." So telling for the next episode and the rest of the season.

When he says, "Okay, I will," of course he doesn't mean what happens. He doesn't have control over turning evil again. And yet the rest of the season is dealing with that total unknown, that Surprise, about Angel.

Buffy And Driving

On the lighter side, Buffy and Joyce talk about Buffy getting a Driver's License. This theme of Buffy and driving continues in the background of the series. It's the most key in Band Candy, where Joyce does let Buffy have the keys, but she's under the influence of the candy. Then Buffy bangs up the car, through no fault of her own, and after that Buffy doesn't drive.

I think that is something that the show creators and writers found useful. We don't want to watch Buffy driving around. It's so much more dramatic to have her running. (For instance, when she runs to try to stop Riley from leaving in Season 5. Much less drama if she can drive to the spot where his helicopter takes off.)

Amends, Happiness

Jenny tells her uncle that Angel still suffers and even makes amends. In Season Three, we will see the episode Amends, which is all about Angel's past. Jenny, in a way, serves his a guide.

Also, the uncle says, "If that girl gives him one minute of happiness it's one minute too much." On first watch, I took it as the uncle feeling Angel didn't deserve any happiness. But "one minute of happiness" also refers to the curse and will reverberate through the rest of Buffy and through Angel the series.

Affection And Jealousy

I love The Judge's comment about Drusilla and Spike sharing affection and jealousy. He scorns that because it's human. One of the reasons I like Spike so much, and fans tend to like him, is that he does share human feelings and isn't afraid to own it. He is not cowed by The Judge. He just says, "Of course we do."

And we will see how affection and jealousy weave through Spike's and Drusilla's relationship. Spike wears his heart on his sleeve, so we feel he's more invested and more vulnerable. But there is some from Dru as well.

Later we'll see Spike is jealous of Angelus and Drusilla. It's part of what leads him to team up with Buffy. And we'll find out in Season Three, Lovers Walk, that Dru starts seeing a chaos demon. Which sparks their break up. But the underlying cause is Dru feeling that Buffy is too much a part of Spike's psyche. So you definitely see that affection and jealousy continue.

Spike Worries

I also like that Spike is not all that enthused about The Judge or the party. He tells The Judge, "Hey, remember who brought you here." These things foreshadow Spike at the end of the season deciding he doesn't want to end the world.

He truly is not the guy who wants to bring forth Armageddon and see the world sucked into hell. He likes being a vampire, he likes doing violence. Spike loves the world. All of that is foreshadowed in this episode.

Xander's Imaginary Relationships

In Xander's fantasy about Buffy and Angel in the future being so unhappy, Angel with the big blood belly stis in front of the TV.

Then in Season Six, Hells Bells, Xander has this vision of his future married to Anya. In his nightmare vision, Xander sits in front of the TV with a beer. He's not able to work, apparently after being injured fighting at Buffy's side. It's a very dark picture of marriage. I find it striking that as far back as Surprise, we glimpse his view of long-term relationships. I also think it's no accident that this happens in the same episode where his mother seems not to know who he is on the phone.

Humanity

Giles says The Judge burns humanity out of people. A true creature of evil can survive, but no one else. This is chilling because in Innocence, The Judge will be unable to cause any harm to Angel. Angel is completely, when he becomes Angelus, impervious to The Judge.

Whereas Spike and Drusilla – I don't believe we ever see them touch The Judge. There is humanity in them.

Angel's Last Breath

Finally, Angel shouts Buffy's name not just once but multiple times. This is echoed in I Only Have Eyes For You later in the season, where there's the Sadie Hawkins dance. Ghosts take over Angel and Buffy to replay a tragic love and a murder-suicide. James loved his teacher and shot her and then himself. And he's saying how can she forgive him. She does forgive him and tells him she died saying his name.

And here we have Angel dying, his human side, his soul, dying as he gasps Buffy's name. Some of the most powerful storytelling in all of Buffy.

Questions For Your Writing

- Review the ends of your chapters or your scene or act breaks. Can you add hooks? If you have hooks, can you make them more compelling?
- Do you use conflict to convey backstory? Or are you having characters just tell each other information, which is less compelling? If the latter, try rewriting.
- Are there scenes where humor (or more humor) might highlight the tension and drama?

- If you're writing in serial form, does each installment also have its own major plot turns?
- Do you use dream sequences? Do they move the story forward? (Try taking them out – if it makes no difference, they're not moving the story.)

Next Week: Innocence

NEXT I'LL TALK about Innocence, the second part of this two-part storyline. The chapter includes the elements of heart-wrenching sub-plots, the pluses of writing yourself into a corner, and how setting affects your story.

I feel like these two episodes are where Buffy truly becomes what it is. It's been amazing so far, but Surprise and Innocence takes the series to a new level.

CHAPTER 2
INNOCENCE (S2 E14)

THIS CHAPTER TALKS ABOUT INNOCENCE, Season Two Episode Fourteen, where Angelus returns and devastates Buffy. Written and directed by Joss Whedon.

In particular, we'll look at:

- How setting affects the characters and a story's emotional resonance;
- Making the audience love your characters;
- Why writing yourself into a corner can be a great thing; and
- Incorporating a heart-wrenching subplot in the midst of an epic main plot.

Okay, let's dive into the Hellmouth.

―――

OPENING **Conflict And A Hook**

Innocence is the second half of the two-part episode that began in Surprise. Because this is the second part of the two-part story, we've already covered the Opening Conflict, the

Story Spark or Inciting Incident, and the One-Quarter Twist, then ended with a Midpoint Commitment by Buffy, our protagonist. She and Angel threw caution to the wind and made love after that harrowing experience with The Judge.

We also hinted at a major reversal for Buffy at the Midpoint. It's where Angel is out in the alley, gasping Buffy's name in terrible pain.

This episode, Innocence, though, starts with its own opening conflict. Because we don't start right in the alley with Angel. We start in the factory with Drusilla and Spike.

Immediately there is conflict.

Spike: I'm not happy, Pet.

He goes on to say that Angel and the Slayer are still alive. Plus, they know where Spike and Drusilla are, and they know about The Judge. Spike thinks that they should vacate the factory.

Drusilla disagrees, saying, "Nonsense." Angel and the Slayer won't bother them at the factory or come back.

Drusilla: My Angel is too smart.

Spike also complains about The Judge, calling him Big Blue. He says Big Blue's just sitting there not doing anything. Spike wants to know when can they go out and end some lives.

All of this dialogue gets in some quick exposition, catching the audience up on much of the plot from the last episode. It ends with a hook as Drusilla cries out and falls on the floor is if she is in pain. She says Angel's name. But a second later she smiles.

Buffy's Reversal - Angel Changes

We fade to Buffy, asleep in Angel's bed. She opens her eyes, hears the rain falling, and sees she is alone. Thunder claps. She looks around and says, "Angel?"

Out in the alley, we are back where we ended the last episode. Angel has fallen on the pavement and says, "Buffy."

A woman in a leather coat, who was smoking in a doorway,

comes over to ask if he's all right. He stands suddenly and says, "Yes. The pain is gone now." He turns and bites her, then exhales smoke. He is in vamp face, and he says, "I feel just fine."

That is 2 minutes 40 seconds in, and we go to credits.

This is a total reversal for Buffy. Angel has become evil. I also see it as a Story Spark or Inciting Incident for the episode. It gets the Part 2 main plot rolling because Angel changes.

As we'll see, this episode has its own major plot points and tracks the major turns for the two-episode arc. That's part of what keeps these two episodes moving so well.

The Day After

After the credits, Buffy comes in through the back door at home. It's a sunny day. Joyce says, "So did you have fun last night?"

We see momentary panic on Buffy's face. She says, "Fun?" and Joyce says, "At Willow's." Because last night Buffy, Xander, and Willow all called their parents and told them they were staying at one of the other's houses. Buffy covers. She's a little awkward but says yes, and Joyce asks her if something is wrong. Buffy says no. And Joyce says, "I don't know you just look – " and she shakes her head and leaves.

Ready To Rescue Buffy

Xander enters the library and says he had no luck at the bus depot finding any parts of The Judge. This catches us up on what our friends were doing at the end of the last episode. Jenny and Willow look somber. Giles tells Xander that Buffy and Angel never checked in the night before. This means The Judge is very likely operational.

Xander says they need to go and try to help Buffy and Angel, go to the factory.

Cordelia: And do what except be afraid and die?

Xander tells her no one is asking her to go. But Giles says she may have a point. If Buffy and Angel couldn't stand against

The Judge, if they were hurt, the others don't stand much chance.

Willow agrees with Xander and thinks the others are being terrible. They both head toward the door, but Buffy walks in.

Xander: We were just going to rescue you.

Willow (with a sidelong look at the others): Well, some of us were.

Buffy tells them The Judge is assembled. She's very upset to hear that Angel didn't check in with the others. She tells them that she and Angel had to hide. Willow reassures her, saying she's sure Angel will come by.

Giles asks about The Judge. Buffy says she kicked him. She barely touched him, but it burned. And Giles says eventually The Judge will be able to reduce humans to charcoal with a look.

Willow and Buffy talk. Willow is worried that Angel went after The Judge, and Buffy says no, maybe Angel just needed – and she breaks off and says she just wishes he'd contact her. She needs to talk to him. They're talking in the hall, and as they head up the stairs Jenny comes around the corner. Clearly, she was listening.

Art, Literary, And Commercial Writing

In the commentary, Joss Whedon noted that there was another scene right here that got cut. In it, Buffy sat in class and remembered the sex with Angel from the night before. Joss said it was very surreal and arty and it got cut mainly for time. And because it really didn't add to the narrative.

But he also commented that when he tries to actually be artistic, "I tend to confuse people," and that it's better when he just tells the story.

This comment reminds me of the distinction between literary fiction writing and commercial and genre fiction. It's not really a bright line. I best heard it described as a sort of continuum. At the literary extreme it is all about the writing.

The style of the writing and the beauty of it. The art of the writing itself. At the other end it is all about the plot and the story.

Most stories don't all the way fall at one end or the other. But people do tend to like things that lean a certain way. Some people love the beauty of the writing. Some people just want the story. That's the main distinction between literary and commercial fiction (or, as I like to think of it, more plot-based fiction). I found it interesting because I think Joss Whedon's stories are so amazing. I love his dialogue, his characterization, but all of those really go to the story more than the style. Amazing as his dialogue is standing on its own, it serves the story. It is rarely there just to be good dialogue.

So I found it interesting that he said when he tried to do this very artsy scene, he ended up cutting it. And feeling like it didn't work as well because it didn't move the story.

Incorporating Villains

We switch to the factory at about 7 minutes in. Drusilla is lying on her back on a table, dreamily naming all the stars. Spike asks if she has seen any more. What happens to Angel?

A sarcastic voice comes from behind Spike as Angel – now Angelus – walks in and answers Spike's question. He says, "Well, he moved to New York and tried to fulfill his Broadway dream."

Whedon said the idea of Spike and Drusilla as villains was to get the villains more incorporated into the real lives of the characters. In Season One, the Master was always separate from our usual cast of characters.

Now Spike, Dru, and Angel are going to be incorporated into our characters' lives. Whedon also loved the triangle idea of Spike, Dru, and Angel because it shows vampires as more complex than before.

The Judge Judges Angelus

Spike doesn't yet realize Angel changed, though Angel

makes fun of Spike rolling through the streets on his wheelchair and is sarcastic in a way that we have never seen Angel be. Spike tells Angel to look over his shoulder. He points to The Judge. The Judge touches Angel, and nothing happens.

Spike says something like, "What are you doing? Just burn him."

Angel: Gee, maybe he's broken.

The Judge says Angel is clean, there's no humanity in him. And Whedon said this was a way to show the audience that Angel really had gone bad. He was not faking it There wasn't some ulterior plot where Angel pretended to be bad. Which is also why they had Angel kill someone in that scene before the credits, the teaser. He did not want the audience to have any question.

So once The Judge has said this, we get a commercial break. (Another great hook.)

When we come back, Spike is happy. He says to Angel, "No more of this I've-got-a-soul crap?" And he's laughing and Dru is dancing, and Spike says it made him sick to see Angel as the Slayer's lapdog.

Angel growls at Spike and lunges at him, but then he kisses him on the head. Spike says, "Now it's three against one, which is the kind of odds I like to play." Angel, though, is not ready to end the world yet when they tell him of their plan with The Judge. He says give him a night. He needs to go after the Slayer first, and he guarantees she won't be anything resembling a threat after he's done with her.

Cordelia And Xander Subplot

Back at the library, Willow is on the phone with Buffy trying to reassure her that Angel must have a plan, that's why he's missing. And he's not dead. The others are going through all of the books looking for answers about The Judge.

In the stacks, Xander asks Cordelia if she's found anything. She says no weapon forged, it takes an army to take him down –

all the same things. Xander apologizes for snapping at her when she didn't want to go after Buffy. And she says, "Well, I'm reeling from that new experience." She also says he was all ready to rush out and die for his beloved Buffy, and he'd never die for her. He says he might die from her, does that get him any points? When she says no, Xander says, "Come on, can't we just kiss and make up?"

Cordelia doesn't want to make up. She smiles, though, and says, "But I'm okay with the other part."

They kiss.

In the commentary, Whedon said one of his favorite things on the show is the changing relationships. And the idea of Cordelia falling for Xander was a perfect sort of romance because they are so wrong for each other. He liked developing Cordelia, who was kind of just the mean girl in Season One, and now she is showing real vulnerability. (He also said that there is nothing more painful in the world than when Alyson Hannigan does her big eyes, which happens in a second.)

Cordelia and Xander are kissing and when they break apart, we see Willow standing there at the end of the row of books. Just looking stricken. Xander runs after her. Cordelia looks upset. I feel like she feels for Willow.

Willow runs out into the hall. Xander follows her.

Willow And Xander Subplot

I love that in the midst of this huge turmoil for Buffy and Angel, with The Judge planning to end the world, we get this subplot with Willow and Xander. And I think it works without being distracting or slowing the momentum of the main plot for a couple reasons.

One is that we love Willow so much and we feel for her in the circumstance. The other is, as we'll see, this subplot always intertwines with the main plot. Cordelia and Xander didn't just randomly argue. He snapped at her over everyone thinking Buffy and Angel might be dead or hurt and Xander wanting to go after Buffy. Despite that it probably would've been a foolish thing to do, as Cordelia pointed out.

Then in the stacks they're researching The Judge. Willow is probably coming back there also to get more books. Then she sees them.

Out in the hall we have some fantastic dialogue.

Willow: I knew it. I knew it. Well, not knew it in the sense of having the slightest idea. But I knew there was something I didn't know. You two were fighting way too much. It's not natural.

Xander: I know it's weird.

Willow: Weird? It's against all laws of God and man. It's Cordelia. Remember, the We Hate Cordelia Club, of which you are the Treasurer?

Xander says he was going to tell her, and Willow says, "What stopped you? Could it be shame?"

And Xander tells her she's overreacting. Then we get the lines that lead to the most heartbreaking thing from Willow:

Xander: We were just kissing. It didn't mean that much.

Willow (no longer yelling, her voice is soft and it breaks): No. Just that you'd rather be with someone you hate than be with me.

And she runs out. Xander looks after her, looking helpless. We get this beautiful plaintive music and it carries over to the next scene where Buffy is walking toward her house. She stops in front of it, then turns away and heads to Angel's apartment.

Escalating Emotional Pain At Angel's

This scene is another example of escalation. If you remember back when I talked in an earlier Buffy and the Art of Story book about Nightmares, there was a scene with Buffy and her dad. Every line escalated the conflict and emotional pain when each time you didn't think that it could get any worse. The writers just kept turning it up again and again.

That's what occurs here, too.

Buffy enters Angel's apartment. It seems like it's deserted. She walks toward the bed and sees his shirt lying there. So she knows that he's been back. It doesn't look the way it did when she left. She is already distraught, and he walks out behind her, shirtless.

She hears him and turns and hugs him and says, "Angel, my God."

He does hug her back, and he says he's sorry. And he sort of sounds like himself. He says he didn't mean to frighten her. At the same time, he is not quite himself. Because he acts like he's surprised that she's upset or that she was worried. This adds to Buffy's unease. She should feel better because here Angel is. Yet he's acting odd. Like it's no big deal, which she will say.

Buffy: You just disappeared.

Angel: What? I took off.

She meets casualness with more intensity.

Buffy: But you didn't say anything. You just left.

Angel (starts putting his shirt back on): Like I really wanted to stick around after that.

Buffy: What?

We can see in her face she can barely comprehend what he is saying. And he calls her kiddo and says she has a lot to learn about men, but he guesses she proved that last night. All of this as he is just casually buttoning up his shirt.

Buffy (looks devastated): What are you saying?

Angel: Let's not make an issue of it. Let's not talk about it at all.

And he puts his coat on.

Actions And Tone Underscore Angel's Cruelty

All of Angel's actions, his tone, and his words, are so dismissive and casual. It's like he's putting on his clothes and he can't be bothered to stop what he's doing and really look at her and focus on her. At the same time, it's intimate. That act of getting dressed in front of her.

Buffy is trying to process this and she says, "Was it me? Was I not – good?"

I feel it just keeps getting more horrible because he chuckles and says oh, she was great, really. He says, "I thought you were a Pro." It's a tone we've never heard him use with her.

And she says, "How can you say this to me?" He tells her lighten to up, it was a good time. It doesn't have to be a big deal.

When Buffy says it is a big deal, Angel again ratchets up the emotional pain and the awfulness.

Angel: It's what? Bells ringing, fireworks, a dulcet choir or pretty little birdies?

He giggles when he says this. That is somehow even more unnerving, Angel giggling.

Angel: Come on, Buffy. It's not like I've never been there before.

He moves his hand toward her face like he's about to tap her nose or chuck her under the chin or something, like a little girl. She jerks away and says in this low voice that's almost a whisper, "Don't touch me."

Buffy's Grief

Angel kind of points his finger at her and says he should've known she wouldn't be able to handle this. He heads for the door. And she says, "Angel."

He turns toward her with this awful grin and she says again, almost in a whisper, "I love you." It sounds desperate. How can this be happening? Even though he's just said these terrible things she wants to bring him back to where they were last night.

Angel does worse than not responding. He says, "Love you too," and he points his finger toward her as he says it, just making a joke of it and mocking her. He opens the door. Before leaving, he adds that final terrible thing. "I'll call you." And walks out.

We can't quite see his eyes rolling, but from his profile and expression we know that's what he's doing.

Buffy's swallows hard and starts to cry. This is so devastating. Because we know – it's dramatic irony – that Angel has been turned. But Buffy doesn't, and to her it is this man that she loved rejecting her. This lovemaking that mattered so much to her and that she thought was this deep connection with him doesn't matter to him at all. We saw all that wedding imagery, the exchange of rings. And worse than not mattering, it's a joke. He's making fun of her.

This is about 15 minutes, 30 seconds in. This is almost a One-Quarter Twist for Buffy's personal story in this episode. It comes from outside of her, outside the protagonist, and sends the story in a totally new direction where she has to deal with this emotional loss.

Setting Matters

In the DVD commentary, Joss Whedon said that initially they wrote and shot the scene with Buffy running into Angel at her house. And he said it wasn't working. It was in the wrong place. You needed to see the two of them in Angel's bedroom. It needed to be intimate. You needed to see Angel with his shirt off instead of two characters in woolly coats standing outside.

And Whedon said it showed he had a lot to learn as writer and a director. When they shot it again, it worked amazingly, as we see.

If you're writing a novel or short story, you don't have actors playing the parts, but you do have characters. So it's a good lesson. If the scene – your dialogue, your conflict – is not working, you're not getting the emotion you want, it's worth looking at whether that scene is in the right place. Have you used the setting to the greatest emotional impact?

And maybe that's a better question. Not that there is one right place. (Although that particular scene, I think there was a right place and that was it.) I don't know that all scenes have that one perfect place. But look and ask if this setting will bring out the most emotion, the most of the characters feelings? That can make a huge, huge difference.

In terms of emotional resonance, Joss Whedon said he thought this scene with Buffy and Angel was the best scene that they ever did on the show.

Writing Characters Different From Yourself

Whedon also said he felt like an ugly person writing the scene because he could make Angel say these terrible things. I think that goes to the question of how do you as a writer write things that you don't want to write. Or write a character who is mean in a way that you typically are not?

As an example, one writer I knew said over and over that she didn't think she could write a character who was a genius because she wasn't one. (Similarly, you might feel you can't write a character who is spontaneously witty and funny if you're not the kind of person who just pops off one-liners.)

But as the writer, you have time. You can spend fifteen minutes figuring out that next horrible line, or that next very funny line, or sorting out this amazing deduction the character makes. Whether it takes you five minutes, fifteen, or fifty, on the page the character says it immediately.

So while you may need to spend more time and effort creating a character who is not you, or who is ramped up from what you would ever do or say, the reader or viewer doesn't see that. They just see this fantastically funny or mean or brilliant character.

Writing Yourself Into A Corner And Out Again

We then switch to Jenny and her uncle. Whedon said this is a scene that he loved because he had to solve so many problems with it.

First we have Jenny saying to her uncle that she couldn't keep Angel from Buffy. And she argues that Angel could help them stop The Judge. That he might be the only chance. But the uncle tells her it's too late and explains the curse. He says Angel was meant to suffer, not to live as human. So "one moment of true happiness, of contentment, one moment where the soul that we restored no longer plagues his thoughts, and that soul is taken from him."

Jenny realizes that if that happened it means Angelus is back. The uncle says yes, he hoped to stop it but he realizes now it was all arranged to be part of the plan. Jenny says that Buffy loves him. And the uncle says now she'll have to kill him. Jenny says unless Angel kills Buffy first. That it's insanity and people will die.

The uncle previously said that vengeance is a living thing. And now he says, "Yes. It is not justice we serve, it is vengeance."

I love this quote. I saw this whole thing as part of the theme of the episode and a real comment on the idea of vengeance. How twisted it can become when our aim is revenge. And how vengeance and justice are not the same. I've always admired that quote.

But it turns out that quote came from necessity. Whedon said he had some serious problems in terms of the Jenny storyline. He commented that though she was sent there to supposedly watch Angel, Jenny hadn't really done anything. That was partly because they didn't decide that Jenny would be part of this clan until later.

He also said the whole curse doesn't make sense. It's a terrible plan to have Angel's soul be yanked away the moment he is truly happy.

So the writers pretty much wrote themselves into a corner. Whedon said luckily he had experience dealing with that kind of thing because he worked for a long time as a script doctor. That's where you get handed a script, and there are elements that the producers or directors love. But there are things that just aren't working. It's the script doctor's job to make those work, including to make elements that do not fit or things that are not built in somehow work.

He took a walk along the Santa Monica Pier and was desperately trying to connect up all these things about the curse. Why would Angel lose his soul? It doesn't make any sense. And he came up with that idea of vengeance as this living thing. This sort of arbitrary god.

I just love that this wonderful commentary on vengeance came out of those problems. And it really does hold it together.

It also is a great example of what I talked about in the last chapter – doing world building as you need it on the fly. Sometimes you get to this place where you don't know what to do. But I think that forces a sort of creativity. And sometimes it makes you come up with something very powerful.

Willow's Back

At the school, Willow comes back. She's walking slowly. We see from her body language how bad she still feels.

Xander is out in the hall, and he says he's glad she came back. They can't do it without her. And we get a great quote from Willow that shows how mature she is and how emotionally aware. She's able to say how she feels, yet still be there to help. And to continue being friends with Xander.

Willow: Let's get this straight. I don't understand it. I don't want to understand it. You have gross emotional problems and things are not okay between us. But what's happening right now is more important than that.

Xander nods, and he says okay. Willow asks where they stand about The Judge.

Right here is a great example of how this Willow-Xander subplot is woven into the main plot. So the main plot doesn't stop in its tracks while we go to one side to deal with Willow and Xander. It is part of it.

Because Xander says they're where they were when she left. No weapon forged. It took an army.

Willow: Yeah, where's an army when you need one?

Now Xander gets an idea. But we don't find out yet what it is because the lights go out.

Angelus Reveals Himself

They start to head for the library, but Angel calls their names. He's standing near the exit in the dark so they don't see his face.

Willow asks if he saw Buffy, and he says yeah. He sounds like himself. He says he has something to show them and tells Xander to go get the others. Willow walks slowly toward Angel, asking what it is. And he says, "It's amazing."

Something in his tone makes Xander turn around. Jenny comes out of the library with a cross and tells Willow to get away from Angel and walk to her. But it's too late. Angel grabs Willow from behind. Jenny says he's not Angel anymore.

Angel: Wrong. I am Angel, at last.

And he says he has a message for Buffy. From behind him Buffy says he should give it to her himself. He spins around, still gripping Willow by the throat, and says it's not the kind of message he can say. It involves her finding the dead bodies of all her friends. Buffy tries to say that some part of him must remember who he is.

Angel: Dream on, schoolgirl. Your boyfriend's dead.

As Angel's talking to Buffy, Xander takes the cross from Jenny and creeps up behind Angel. Buffy is telling him to leave Willow alone and deal with her, and Xander thrusts the cross at Angel, surprising him. Angel reflexively jerks away and throws Willow to the side. Then he grabs Buffy by the shoulders and says, "Things are about to get very interesting." He kisses her, flings her against the wall, and stalks out.

This is nearly the episode Midpoint, and it seems like a major reversal for Buffy. But it gets worse. That Midpoint is still coming. It will also be the three-quarter plot turn for the entire story arc. But first, we cut to a commercial.

Giles Leans Toward Panic

In the library, Giles is leaning towards blind panic. It was enough with The Judge, he wasn't prepared for Angel crossing over. Willow asks if Buffy's okay. Buffy shakes her head and says she should've known. She says, "I saw him at the house and he was different."

Interesting that she says "at the house." So it seems like this scene must've been filmed before they realized it should be in Angel's apartment.

Buffy goes on to say she should have known because of the things he said. Giles says, "What things?" And Buffy says, "It's private.:

The next moment, we get what I see as the Three-Quarter Turn of the double episode arc.

The Three-Quarter Turn In Surprise-Innocence

It's about 22 minutes in, right about three quarters through this whole story.

Giles is pushing Buffy to tell them what Angel said to her and what happened. And he says if only they knew what set off Angel's change. And Buffy says, "What do you mean?" Giles says some event must have set it off and "if anyone would know, Buffy, it should be you. Did anything happen last night?"

This is a major reversal for Buffy. So it's the episode Midpoint for her because she realizes that their lovemaking somehow caused this. She couldn't be more devastated.

We would've thought nothing could get worse for Buffy. First, she thinks Angel rejected her and was fooling her all along, toying with her. And it's terrible emotionally. Then she finds out, well, he *really* is not who she thought. And because he's become Angelus, she has not only lost Angel, but Angelus, this evil being, poses a threat to everyone. And now it is so much worse because she feels personally responsible. She feels she is the one who did this.

As Giles pushes her, she says, "Giles, please, I can't," and leaves. He calls after her, saying something like, "We can't afford to be emotional at this time."

Willow says, "Giles, shut up." And we see that Willow has put together what happened.

In the commentary, Joss Whedon said a couple things about these scene. One is that he loves Willow's bond with Buffy. That it is kind of transcendent. And I agree.

Visiting The Scene

Whedon also commented on scenes in the library, where there's almost always information coming out and there are a number of people there. So he goes there and walks through it. Figures out exactly where everyone will be. I think that is a great idea.

I don't have sets to go to. But sometimes when I am struggling with a scene, I draw on a piece of paper the room or the neighborhood. I am not an artist by any means. I would not share those drawings. (They're really bad line drawings.) But I have done that to help me get that sense of who is there and what are they doing.

Likewise, I have gone to places and just sat there and looked around. Or taken a video of them and figured out, okay, yes, this is the bench. This is how far it is from the Picasso sculpture. This is what my character would see and observe and hear and so forth. That can be really valuable.

Xander's Plan

Cordelia says how terrible things are. She lists all the awful things, including not just The Judge being operational but Angel turning and the Slayer being a basket case. And she ends with:

Cordelia: I'd say we've hit bottom.
Xander: I have a plan.
Cordelia: Oh no, here's a lower place.

Xander has figured out a way to deal with The Judge, and he needs Cordelia's help.

Back at the factory warehouse, Angel goes on about the look on Buffy's face being priceless. When Spike says, "So you didn't kill her," he says of course not.

Another great quote:

Spike: I know you haven't been in the game for a while, mate, but we do still kill people. It's sort of our raison d'être you know.

Drusilla says Angel doesn't want to kill Buffy. He wants to hurt her, "just like you hurt me." She says it with a little laugh. And Angel says, "No one knows me like you do, Dru."

Angel tells Spike he doesn't get it. Spike tried to kill Buffy and look at him. Angel laughs at Spike in wheelchair and says that force won't do it.

Angel: To kill this girl you have to love her.

Buffy Learns Through Her Dream

Back at home, in her bedroom Buffy looks at the cross on the necklace that Angel gave her, and the ring he gave her. She sobs and curls up on her bed. We drift into her dream.

Buffy and Angel are in bed. We see the rings on their hands. It is almost that artistic type of approach to a lovemaking flashback that Whedon talked about cutting, though it is clear what's happening. Angel whispers, "I love you," and it's very sweet. We see him touching her face. It emphasizes for me the horribleness of how Angel treats her the next day.

Then Buffy in the dream is at a grave. Angel stands there in the sun. He looks at her and says, "You have to know what to see." Buffy turns and sees Jenny all dressed in black, pulling a veil down over her face.

This is an example of a dream moving the story forward. It also fills in the scene that we missed with Buffy and Angel when they are finally making love. It works in a very television, PG sort of way. (The only real option for network TV at the time.) We get that emotional moment that we missed and saw the aftermath of. This also moves the story because Buffy connects Jenny with what happened.

Buffy Confronts Jenny

In the next scene, the music becomes intense with a driving beat. Buffy strides into school and straight into Jenny's classroom. Giles is talking to Jenny. Buffy ignores him, grabs Jenny by the throat, and pins her on the desk. She then immediately lets go but says, "What do you know?" Giles sends the students away, saying he'll deal with it.

Buffy: Did you do it? Did you change him? Did you know this was going to happen?"

Giles yells at Buffy and says she can't go around accusing everybody. But Jenny says, "I didn't know exactly. I was told –" And Giles is just shocked. Jenny tells him she's sorry, but Angel was supposed to pay for what he did to her people. She tells Buffy she didn't know what would happen until after. She swears she would've told Buffy.

Buffy: So it was me. I did it.

Jenny: I think so.

She explains about the moment of true happiness.

Giles: I don't understand. How do you know you were responsible –

Buffy just looks at him. He looks back, takes off his glasses, and says, "Oh."

When You Don't Need The Monologue

Buffy tells Jenny to curse Angel again. Jenny says she can't. The magics are long lost. If she can't help, Buffy wants Jenny to take her to someone who can.

We cut to the uncle. He hears the door open behind him and says, "I knew she would bring you. I suppose you want answers."

But it's Angel. He says, "Not really."

Joss Whedon said that he had this long scene planned where Angel tortured the uncle and kind of monologued. Then he cut it because he realized even before they shot it that as soon as Angel spoke it's over. We all know what will happen.

Subplot: Oz Doesn't Kiss Willow

We cut to a rainy night outside a military base. Willow and Oz wait in his van. (In a previous scene, Xander said they needed transportation bigger than a car. And Willow said, "No problem, Oz has a van.")

She and Oz wait while Cordelia and Xander sneak into the base. When they're caught, Xander pretends he's a soldier on leave bringing his girl in to impress her. (He uses what he remembers from when he was a soldier on Halloween to fool the guard.) They get into the armory to steal something, but we don't know what.

Oz and Willow talk while they wait and Willow suddenly says, "Do you want to make out with me? Oz says, "What?" and she says forget it, she's sorry.

But then she says, "Well, do you?" Oz tells her that sometimes in class he's thinking – and he says I'm not thinking about class because that would never happen -- but he thinks about kissing Willow. He says it's like freeze-frame. And he makes it sound so amazing. She kind of looks at him expectantly and he says no, he's not going to kiss her.

Willow doesn't understand why. And we get a wonderful line from Oz.

Oz: Well, to the casual observer, it would appear that you're trying to make your friend Xander jealous, or even the score or something. And that's on the empty side. See in my fantasy, when I'm kissing you, you're kissing me. It's okay. I can wait.

Making The Audience Love Oz

Joss Whedon said that Oz was based on someone he knew who was very laid-back and cool. Whedon wanted a character that was so cool that he sees how cool Willow is even when she's hidden in that big Eskimo outfit in Inca Mummy Girl. But the audience was not loving Oz. He said they were very vocal about it.

They wanted Willow with Xander because Willow was so into Xander. And he wrote this scene that makes Willow love Oz. He said Willow really falls for Oz at that moment when he explains why he isn't going to kiss her and says he can wait. We see that in Willow's face, and because Willow falls for Oz the audience falls for Oz.

Three-Quarters Through Innocence

We now switch to the uncle's home. Buffy, Jenny, and Giles are there. Jenny runs to the body. "Was it good for you too?" is written on the wall in blood.

Giles tells Buffy Angel is doing it deliberately to make it harder for her. And she says he's only making it easier. She knows what she has to do. Kill him.

This is about 34 minutes in. That is close to three quarters through this episode. Normally our Three-Quarter Turn grows out of the protagonist's actions at the Midpoint and turns the story in yet another new direction. Or it can grow out of a reversal and turn the story again. Here, this grows out of the reversal that Buffy suffered and out of all of her decisions. And it spins the story because now she knows she has to kill Angel.

We cut to commercial.

The Judge Is Ready

When we get back, we're in the factory. The Judge says he's ready.

Angel to Spike: Too bad you can't come with. I'll be thinking of you.

Spike: I won't be in this chair forever.

And this is great: not just foreshadowing, but already developing this triangle. This tension between Spike and Angel.

We see Xander putting a large rectangular box on a table in Giles' office. He says, "Happy Birthday, Buffy," and hopes she likes the color. We still don't see what's inside. It looks a bit like the box The Judge's arm came in at Buffy's party, though it's newer and it's more of a regular shape. But it's a nice echo back to that. Because that was Dru's birthday present, and now this is Buffy's.

Jenny appears and wants to help. Buffy tells her to get out. Jenny says something to Giles and he says, "She said get out," and turns his back on her. It is so sad but I love Giles in this moment because he puts Buffy first.

They go to the factory and don't find anyone there. Spike is hiding and listening to them. They talk about where The Judge might be, that he needs bodies and the Bronze is closed. They figure out the most people will likely be at the mall. Which would have probably been true back then.

We switch to the mall. People stand in line at a concession stand. There's an open area almost like a food court.

Angel, Dru, The Judge, and other vamps enter. They're up at the top of the stairs, on a somewhat higher level than that food court area. The Judge burns a man. It's almost like a lightning bolt that comes out of his fingers crackling with electricity. And this man just a few feet away burns up.

The Climax Of Surprise And Innocence

We are now at the climax of our two-episode story arc. It's 36 minutes 50 seconds in. Buffy enters with her friends. Giles is carrying the box on his shoulder.

We switch to The Judge, Angel on one side of him, Dru on the other. Angel is smiling. The Judge shoots bolts of electricity that are zigzagging through the crowd. Just as we close up on Angel smiling, an arrow hits The Judge's chest.

The Judge: Who dares?

We Pan to Buffy. She is standing on the counter holding a crossbow and says, "I think I got his attention." The Judge tells her she's a fool. "No weapon forged can stop me."

And Buffy says that was then. She hands down her crossbow. Someone else hands her the rocket launcher. She puts it on her shoulder and says, "This is now."

As it powers up, people run. Drusilla and Angel look at each other and dive off that upper level to get out of the way. It's all in slow motion. The Judge says, "What's that do?"

Buffy fires. As the blast hits The Judge, Angel and Dru hit the floor. Dru squeals and runs as pieces of The Judge rain down everywhere. Angel, looking exasperated, runs the other way.

I love all of this because it so fits Buffy, who is not constrained by the old rules. She gets this rocket launcher that didn't exist when The Judge was previously dismembered. Also I love that it's an ensemble effort. Everybody together researched, and Xander had this idea, and Cordelia helped get the weapon. Oz and Willow brought it back. Everybody took part in this.

It wasn't just the one girl in all the world.

Falling Action In Surprise And Innocence

Now we are at the Falling Action for this main part of the plot with The Judge. We have to tie up the loose ends. "Falling" is a bit literal here, because Angel and Drusilla do fall with the blast.

Buffy says this was her best present ever. But she says they can't be sure he's dead and tells the others to pick up the pieces and keep them separate.

Cordelia: Pieces. We get the pieces. Our job sucks.

But she goes off to do it. Now we have to deal with Angel.

Part Of The Climax?

In a way, this next scene is part of the Climax. Though we started that Falling Action of tying up loose ends, this is the Climax of the Buffy and Angel part of the story. Buffy sees him leaving. He glances back, sees her, and ducks into a side hallway. She follows him toward the back where the movie theater is. There's no one else around.

Angel again says horrible things to her. He tells her the worst part was pretending to love her and says, "If I knew how easily you'd give it up, I wouldn't have even bothered." But she says it doesn't work anymore. He's not Angel. And he says she'd like to think that but it doesn't matter. The important thing is she made him the man he is today. They fight.

We switch to our friends in the food court. Oz points to the ground and says, "Arm."

It's funny, and in the commentary, Joss Whedon said that juxtaposing these types of scenes is key.

Angel continues to say these kinds of intimate, awful things to Buffy that could've fit with what she originally thought was happening. That Angel just did not love her and was mocking her. Although now she knows it's Angelus, it still makes it so much more than just a physical fight.

She throws him into a glass case, kicks him against the wall. He's sort of cowering. Buffy pulls out a stake and then looks at his face. And even though he has that horrible mocking grin still on his face, she can't do it. She starts lowering the stake.

Angel: You can't do it. You can't kill me.

She kicks him really hard in the crotch. He groans and falls to his knees. She walks away.

Buffy: Give me time.

This is the climax of the Buffy and Angel plot. And now we get the Falling Action from that.

More Falling Action

Giles drives Buffy home. He pulls up in front of her house and tells her it's not over. Angel will come after her particularly. Buffy is staring straight ahead through the windshield.

Buffy: You must be so disappointed in me.

She finally looks at him and he says he's not disappointed. And Buffy says it's all her fault, and he tells her he doesn't believe it is. And says, "Do you want me to wag my finger at you and tell you you acted rashly? You did and I can." But he knows she loved Angel, and Angel proved more than once he loved her. She couldn't have known what would happen. And then he continues:

Giles: The coming months are going to be hard. I suspect on all of us. But if it's guilt you're looking for, Buffy, I'm not your man. All you will get from me is my support. And my respect.

And her face just crumples.

Buffy Got Older

The scene cuts. We see an old black and white movie. A couple dances. The woman is singing "goodnight, my love" and something about their moment together now is ending. (I looked this up. The movie is called Stowaway. It's from the 1930s.)

Joyce brings out cupcakes and asks what Buffy did for her birthday. And Buffy says, "I got older."

Joyce looks a little concerned, but says, "You look the same to me." She lights a candle on one of the cupcakes and tells Buffy to make a wish.

Buffy looks at the candle and says, "I'll just let it burn."

I thought the previous line, "I got older" was one of the most heartbreaking I'd ever heard. Then when she says "I'll just let it burn" it's so much sadder. Joyce strokes Buffy's hair and Buffy leans into her mom.

The song finishes, and that is the end of the episode.

The Meaning Of Innocence

Joss Whedon commented that part of the meaning of Innocence in the title is that Buffy is in a sense innocent. She hasn't lost anything of herself even though she's gone through this painful maturing process. And he said that's why Joyce says she doesn't look different. He wanted to show that Buffy is still the same good person that she was before.

Sex In Buffy The Vampire Slayer

Before we get to Spoilers and Foreshadowing, there are a few more things from the DVD commentary that deal with the issue of what *Buffy* as a show is saying about sex. (Which I wrote about previously when covering *Ted*.) Here, Whedon talks first about how he created the movie *Buffy the Vampire Slayer* to deal with that trope of the blond girl always being the victim. Also, that it always seemed like the girl had sex and got punished for it by being killed.

But in the series, they had to make Buffy younger, so that she could be in high school longer. So they made her a sophomore, and he felt like they had to deal with her first first time having sex. This storyline is the horror version of "I slept with my boyfriend and now he doesn't call me." Plus, he is killing people.

And Whedon said he really struggled with that because he didn't want to kill the girl who has sex. And yet the show does in a way punish her. But he said the thing is, in horror, eventually you end up punishing characters for everything they do. The distinction he tried to make from the trope is that the consequence to Buffy here, the punishment, is emotional. And she grows from it. She learned from it. And she doesn't get ax-murdered because she had sex.

The Most Important Buffy Episode

He also said that this two-part episode was the most important one that they did in *Buffy* on two different levels. For the network it was key because they had just moved *Buffy* to a new night and time, one that was better for any show. And the network was worried not enough audience would respond or come to the show to justify that. But Surprise and Innocence did.

To the writers, Whedon said it was most important because of the emotional resonance. And it showed how much the show had evolved. That it was a much harder-edged story than they had ever done.

He also commented on Angel changing – that was to avoid the Sam and Diane issue from the show *Cheers*. Where once the couple finally gets together, they become boring. So he came up with the idea of Angel turning evil almost the instant that they get together.

Finally, he talked about Surprise and Innocence being the mission statement of the show. It is at once mythic – it's the Hero's Journey, Buffy losing Angel and having to fight him. And it is the personal story. I slept with someone and he doesn't call me anymore.

Spoilers and Foreshadowing

THE END OF THE WORLD

I said in the Spoilers and Foreshadowing section for Surprise that Spike doesn't want to end the world. He likes the world. And I mentioned that by the time we get to the end of Season Two, that's where he says he likes the world.

In this episode, though, he does seem kind of gung ho about the end of the world. At least, he's irritated that Angel is delaying it. I read this, however, as not necessarily that Spike wants to wipe out the whole world. But he would not mind wiping out a bit of humanity, including a lot of Sunnydale. Because in the beginning of this episode he is so despondent and he feels like Sunnydale is just cursed for him and Dru.

I think that is the source of his saying "come on, let's start the end of the world."

The Moment Of True Happiness

Throughout *Buffy*, the characters will interpret Angel's curse and the one moment of true happiness as sex. Specifically, sex with Buffy. In Season Three when Angel comes back, that worries everybody. They fear Buffy and Angel will have sex again and Angel will lose his soul.

In *Angel* the show for a long time the curse is interpreted by almost all the characters (I actually think all of them) as Angel having sex with anybody. But we do get an episode where it's finally clarified that it isn't just sex. It is true happiness. Great love, true happiness. All of that together.

In *Buffy*, it is a fantastic development because this will forever stand in Buffy's and Angel's way. They will struggle with how to deal with it and be together or even be friends.

Buffy And Angel At The End

Now I'm really going to jump ahead, all the way to Season Seven. As we near the finale, I've always been confused by Angel coming back. Not that he comes back. But that conversation they have where he seems to be saying maybe Buffy will eventually choose to be with him. I don't get that because it was already settled both in *Buffy* and in *Angel* why they can't be together.

So I find it very odd because there's no solution for them that we have seen in either show. But it could be that his statement is justified in a way that I'm just not grasping right now.

Buffy's Abandonment Fears

The emotional fallout of this episode really resonates and informs Buffy's other relationships. When I wrote about spoilers in the episode Nightmares, I said I didn't find Buffy's abandonment fears all that believable by the time we get to Season Four's Fear Itself. And I mentioned how I really dislike the Parker Abrams story arc. (Where Buffy falls for Parker and sleeps with him and then pines over him for what seems like forever.)

Now that I'm doing the podcast and looking so closely, I realize that maybe I was too literal about Parker. Because he's the next person Buffy sleeps with, and he is such a jerk. It plays out in a very mundane way. He sleeps with her and then just doesn't call her again. And I realize now that maybe the reason Buffy has so much trouble getting over him is that it isn't about Parker.

It's about Angel. And in fact, Spike taunts her with the comparison between Parker and Angel in the episode where he gets a ring with a gem that makes the wearer invincible.

The Audience And Oz

Finally, I found it really interesting that Joss Whedon talked about the audience not wanting Willow to be with Oz. Then he wrote that scene where Willow really falls for Oz, and so the audience loves him too. He must've thought he needed to do that because otherwise Phases, where Oz finds out he's a werewolf, wouldn't have the emotional impact it does.

Questions For Your Writing

- Look over a scene where your characters feel strong emotions. Is there a setting that might impact your characters (and so your readers) more intensely?
- If your main character feels great love for someone else (any type of love, it doesn't need to be romantic) will your readers understand why? If not, can you bring that out through dialogue or action that still advances the subplot or the main plot?
- Find a spot in your story where you feel stuck or hemmed in by what you wrote up to this point. Can you find a creative way to move the plot forward or explain the obstacle so that it underscores a theme or further develops a character?
- Do your subplots intersect with the main plot in interesting ways or move it forward?
- Are your characters invested in your subplots?

Next: Phases

NEXT WE'LL TALK about Phases, where Willow wants to move her relationship with Oz forward but, unknown to her, he just figured out he's a werewolf. This episode raises key questions about protagonists, themes, and giving your audience clues without revealing too much.

CHAPTER 3
PHASES (S2 E15)

THIS CHAPTER TALKS ABOUT PHASES, Season Two Episode Fifteen, where Oz discovers a beast within. Written by Rob DesHotel and Dean Batali and directed by Bruce Seth Green. In particular, we'll look at:

- Why Buffy is the protagonist of this key episode for Willow and for Oz;
- Humor and character development that hide clues from the audience; and
- Philosophy, theme, and who Buffy believes she's allowed to kill (or not) because she's the Slayer.

Okay, let's dive into the Hellmouth.

BEFORE CONFLICT, **Call Back**

Remember that our opening conflict, which sometimes relates to our main plot and sometimes doesn't, exists to draw audience members or readers in before we get to that Story Spark or Inciting Incident that sets off the main plot.

Here, the episode begins with three opening conflicts and the Story Spark, all in the teaser part of the episode before the credits. (Also known as the cold open.)

What's kind of amazing is that even before we get to that, we have a short call back to The Witch. All of this in less than 5 minutes.

Oz is in the hallway looking at a cheerleader trophy. In The Witch, Amy's mom became trapped in that trophy. None of our characters knows that, although they do know that the statue or trophy is of Amy's mom. As Oz stands in front of it, he's kind of moving from side to side.

Willow walks up, and he says something like, "This cheerleader trophy. It's like its eyes follow you wherever you go. I like it."

Opening Conflicts In Phases

Now we go to our opening conflict. The first one is between Willow and Oz.

Willow asks did he like the movie last night. She is really asking did he have a good time with her, but he answers the literal question. And does a very short mini critique on movies.

Oz: You know, movies today, they're like popcorn. You forget them as soon as they're done. But I really like the popcorn.

Willow: Well, I had fun.

She's doing a little bit of hinting, trying to see how he feels. He is not getting it. They continue this kind of awkward back-and-forth until Buffy appears. Willow says something very awkward like, "Oh, there is my friend, and I will go to her."

New Character Conflict (Larry)

We now get a second hint of conflict here, which is when Larry, a new character, knocks a girl's books out of her arms. As she bends over to get them, he looks at her butt and makes a sleazy comment. He also looks at Buffy and Willow as they walk away and says to Oz something like, "I'd love to get some of that Buffy-Willow action if you know what I mean."

And we get a great quote from Oz:
Oz: That's great, Larry. You've really mastered the single entendre.

Larry gives Oz a hard time about dating a junior and asks how far he's gotten.

We cut to Buffy and Willow. Willow says, "Nowhere!" So clearly Buffy has asked a similar question, but with a much different intent.

Note in that conflict with Larry and Oz, a lot happens. We establish Larry as this new character who harasses girls. We also doubled down on Oz's humor. Later on, Oz will make a similar dry comment that seems like it's there to show his humor and wit again, but it's actually a clue to what's happening.

Relationships

Willow tells Buffy she doesn't want to be the only girl in school without a real boyfriend. Buffy looks sad and Willow immediately picks up on it. She says she's sorry, and asks how Buffy is doing. Buffy says it's hard, but it would help if the three of them could get together and share the misery as they often do.

Willow makes a snippy comment about Xander and Cordelia. But she does agree that they should get together.

So we've done a really nice thing there by getting in some very quick back story about Angel and Buffy, Willow and Oz, and Willow finding out about Cordelia. If you hadn't seen the prior episode, you wouldn't necessarily understand all of what happened. But you would get the sense of where these characters are. And what these relationships are about.

Next we see Cordelia and Xander making out in her car in a wooded area where students go to park.

Xander breaks away and says, "What does she see in him?" Cordelia says all he does is talk about Buffy, Buffy, Buffy or

Willow, Willow, Willow. And she tells him to shut up. And they kiss.

This adds to the conflict and provides more quick exposition. Because we get this tension between Cordelia and Xander where Xander always seems to be focusing on anything and anyone other than Cordelia.

The Story Spark

At 4 minutes 33 seconds in we get our Story Spark or Inciting Incident that sets off our main monster plot. Usually this comes about 10% into an episode, and it does that here. (The episodes are generally 43-44 minutes.) We hear growling, and we see this beast. Cordelia and Xander, though, are at the moment unaware of it.

This is the spark that sets off the werewolf story. It also gives us a classic horror set up.

After the credits, Xander says he thinks he heard something. Cordelia didn't, and she's mad at him, again thinking he is just being distracted. Then a claw comes through the cloth convertible roof. She throws the car in gear and drives away, throwing the beast off the roof. Xander says, "Told you I heard something."

The next day, Buffy looks at the shredded top of the convertible. Xander says it was a werewolf. Cordelia says it's so awful and follows up with, "Daddy just had this car detailed." Giles tells them that animal carcasses were mutilated last night, though no people were injured yet. He guesses the werewolf will be back at the next full moon.

Willow points out that last night was the night before the full moon. I love that Willow knows something, or pays attention to something, that Giles missed. He's very intrigued because this is one of the classics. All the others give him these looks.

Self-Defense Class

We switch to gym class and a session on self-defense. The teacher tells them to get in their assigned groups.

Xander is near Larry and notices that Larry has a scar. Larry says last week a huge dog jumped out of the bushes and bit him. He needed thirty-nine stitches. Oz says he's been there. He holds up his index finger and says cousin Jordy just got his grown up teeth in, and he does not like to be tickled. Larry rolls his eyes.

This is that moment I was talking about. We have set this up as an episode where we get to know Oz better. And this seems like just the third example of showing Oz's personality. But really we've just learned about the incident that turned Oz into a werewolf.

Larry goes over to Teresa, another student I don't think that we've seen before. He says something gross to her and then:

Larry: Oh, we're in the same group. I may have to attack you.

Teresa: Oh, there are a few people in our group.

Buffy is one of them. She gives Larry this great look. Willow, though, pulls Buffy aside and reminds her she's supposed to be a "meek little girlie girl like the rest of us."

Buffy's attempt to be the meek little girlie girl doesn't work. The teacher has the boys stand behind the girls. She's trying to show the girls how to flip an attacker behind them over their shoulder. Buffy pretends to try and be unable to. Larry says she's turning him on, and she immediately flips him onto his back on the mat.

I don't think it's too much of a spoiler to say this: Buffy – never great at undercover.

Giles Explains Werewolves

In the library, Giles explains more about werewolves, using a globe and a model moon. He talks about how the moon brings out the darkest qualities and the werewolf is an extreme representation of inborn animalistic traits. Pure instincts, predatory.

Buffy: Typical male.

Giles: Don't jump to conclusions.

Buffy: I didn't jump. I took a tiny step and there conclusions were.

That line may be one of my favorite Buffy quotes ever.

Giles, though, points out that this could be a woman, not a man. He also tells them they will not be making any silver bullets. This is a being who is human most of the time and might not even know about being a werewolf. They need to bring the werewolf back alive. Buffy agrees.

About 11 minutes in, Giles and Buffy are in that parking area. They've split up to look around. When they meet again, Buffy starts to tell Giles gossip about who she saw making out with whom. He wants to go around and ask people if they've seen anything.

Buffy: Giles, no one's seen anything.

The One-Quarter Twist In Phases

We are now getting to our One-Quarter Twist. This is the first major plot turn. It generally comes from outside the protagonist and spins our story in a new direction. Usually, we see it about a quarter way through the story, though in network television (as opposed to movies or books) it shifts around a little bit more. I think because it is timed for commercial breaks. Here, we get it right before the commercial at about 12 minutes. So that is a bit past our one quarter mark.

Buffy is walking through a more wooded area. She steps on something and gets caught in a rope net or trap that pulls her up. She's hanging from a tree branch and trapped. We hear a man's voice say, "Gotcha." This guy with a gun appears, and we cut to a commercial.

So we have this hook almost literally with Buffy hanging there.

Now that this turn happened, the story takes a new direction. It shifts from Buffy trying to figure out who the werewolf is and stopping it to Buffy racing against this guy (who tells her his name is Cain) who wants to find the werewolf first and kill it for its pelt and teeth.

Predatory Behavior

Cain is another example in this episode of a character who is almost a caricature of the predatory male. I should say of predatory male behavior. We also saw that in Larry, and Giles alluded to it, though he was talking about the werewolf.

Cain tells Giles he's impressed seeing him with Buffy –it's "good to get the fruit while it's fresh." So gross. Which Giles immediately points out. And Buffy says it's not what Cain thinks, they're hunting werewolves. Cain laughs at that and says, "Well, this guy looks like he's auditioning to be a librarian" and she's a girl.

He tells them he has a tooth from each of his kills, and he sells werewolf pelts. Buffy says doesn't he care that a werewolf is a person twenty-eight days out of the month? And Cain says that's why he only hunts them the other three.

Cain does give them some good information. He tells them werewolves are drawn to locations with a lot of sexual heat. Buffy claims she has no idea where that might be. But of course, as soon as Cain is gone, she tells Giles she knows where to look.

Angel Attacks, Willow And Cordelia Commiserate

First, though, we cut to Teresa walking home in the dark. She thinks she hears something. Growling. She's looking back over her shoulder as she runs, and she runs right into Angel. He plays the nice guy, reassures her there's no one behind her. And says something like, "Oh don't I know you? You go to school with Buffy."

Teresa is very relieved that he knows Buffy. This makes him seem familiar and safe. He says he'll walk her home.

Now we switch to the Bronze.

Cordelia and Willow are sitting together and talking as band plays. Cordelia is complaining about Xander. It's always Buffy did this and Willow says that. And then he acts all confused when she calls him on it. Willow says she and Oz are in some kind of holding pattern, but without the holding. They both agree that the problem is that Oz and Xander are a couple of guys.

I really like this character development. Despite Willow's snarky comment about Cordelia earlier, we see them becoming friends. And this to me is one of the strengths of the show. While it does use classic setups for conflict like love triangles, it almost never falls back on the clichés. So we don't have Cordelia and Willow feuding with each other over Xander. Instead, though Willow is upset about Xander and Cordelia and Cordelia knows that, they are commiserating. They're there for each other.

And it's particularly interesting because in our pilot, Cordelia was so mean to Willow. She clearly viewed Willow as far beneath her socially. This reflects that none of our core characters are defined by only one relationship or one role in their lives.

Werewolf At The Bronze

A werewolf drops in, or jumps in, right in front of Willow and Cordelia seemingly from nowhere. (I guess he jumped down from that kind of catwalk balcony area on the second level of the Bronze.) Everyone screams and runs.

Giles and Buffy pull up in Giles' car. Buffy goes inside. The Bronze now is pretty much deserted. She looks around the stage for the wolf. She has a chain with her, and when she sees the wolf, she swings the chain until it wraps around the werewolf's neck. But it gets away from her.

Cain comes in right after that and makes a comment about what happens when a woman does a man's job. Which does not phase Buffy, irritating as it is. But then he says something that does hit her: if the wolf harms anyone it's on her head. (Of course, he says "pretty little head.") Buffy tells him she lives with that every day. And we see how it weighs on Buffy that every time she can't stop a demon, monster, or Angel, somebody can be killed.

Outside of the Bronze, the wolf is following a scent. He finds Teresa's body. Angel is standing over it in vamp face. They growl at each other. Angel backs off.

This scene seems to me to be here solely to provide that classic vampire meets the werewolf moment. And to give us a little more time with Angel. I really enjoy it despite that it doesn't move the narrative along.

Ideally, we want every scene to have some significant character development or move the story. This does neither. But it's fun, and it's quick, and I think it works because the story overall has so much emotional impact.

Midpoint Reversals In Phases

Now we're coming up to our Midpoint. Usually we see a major commitment by the protagonist here, or she suffers a major reversal.

Here, we have something a little bit different and interesting. We have two reversals for Buffy. One that appears to be a very direct reversal for her, and one that is somewhat indirect. Because its first impact (that we see) is on Oz and, by extension, on Willow.

Buffy and Giles patrol the parking area again at 21 minutes 4 seconds in. So just a little before halfway through the episode, very close to our Midpoint.

Buffy gets in the car, and they hear a radio news report about Teresa that says she was killed. It's linked to the recent animal attacks. We can see in Buffy's face and body language how hard that hits her. She says (either here or little bit later) that she should have killed the wolf when she had the chance.

This seems like our Midpoint Reversal. And then the show surprises us with another one at 21 minutes 18 seconds in.

The wolf is lying in a field. Dawn is breaking, and the wolf changes into Oz. (I was truly shocked the first time I saw this.) Oz opens his eyes, sits, looks around. He's naked. And in his very understated way, he says, "Now that's odd."

What Happened Last Night?

Now that I'm re-watching so closely it occurs to me that this is the second night the werewolf has been out. On the first night did Oz just come back into bed as a werewolf and put the covers over himself, wake up as Oz, and not know anything happened?

I guess that's the implication here. Because he is surprised. At any rate this reversal, as I mentioned, directly impacts Oz and it impacts Willow. And I do see it as well as a reversal for Buffy. Now the werewolf isn't only a human being, which already was a concern for her. It is a human being that her best friend has fallen for.

What Makes Buffy The Protagonist?

Which brings me to the question: why am I framing this from Buffy's perspective? Why do I see her as the protagonist?

Our protagonist, ideally, should:

1. have a goal that she actively pursues
2. be the main point of view character and
3. have the most at stake.

Goals And Viewpoints

Here, out of Buffy, Oz, and Willow, only Buffy has a goal she actively pursues throughout the episode. Up until this point Oz hasn't had any goal. Buffy has had the goal to find and stop the werewolf.

There is a Willow-Oz subplot. And while you could see Willow as the protagonist of that subplot, she is not actively pursuing a goal for much of the episode. She is unhappy that the relationship is not moving forward. She doesn't know where she stands with Oz. And this grew out of the last episode where he didn't want to kiss her because he felt she was trying to get even with Xander. Now she is feeling like okay, he said he wanted to wait, and he said he'd give it time, but it's too much time. Still, Willow isn't actively pursuing that through much of the episode.

She does start to do that, though. So I'll take back what I just said. I think it is a subplot with Willow as the protagonist. It's just we've only gotten to the initial conflict or maybe the Inciting Incident part of it. We haven't yet gotten to where Willow is actively doing anything.

Buffy, though, is the only one actively pursuing a goal for our main plot. She also is our main point of view character. We follow Buffy the most often. We do get a very small amount of Oz's point of view. We get more of Willow's, and a tiny bit of Cordelia's.

But Buffy is the one of all of them who has the most screen time and whom we follow the most.

What's At Stake

Who has the most at stake is a little bit fuzzier.

Certainly, Oz has a lot at stake here. Cain could kill him. Willow has a lot at stake. Both emotionally, because she has fallen for Oz, and physically, because Oz as a werewolf poses a danger to her.

But Cain tells Buffy it's on her head if anyone gets killed, and she fears that maybe she should've killed the werewolf. That gives her the most at stake in the sense that she is charged with protecting everyone in Sunnydale. Not just herself, and not just her boyfriend or her friend's boyfriend.

This also threatens her philosophy and worldview as the Slayer, and I'll talk a little bit more about that right before the Foreshadowing and Spoiler section.

The werewolf is a particular challenge. Because the werewolf is human for most of the month and only a werewolf for three days. It puts the werewolf in this gray area that threatens Buffy's mission. Or at least her view of her mission and herself as the Slayer.

Another Great Hook

So we have found this thing out about Oz, huge reveal, and of course we cut to a commercial. It's one of those great hooks that Buffy uses to keep us coming back. Always a thing to think about when you're ending your chapters.

After the commercial, Oz is on the phone with his Aunt Maureen.

Oz: Is Jordy a werewolf?... And how long has that been going on?... No reason.

Impact On Oz

Then we get the impact on Oz. He is walking through the halls. The sounds around him, from his point of view, are a bit hollow – much the way Buffy heard the world when the bounty hunters were coming after her. So we see that maybe it was only talking with his aunt that made this sink in with Oz. Before that, he knew something was off because he woke up in a field naked but he didn't know for sure that he was the werewolf.

He walks into the library in the midst of a conversation. Buffy says she can't believe she let the wolf go, that Cain was right, and she should've killed it when she had the chance. Oz asks if anyone got bitten or scratched and Buffy says Teresa's dead. Oz looks stricken and Giles says there's one more night.

As Oz says, "Another night," his whole body sags. He puts his hands on the library table. His shoulders hunch. We have truly never seen Oz appear distraught before. So while this is a relatively small body language change, it telegraphs so much because normally Oz is unflappable.

Identifying The Werewolf

Xander says he can find the werewolf because of his experience with being the hyena. And he goes into this whole thing about how he knows that urge for freshly killed meat. Buffy and Willow remind him that he said he didn't remember any of that (from The Pack). He kind of rushes past that. He looks around and says, "Wait a second. The answer is right in front of us."

Xander's looking at Oz, and Oz looks frightened. But Xander says, "I'm Larry." He says it's clear given how Larry behaves. Xander is going to go talk to him.

It's an interesting choice for the audience to know the truth here. That is dramatic irony, where we know something that our main characters do not. Here I think it's partly for the humor in the next scene. We get that there is this misunderstanding going on, but Xander doesn't.

But it is also for the intensity and the emotion in this scene. We feel Oz's tension in a way that we could not if we didn't know what Oz knows. Because the other characters don't really pick up how upset Oz is.

The Limits Of First-Person Point Of View

I'm kind of jealous that I can't use dramatic irony in my current series because it is first-person and limited to my character Quille's point of view. My previous series (the Awakening supernatural thriller series) featured multiple points of view so I could do that. The audience could learn something key from a minor character that my main characters didn't know. That can be so great for ratcheting up the tension.

But in first person, the audience can only know what the main character, or the viewpoint character, knows.

Willow Tries Again

Willow does notice that there is something going on with Oz because she asks if he is okay, and she attributes it to him knowing Teresa. She says she knows he knew Teresa. And he says he is trying not to think about it, it's a lot. Willow says he could help her research, but he tells her he's busy, he's gotta go.

Buffy overhears and looks sad for Willow. They both take it as Oz not being as interested in Willow as she is in him. Or at least as Oz just not picking up on things and not moving the relationship forward.

Larry And Xander

We then get this scene with Larry and Xander in the locker room. Xander says to Larry, "I know your secret. I know what you're hiding." Larry threatens Xander, but Xander says hurting him won't make the issue go away. And Larry says what, he wants hush money?

But Xander reassures him he knows what Larry's going through, and he just wants to help. That Larry should talk about it. And Larry says that's fine for Xander but Larry has a reputation. "How are people going to look at me after they find out I'm gay?"

Xander now looks shocked. But Larry feels great now that he said the words. He's grateful to Xander for helping him and says that knowing Xander went through what he did, went through the same thing, made it easier for him to admit it. Xander laughs very awkwardly, looks a little panicked, and says, "No, I'm not – "

And Larry says, "Don't worry. I wouldn't do that to you. Your secret is safe with me."

This scene, looking at it twenty-some years later, can be read a couple different ways. At the time, in a number of shows you would have what some call Gay Panic. Where the joke was supposed to be hey, it's okay to be gay (think of *Friends*), not that there's anything wrong with that, but the guy panics at the idea that anyone would think that *he* is gay.

The reason I feel like there is more to it than that, or it is not meant to be that, is Larry says he does not think people in Sunnydale High would be accepting. So he feels he needs to hide. It could perhaps be a dangerous thing to admit. Sunnydale High isn't the safest place to be.

Also, I don't read Xander -- and I could be wrong – saying being gay is scary thing or that's it's a bad thing. But some audience members might feel that we should just have left out this scene.

Back at the library as they are researching, Buffy suggests to Willow that maybe she needs to do something daring and make the first move with Oz. Separately, Xander tells Buffy that Larry's not the werewolf. And Buffy talks about how bad she feels about not being able to save Teresa.

As they talk, she realizes that the news reports did not say that Teresa was mauled, which would be consistent with the werewolf.

Teresa Delivers A Message

We cut to the funeral home. Teresa is lying in the coffin. Buffy moves a scarf on her neck and we see a vampire bite. First, Xander is saying, "Oh this is good. It's not a werewolf." And then he says something like, "Oh. There's no good here," because it's just something else Buffy couldn't save Teresa from. Xander says she can't blame herself for every death.

Teresa rises from coffin. She and Buffy fight. Buffy is about to stake her.

Teresa: Angel sends his love.

This catches Buffy off guard. And Teresa is able to overpower her. Proving Angel's point that he made to Spike in Innocence – that to kill Buffy, you have to work from the inside. You have to love her. Get into her heart.

Teresa's on top of Buffy, about to bite her and Xander stakes Teresa from behind.

Xander And Buffy

Xander helps Buffy up and hugs her and holds her.

Xander: He's not the same guy you knew, Buffy.

She gives Xander this look that could be interpreted as romantic and walks away.

Xander: Oh no, my life's not too complicated.

That part of the scene has never quite worked for me. I really feel like this is here because maybe there were fans still shipping Xander and Buffy. Or the network thought that this should be held out there, the idea that maybe they'll get together. It's one of the rare times there is a moment in Buffy where what the characters do just doesn't work for me.

Moving Toward The Three-Quarter Turn In Phases

We are now at 33 minutes in. We're moving toward the Three-Quarter Turn in the plot. That's the next major plot turn. It should grow out of that Midpoint Commitment or Reversal and spin the story in another new direction.

Before we get there, we see Cain. He's in his truck and he's making silver bullets. The full(ish) moon is rising. (It's the night after the full moon, but it still looks full.)

Oz is at his place. He's gotten out these rusty metal cuffs and chains from a box. Someone knocks on the door. It's Willow. We're at 34 minutes in, and we're getting a turn where Willow puts herself directly in the path of the werewolf.

I see this as arising from that Midpoint Reversal where we learned Oz was turned into a werewolf. And it was a reversal for our protagonist, Buffy, because now it was not just a human she had to fight but someone she knew and cared about.

I talked earlier about the the idea of Teresa's death being a reversal for Buffy because she couldn't save Teresa. Now we realize that was not a reversal for this episode because the werewolf didn't kill Teresa. So it doesn't really serve as an episode Midpoint Reversal for Buffy. Yet it is still a personal reversal because Angel killed Teresa. Not just a generic vampire that Buffy never ran across but Angel. Buffy still feels she was responsible for his turn into Angelus.

On Not Letting A Character Talk

Next we get a great Willow ramble.

She's angry. Oz tries to tell her this isn't a good time. But Willow says she had this whole thing to say worked out. She had it written down, but it didn't make any sense when she was reading it back. So she just kind of free forms with the things Oz did that made her think he really liked her, including something I love – that he tucked her tag back into her shirt. But now he's backing away. She goes on and says that Buffy says a girl has to make the first move.

Willow: And now that I'm saying this, I'm starting to think that the written version sounded pretty good but you know what I mean.

This is a great example of a genuine misunderstanding and difficulty communicating. We've all seen those scenes on TV or in movies where someone comes in to tell something vital that maybe could stop the other person from getting killed. And the other person won't let the character talk.

Most of the time I see those and find them frustrating and artificial. Because in real life, if I came in to tell you something like that and you were insisting on talking about something else, I would stop you. I'm a fairly soft-spoken person when I'm not arguing in court. But I would just cut that person off. I'd probably put my hand on their chest and say Stop. Or put my hand up and say Stop, or I'd yell over that person. Whatever it took to get their attention.

And yet so often in TV and movies the character doesn't do that. They just let the other person keep them from speaking.

Conflict Arising From Characterization

Here, though I believe this scene. Willow is so angry that she's going into all of this. We established that Oz is still in shock. He is still processing this. So I feel like he just doesn't have the words to tell her. Also, I don't think he's ready to tell her. And she's angry that he's home when he told her he was busy, so the situation increased her anger. She says that now he's here doing nothing rather than being with her. Oz tells her he's going through some changes. She says she's going through a lot, too. And Oz says, "Not like me." And then she sees the chains and the handcuffs and kinda trails off, and she's very confused.

The other thing that makes Oz not cutting Willow off work is that we've established that Oz is a man of few words. He doesn't ramble. He doesn't express emotions in a big way. So I think that goes to the idea that he doesn't quite know how to jump in and stop this. Or he's not quite ready to do it. But finally he tells Willow get out.

The Change Puts Willow In Peril

Oz staggers behind the couch. We see him changing into the wolf. Willow can't see it until he rises up and he is the wolf.

The special-effects here, especially looking back twenty-some years, are not great. Even at the time the wolf looked a little goofy. But I'm willing to go with it. Especially because Willow is in peril. She sees him, screams, and runs outside.

She gets over this fence just before he catches up. Once she's over he tries to follow. Willow hits him with a garbage can.

And we do a quick cut to Cain, who hears a werewolf howl. This moment reminds us of the danger Oz is in from Cain.

At the library, Buffy tells Giles about Teresa.

We cut back to Willow running through the woods. She stumbles and falls. The wolf catches up with her. But then stops, sniffs the air, and follows a scent to this piece or pile of raw meat.

Willow runs into the library and says, "It's Oz, it's Oz." Then we get a nice back and forth:

Giles: Are you certain?

Willow: Can't you just trust me on this?

(That whole sequence, watching it now when I know what's going to happen, makes me wonder about the layout of Sunnydale. Where exactly are these woods? Willow runs on the sidewalk and then she's in the woods and then she's in the library. I don't know.)

The Climax

So we are at the Climax, where we bring the main plot to a close and bring our opposing forces together. 37 minutes 47 seconds in Cain aims his gun as the wolf bends over the meat. So he left that as a way to lure the wolf.

I like this because Cain inadvertently saved Willow. And it is somewhat set up because we saw earlier when Cain caught Buffy, he was trying to catch the werewolf with a trap. So it fits. Otherwise, it would seem too convenient that Cain does this just in time to save Willow.

At the last second, Buffy kind of comes out of nowhere and kicks Cain. Then she fights the werewolf, trying very hard not to get scratched.

Giles has a tranquilizer gun, but he can't use it because Buffy and the werewolf are spinning around and around. Willow ultimately ends up with the gun and shoots Oz.

He falls.

Willow: I shot Oz.

Giles: You saved us.

Willow's Character Growth

Though Buffy is pivotal to all of it and to the resolution, as is Giles, Willow is the one who shoots.

I see this as key for Willow's character. It shows that Willow is so strong in the sense that she is able to grab that gun and shoot Oz despite her feelings for him. She is not letting her emotions or her love for him blind her to the danger. And she's making a choice to stop him.

Now, is it a deliberate choice? Most people are acting on instinct in these kinds of moments. But her instinct still is to protect herself. Protect her friends and others by stopping Oz.

The Falling Action

We move to the Falling Action. That is the part of the story where we tie up the loose ends.

Cain says no wonder the town is overrun with monsters. No one's man enough to kill them. Buffy has his rifle. And she says,

"Don't be too sure of that," and she bends it into a loop so it's unusable. She hands it back to him and says something like, "Don't let the door hit you on the way out."

Giles reassures Willow that while Oz will be a little sore tomorrow, he will be okay.

At school the next day Buffy and Xander are sitting at a table near the vending machines. Xander says it'll be so weird. He doesn't know how to look at him now that he knows so much about him. Buffy says he's still a human being most of the time, and Xander says, "Who are we talking about?"

And we realize he was talking about Larry and knowing Larry's secret.

The Danger Of Secrets

Another guy knocks a girl's books out of her arms as we saw Larry do in the beginning. She bends over to pick them up. The guy starts to make a comment. But Larry helps her retrieve her books and is really nice to her. Larry's story encapsulates one of the themes of the show. Which is about being who you are and the danger of secrets.

We saw Larry with his secret. He was behaving in this terrible way, either as a cover or because he couldn't admit something about himself. He even says to Xander (when he thinks that Xander is telling him he's gay) that, "Hey, maybe all those times I beat you up it was because I saw something in you that I didn't want to accept in myself."

So that is part of the message.

And with Oz, we see that in a different way. Oz is this huge danger to Willow, to everyone, until he becomes aware of who he is and can take precautions to deal with it. So during the time when Oz is human, everything's fine. And we'll see in the next scene he's going to have to lock himself up on those three nights.

Xander says to Buffy – at first as a joke and then for real – that he is worried Willow's not safe with Oz.

Xander: If it were up to me –
Buffy: Xander, it's not up to you.

Oz And Willow Move Forward

We cut to Oz and Willow. This is where we tie up what's going to happen with Oz. He says Giles told him he'll be okay. He just has to lock himself up three nights a month.

Oz: Only he used more words than that. And a globe.

Oz says he didn't tell Willow because he didn't know what to say. It's not every day you find out you're a werewolf. He says maybe it's best if he stays out of her way. But Willow says she's kind of okay with him being in her way. They agree they will keep seeing each other. She walks away. Then she comes back and kisses him.

This is the end of a three-beat involving Willow making the first move.

Initially we got Buffy saying maybe you need to do something daring and make the first move. Then we got Willow trying to make the first move, and I guess she does make it. She shows up at Oz's, but she can't follow through because she finds out he's a werewolf. So that is the second reference to Willow making the first move. And now we get Willow actually making that first move.

They're both very happy.

Werewolf In Love

Oz, after she's walked away, turns, looks at the camera, and says to himself, "A werewolf in love."

I don't love this moment. It's rare that Buffy breaks the fourth wall between the show and the audience. I'm not sure it ever does it other than this.

What's interesting is I always forget that this is here. Every time I watch this episode, I'm surprised by it. I think in my head I edit that scene out. It ends for me when Willow kisses him and she walks away and they both look so happy.

There is no DVD commentary for this week. But before we

get to Spoilers and Foreshadowing, I want to share a couple things from *Buffy the Vampire Slayer and Philosophy: Fear and Trembling in Sunnydale*, edited by James B. South.

You're Not Who I Thought You Were

First, an essay by Tracy Little (*High School Is Hell: Metaphor Made Literal In Buffy the Vampire Slayer*). Little pointed out that a theme of You're Not Who I Thought You Were is woven throughout Season Two. And we saw that already. We saw it with Giles in A New Man, with Buffy realizing there is this hidden side to Giles. We just saw it with Angel turning to Angelus. And in Ted, Joyce's boyfriend. Also, Buffy's friend Ford, whom she had such a crush on, in Lie To Me comes to Sunnydale High and tries to use her. To trade her life for his.

And we also found out last week about Jenny being from the clan that cursed Angel. So again, something hidden, something in a close romantic relationship, often that is unknown. You're Not Who I Thought You Were. Now we have this with Oz.

High School Is Hell

This theme also fits the show's High School Is Hell metaphor because it's the time in life when more and more young adults are realizing that their parents are not necessarily who they thought they were. This can often be a source of great disappointment and even anger. We see Buffy go through that with Giles in The Dark Age (where Giles's past comes back to haunt him in the form of a demon he and his friends raised when they were young).

Also, it is that age where often the first love and first sexual experience occurs. There are intense emotions and hormones and attachments. That very difficult lesson many people learn at that stage – you're not who I thought you were – can also happen later. But it can have so much impact as a teenager to find out that person you've fallen for, that you feel so smitten with, is truly not who you thought. We really see that metaphor again here with Oz, though it plays out in a much less awful way than the Buffy-Angel experience of it.

Feminism And The Ethics Of Violence

The other essay that talks about Oz is *Feminism And The Ethics Of Violence, Why Buffy Kicks Ass* by Mimi Marinucci, goes to the theme of this episode and to why I think that the stakes are so high for Buffy. The essay explores who can Buffy kill. And makes the point that Buffy kills vampires and monsters, but not always. Only when they're a threat. So Marinucci argues this "suggests Buffy does not use violence against vampires, demons, and monsters insofar as they are vampires, demons, and monsters. Instead, she uses violence against willing agents of evil."

This episode is one of the earliest and most explicit examples of this.

We saw a little bit of it when Xander was possessed by the hyena. But here we see it in more depth. Buffy doesn't want to kill the werewolf even before she knows it's Oz. Because the vast majority of the time, the werewolf is human and not a threat. And there's an intent and knowledge question. She didn't kill Xander as a hyena, though he was a threat and a danger, because he hadn't chosen to be a hyena. She didn't think he was in control. Likewise, here, Giles makes the point that the werewolf might not know that it is a werewolf. And, by inference, it didn't choose to be a werewolf.

Buffy's choice further develops her as a hero. Though she briefly regrets not killing the wolf when she thinks it killed Teresa, I think even if Teresa had been killed by the werewolf, she ultimately still would've brought that tranquilizer gun.

Spoilers and Foreshadowing

Cordelia's Feelings For Xander

The scene before the credits with Xander and Cordelia in the car shows that Cordelia has stronger feelings than does Xander. Or at least she's more focused on their relationship than Xander is.

Cordelia's complaints later to Willow in the Bronze emphasize that. Because now that Willow knows, Cordelia is fairly open about her feelings about Xander (though she shares them by expressing irritation that he's always talking about Buffy and Willow). This openness heightens how much we feel for Cordelia in the next episode. Though she breaks up with Xander, we realize that she really does care about him. And this episode builds up to that.

A Female Werewolf And A Possessive Xander

Very minor foreshadowing: Giles mentions the werewolf could be female. And in Season Four we will see a female werewolf that will be key to a whole Oz storyline.

Also, Xander says Oz isn't good for Willow, and he is worried about Willow. And Buffy says, "Xander, It's not up to you." We will see Xander continuing to have these possessive feelings about Buffy and Willow and who they get involved with. Particularly with Buffy. Xander is very negative about her relationships. The only guy he really likes is Riley, and I have to wonder if that's because he senses that Riley is not there for the long term.

You can obviously also argue that Riley doesn't pose any physical danger to Buffy. He's not a vampire. He's not a werewolf. He's not a monster. But it is interesting that he is the one guy that Xander likes to see Buffy with. And certainly this hints at how judgmental Xander will be when Buffy and Spike become involved.

Trust And Faith

Returning to the theme in the episode, and the point from the essay, about Buffy using violence only when she sees a vampire or demon as a threat – Buffy's view on this will be a source of conflict between Buffy and Faith. Next season when Faith discovers Angel's still alive, and Buffy has not told her that, Faith assumes that Angel is evil and tries to kill him.

That is the same episode where Gwendolyn Post, pretending to be a new Watcher, shows up and completely misleads Faith and manipulates her. I see that episode as a huge turning point for Faith, largely because Gwendolyn Post betrays her. But also because she feels betrayed by Buffy not telling her about Angel.

At least in the beginning, Faith has a more black-and-white view of everything than does Buffy. And in some ways that's great. She takes more joy in life than Buffy because she doesn't see all the shades of gray and doesn't struggle as much with the moral complexities of being the Slayer.

This episode foreshadows that a bit. There will be numerous issues where Buffy has to make these decisions about how much of a threat another being poses to humans. And whether it is right for her to kill that being.

Spike And His Chip

Of course, that will be a huge issue with Spike when the Initiative puts that chip in his head in Season Four. It keeps him from harming humans, or at least from killing humans, but doesn't really change who he is. (At least not for much of the series.)

Many different times, different characters will think that Buffy should kill Spike and she will not do it.

Beasts And Aggression

Finally, this episode foreshadows parts of the Season Three episode where Angel comes back, Beauty And The Beasts. There, the show will further explore this relationship between the idea of male aggression and violence and the idea of a beast within. I'm looking forward to talking about it.

Questions For Your Writing

- Does your protagonist have a goal they actively pursue?
- What's at stake for your protagonist?
- Are most scenes written from your protagonist's point of view?
- Do your characters do or say anything that is necessary for the plot but is unbelievable?
- Are you weaving in clues for your audience? Can you use humor or character conflict to distract your audience from catching them?
- Viewed as a whole, does your story have a consistent theme? Is it a theme that resonates with you?

Next: Bewitched, Bothered And Bewildered

NEXT WE'LL TALK about Bewitched, Bothered And Bewildered. It starts as a light, fun episode and includes plenty of humor, but also foreshadows much of series. It also explores serious themes, including love versus obsession and being who you are.

CHAPTER 4

BEWITCHED, BOTHERED AND BEWILDERED (S2 E16)

THIS CHAPTER TALKS ABOUT BEWITCHED, Bothered And Bewildered, Season Two Episode Sixteen, where Xander tries a love spell with disastrous consequences. Written by Marti Noxon and directed by James A. Contner.

In particular, we'll look at:

- Foreshadowing of the season and series in what starts out as a light, fun episode;
- Themes of love versus obsession, leadership, and being who you are;
- Conflict that conveys exposition;
- A plot that forces character growth for Cordelia; and
- Numerous plot lines seamlessly woven together.

Okay, let's dive into the Hellmouth.

OPENING Conflict

We start, as we should, with conflict. Xander and Buffy are

in the graveyard. He shows her a silver heart necklace and asks if she thinks Cordelia will like it. Buffy doesn't quite understand what he sees in Cordelia and gives him a bit of a hard time about it. He says the only other person who interests him is unavailable and gives her a look.

Buffy more or less ignores that and tries to reassure him that yes, Cordelia will like the necklace. And we get the first of some great Xander quotes in this episode.

Xander: This is new territory for me. I mean, my Valentines are usually met with heartfelt restraining orders.

He also says that he wishes dating were more like slaying, with everything clear, no fuss, no muss. A vampire emerges from the grave and goes after Xander. Buffy fights it and she slays it. Afterwards she tells Xander that slaying is a little more perilous than dating.

He says she's obviously not dating Cordelia. And we go to the credits.

Internal v. External Conflict

This opening conflict focuses on internal conflict for Xander. While Buffy gives him a bit of a hard time about what he could possibly see in Cordelia, which is external conflict coming from another character, she is overall supportive and reassuring. He, though, expresses mixed feelings. While he wants Cordelia to like the necklace, he still makes it clear he's interested in Buffy. For the most part, he's saying she would be his first choice. At least that's how I read it.

Ambiguous feelings could lead to weak conflict. But here it's very strong in the sense that Xander's ambiguity will drive the episode. In fact, it's probably key to what goes wrong with the spell.

Cordelia's Friends Turn On Her

After the credits, we see Cordelia struggling with her own conflict. That also will play into our main plot.

At 2 minutes 42 seconds in, Cordelia walks up the steps to

school. She's calling after four girls, including her friend Harmony, to wait for her. They finally turn around.

Cordelia says to Harmony, "Why didn't you call me back last night?" and tells her they need to coordinate outfits for the dance. Cordelia then looks at another girl and says, "I'm wearing red and black, so you need to switch."

The girl, though, responds by asking if red and black is what Xander wants her to wear.

Cordelia: What does he have to do with it?

Harmony: Well, a girl wants to look good for her geek.

She then goes on to ask when Cordelia and Xander are going to start wearing cute little matching outfits because she's going to vomit. She leads the other girls away.

Cordelia stands alone, looking hurt.

Episode Theme: Who Is A Leader?

This begins one underlying theme of this episode about popularity, who is a leader, and who is a follower. Of Cordelia's friends in the series so far, Harmony has spoken the most. She may be the only one who has a name. But she has definitely been subservient to Cordelia, always trying to get Cordelia's approval. Now she's turning on Cordelia and becoming a leader herself. Or so it seems.

Bad Breakup?

At 3 minutes 29 seconds in, in class, the teacher tells the students they need to turn in their papers or get an F.

After the bell rings, Amy asks Willow if she and Buffy are going to the Valentine's dance. Willow looks really excited. Buffy tells her it's okay to say it. And Willow says, "My boyfriend's in the band!" Amy smiles and says that's cool and asks Buffy if she's going. Buffy says something about Valentine's Day is just a gimmick to sell chocolate.

Amy: Bad breakup?

Buffy: Believe me when I say Uh-huh.

Quick Exposition Through Conflict

As we see so often in *Buffy*, we got so much exposition through conflict in these three quick scenes. These weren't huge conflicts, but Willow was so happy, while Buffy clearly feels bad about her breakup. We also get a little bit of humor, all of which gets across that something terrible happened to Buffy romantically. And that Willow has a new boyfriend she's really excited about.

In the previous scene we learned very quickly that Xander is not in Cordelia's social circle and her friends looked down on her for dating him. And in the Xander-Buffy scene we learned quite a bit about his feelings about Cordelia and Buffy. And about his fears of rejection.

Regular viewers know all these things. If we tuned in for the first time ever, we might not understand everything about these characters. But based on these minor conflicts and the exposition they convey, we'd get a pretty good idea what's going on. Who these characters are, what the relationships are between them. And in less than 4 minutes.

The Story Spark

We're leading to our Story Spark or Inciting Incident that sets our main plot in motion.

At the end of class the students line up and hand in their papers one-by-one to the teacher. Amy, though, is empty-handed. But she gives the teacher this look, and the teacher thanks her and mimes taking a paper.

Xander sees this. It happens at 4 minutes 25 seconds in. That is often where we see the Story Spark – at 10% into an episode, novel, or a movie. These episodes are 42 to 44 minutes long so this is right at that 10%.

This moment sets our main plot in motion. Because if Xander hadn't seen Amy using her witchcraft, he couldn't later go to her about a love spell no matter how angry he felt at Cordelia.

In the hallway, Xander tells Buffy and Willow what he saw.

They all agree that Amy is the last person who should use witchcraft given what happened with her mother. So more quick exposition through a little bit of conflict in the sense that they are all concerned.

Tension With Jenny Calendar

Giles comes up and wants to talk to Buffy. At that moment Jenny emerges from her classroom.

She says, "Rupert," but he says, "Miss Calendar," which is what he called her before they knew each other well and dated. She says she wants to talk to him if he has a minute. Buffy is looking down at the floor through this whole exchange. And Giles says he doesn't have time right now, he needs to talk to Buffy about something. Buffy says, "Let's go."

Jenny walks off and both Willow and Xander look sad for her.

In the library, Buffy asks if Giles is okay. He says he'll be fine, though he doesn't really look it, and that he's more concerned about her.

Giles Warns About Angelus And Valentine's Day

In unusually vague terms, Giles warns Buffy about what Angel might do to her because it's Valentine's Day. He says Angel is prone to what he probably thinks of as brutal displays of affection. Giles also suggests Buffy stay off the streets. He'll patrol instead – better safe than sorry. After a long pause, Buffy says it's a little late for both.

Notice how we have a number of conflicts and plot lines in the episode so far. Xander's feelings for Cordelia and fears of rejection. Cordelia's conflict with wanting to remain popular and lead her friend group versus being with Xander. Amy using witchcraft despite that it had disastrous consequences for her mother.

Now we add Angel posing an escalating threat to Buffy because it's Valentine's Day. And as sort of a side note to that,

Buffy's feelings about this awful breakup being heightened and emphasized because of Valentine's Day.

All of these weave together so well throughout the episode, and now we'll get one more. It's not quite a subplot for the episode. But it is a subplot for this half of the season. The dynamic and conflict which creates a triangle between Spike and Angel and Drusilla.

The Triangle

The scene switches to the factory. We close up on a jewelry box that opens to show a beautiful necklace inside. As often is the case, we see the dark relationships mirroring Buffy's relationships and friendships.

Xander is planning to give the heart necklace to Cordelia, fearing rejection. Here, Spike gives this beautiful necklace to Drusilla. She loves it, which makes Spike happy. But just as he is saying nothing but the best for her, Angel drops a bloody heart on the table in front of her. He tells Drusilla he found it inside a quaint little shop girl. He also takes the necklace and puts it around Drusilla's neck. Spike, who is still in the wheelchair, starts to say he'll get it.

But Angel says, "Done." He adds that Spike has to admit it's much easier when Angel takes care of Drusilla.

Angel then ponders how best to send Buffy a message on Valentine's Day. Spike suggests ripping her lungs out. Angel says it lacks poetry, and Spike says it doesn't have to. Drusilla intervenes.

Dru: Don't worry, Spike. Angel always knows what speaks to a girl's heart.

That does not make Spike feel any better.

Roses And A Subplot One-Quarter Twist

At the Bronze, Willow happily watches Oz playing in the band. Xander is fiddling with the box with the necklace for Cordelia. She walks in looking stunning in a red dress.

She goes over to say hello to Harmony and the other girls, but they just turn away from her.

At Buffy's house, Buffy is watching videos with her mom and eating snacks. There's a knock on the door. Buffy goes to the front door, but no one's there. When she returns, Joyce is gone. She's in the kitchen. She found a long black box with a black ribbon at the back door. Inside are a dozen red roses and a card that says, "Soon."

We're moving toward the One-Quarter Twist. That is the first major plot turn that spins the story in a new direction. It generally comes from outside the protagonist. And from that point to the Midpoint the protagonist reacts to that twist.

This story is primarily about Xander and Cordelia. But the roses serve as a One-Quarter Twist in the Angel and Buffy Valentine's subplot, as this pushes Buffy to get more specific information from Giles.

Breakup At The Bronze

At the Bronze, Cordelia is sitting alone looking sad. Xander joins her. She says he looks good. He awkwardly says he let Buffy dress him and then amends it to say Buffy helped him pick out clothes. Cordelia says him looking good makes it harder.

Xander doesn't know what she's talking about, but he goes into a sort of speech that lets us know that maybe, despite all his comments about Cordelia, he is starting to feel something more. He says kissing once or twice could all be just hormones, but maybe there's something more. Maybe something in him sees something special in her and vice versa.

He gives her this necklace. This shows Xander's vulnerability. He is reaching out, trying to take what they had both been treating as just attraction to each other into something greater.

And in typical Joss Whedon fashion, just as Xander is taking this leap and showing this vulnerability, he is crushed. Cordelia thanks him for the necklace and says it's beautiful, seeming very genuine. Giving Xander what he wanted. And then she says, "I want to break up." She's sorry, but they just don't fit. Who are they kidding?

Xander: You know what's a good day to break up with someone? Any day but Valentine's Day.

The One-Quarter Twist In Bewitched, Bothered and Bewildered

That moment is the One-Quarter Twist in our main plot. It's 12 minutes 47 seconds in, so it is slightly past the one-quarter mark in the episode. Everything from here to the Midpoint will be put in motion by this.

At school the next day a random guy laughs at Xander for the way he was dumped. Harmony and her friends also laugh in his face.

Xander sees Amy and pulls her aside. He says the Hellmouth is finally going to work for him. He threatens to expose her using magic to fool the teacher unless she helps him. (It's not clear exactly how Xander's going to do that (expose Amy) since I don't think the adults in Sunnydale are ready to admit that magic exists. But I suppose he could show the teacher that Amy didn't really turn in the paper and she would fail the class.

He tells Amy he wants her to do a love spell. And we cut to a commercial.

A Love Spells Need Pure Intent

When we come back Amy tells Xander love spells are the hardest ones. It's a huge thing to make someone love you for all eternity. And Xander says wait, wait, wait, he doesn't want Cordelia to love him so that he can be with her. He wants her to fall in love with him so he can reject her and she can feel the pain he's feeling.

Amy: I don't know. Intent for a love spell has to be pure.

Xander says it is pure – pure desire for revenge. She finally agrees and tells him she'll need something that belongs to Cordelia.

This shows what I meant by Xander's ambiguity playing into and driving the plot. We're told intent has to be pure. Not only does Xander want revenge, I think he's partly acting out because he wasn't even certain there was more there with Cordelia. Somehow that makes it worse for him because he put himself out on this limb for someone he didn't feel sure was the right person for him.

That's my take on it. It could also be that he really does have these deep feelings he's not admitting to himself. But definitely not a pure intent.

In the library, Buffy gives Giles the card from Angel.

Buffy: Soon what, Giles? You never held out on me until the big bad thing in the dark became my ex honey.

And Giles says she's right, he will tell her what he learned in his research about Angelus.

Symbolism And Hearts

We switch to the hallway. Xander asks Cordelia for the necklace back. She says she thought it was a gift, but he insists. Now we see Cordelia's true feelings and vulnerability. She pretends the necklace is in her locker. But she is actually wearing it under her shirt. So she goes to her locker, opens the door to shield herself, and takes it off. She buttons up her shirt again, gives it to him, and says at least now she doesn't need to pretend to like it.

This is part of what makes us like Cordelia better. We have been building this, that she does have genuine feelings for Xander. It also sets up her having a change of heart at the end of the episode.

I don't think it's any mistake that the necklace is a heart necklace. It's not just an allusion to Valentine's Day, but it's an allusion to Cordelia's change of heart. And perhaps the heart that Angel dropped on the table for Drusilla is symbolic of her heart changing and being more drawn to Angel than Spike.

The Spell

About 17.5 minutes in, in a dark classroom with lit candles all around, Amy calls on the goddess Diana and casts a love spell.

The next day Xander walks through the halls, kind of swaggering, and heads straight for Cordelia. She's sitting with Harmony and her friends. But she's annoyed with him and asks if he's going stalker boy on her.

In the library, Giles lists terrible things Angel did to torment women that he loved. Buffy tells Giles he can skip the part about Angel nailing a puppy to a tree since she doesn't have a puppy.

Xander walks in complaining about how awful his life is. Giles is back in the stacks, researching. Buffy tells Xander she heard about him and Cordelia and it's Cordelia's loss. Then she tells him she'd really like it if the two of them could just get together that night and hang out. Maybe comfort each other.

Xander makes a joke about whether that comfort might include a lap dance, which he finds really comforting. And Buffy says if he plays his cards right and moves closer to him.

Xander says something like, "Okay, you, know you're talking to me, right? Xander." But Buffy says she was surprised how glad she felt when she heard about him and Cordelia breaking up.

Foreshadowing Payoff

So this is probably why we got that moment back in Phases with that little bit of tension between Buffy and Xander. It foreshadows or builds up that Xander might believe Buffy's interest is genuine.

Buffy: It's funny how you can see someone every day but not really see them, you know?

But just as they're about to kiss Amy interrupts.

Out in the hallway, she tells Xander she doesn't think the spell worked right. But she is pretty new at this so they can try again. He glances through the window in the door to the library. Buffy is sending him sultry looks.

He tries to put Amy off. But then she says they don't have to cast spells, they could just hang out.

Amy: You know, it's funny how you can see a person every day and not –

Xander: Not really see them.

Amy: Exactly.

She looks thrilled that Xander knew what she was thinking. Another girl comes up and wants to study with Xander. He says he has to go.

Midpoint Reversal As Xander Tries To Hide

We are now getting to the Midpoint of the episode. Here we normally see a major reversal for the protagonist or a major commitment. Xander is the protagonist here. (I'll talk about why later). But first we have this major reversal, I feel like this is a particularly interesting one. While it is part of the main plot, it is primarily a reversal about relationships. Which really fits because it's a Valentine's Day episode.

Xander goes home to get away from this chaos he created. And there he hurts the last person in the world he wants to hurt. Because when he sits down on his bed, Willow pops out from under the covers.

This is about 21.5 minutes in, so right about that Midpoint. She comes on to him and he tries to hold her off. He asks what about Oz. Willow says she doesn't care. She just wants Xander.

Xander tells her he cast a spell and it backfired. Willow ignores that and continues to step closer to him. She wants Xander to be her first, and they both know that it's right. Xander says this has to stop. And he runs.

At school, Harmony and the other girls shun Cordelia once again. And she asks what did she do now, wear red and purple together? Harmony says Xander is wounded because of

Cordelia, and only a sick pup would let Xander get away. No matter what her friends said.

Xander is back at school to seek help from Giles. All the girls stare at him and follow him.

Xander Confesses

Xander tells Giles he made a mess and cast a love spell. Jenny comes in and says she and Giles really need to talk. But she, too, becomes distracted by Xander, telling him what a nice shirt he's wearing, touching his shoulder, asking if he's been working out. All this as she is trying to convince Giles to give her another chance. Xander nods toward Jenny and looks desperately at Giles.

Giles: I cannot believe that you were fool enough to do something like this.

Xander: Oh no, I'm twice the fool it takes to do something like this.

Giles tells him people under love spells are deadly. They lose all reason. And he tells Xander not to leave the library, he'll find Amy and try to get her to reverse the spell.

Xander pushes the card catalog in front of the double doors, but unfortunately the doors swing outward. Buffy opens one and strolls right in.

Buffy Comes On To Xander

She is wearing a very short black raincoat, apparently with nothing underneath it. She starts to take it off. Xander begs her not to. He's saying if he thought this was real to her it would be different. But she has no clue what it really would mean to him. She's under a spell, and they can't do this.

Buffy gets angry and asks if he's been toying with her. Is it just a game?

Amy joins them and yells at Buffy to get away from Xander, he belongs to her. Buffy then accuses Xander of two timing her. It escalates. Buffy punches Amy. Amy does a spell, calling on the goddess Hecate, and says, "Before me let the unclean thing crawl."

Buffy seems to disappear. Her raincoat drops in a heap on the ground. A very small heap. It's a small coat.

The Buffy Rat

This seems like our Three-Quarter Turn. Like the One-Quarter Twist, the turn at the three-quarter point spins the story in yet another direction. But this turn grows out of the Midpoint, so it doesn't come from outside the protagonist. The last moment could seem like a major plot turn because something terrible happened to Buffy.

But, as we'll see, while it adds a wrinkle in what's going on, it doesn't really turn our main story.

It is, though a great hook. And we cut to commercial.

When we return, a rat crawls out from under the raincoat. So Buffy has not disappeared or been killed. She's been turned into a rat.

Giles and Jenny return. Xander tells Amy to undo the spell. Jenny echoes that, and then adds that when Amy's done, she should leave because Xander belongs with her (Jenny). Amy starts another spell against Jenny, but Xander stops her.

Giles tells Jenny and Amy to sit down and be quiet.

Giles: We have to catch the Buffy rat.

Everyone's Angry

About 30 minutes in, Xander is down on the floor looking for the Buffy rat. Oz strides in and punches him. Which hurts his hand. He says he was on the phone with Willow all night listening to Willow cry about Xander. Oz isn't sure what's going on but he was left "with a very strong urge to hit you," he says to Xander. And then helps him up.

Buffy the rat runs out the door. Giles tells Xander to go home and lock himself away. He'll try to break the spell with Amy and Jenny. He asks Oz to look for Buffy.

Giles is both angry about the spell and that Xander has put

Buffy in such danger. He tells Xander to get out of his sight. Xander looks despondent. Looking down, he leaves.

We're now 31.5 minutes in and in the hallway, girls surround Cordelia, beating her up.

Xander sees. He breaks in to carry her out of the school.

It's Not Love

Giles, talking to Jenny and Amy, says that Cordelia's necklace must have protected her from the spell. Jenny and Amy argue about which one of them has a real love for Xander. Giles yells at them, and Amy says he has no idea what she's going through.

And then we get this wonderful quote from Giles:

Giles: I know it's not love. It's obsession. Selfish, banal obsession. Now Xander's put himself in very great danger. If you cared at all about him, you'd help me save him rather than wittering on about your feelings.

While Giles is talking Jenny disappears out the door.

The Three-Quarter Turn In Bewitched, Bothered and Bewildered

We now get to our Three-Quarter Turn. It's about 32.5 minutes in, so right about three quarters through the episode.

Cordelia and Xander run outside the school. Xander thinks that they've lost the group that was pursuing them. Then they both freeze as they see all these girls and women waiting for Xander, including Willow with an ax. And Xander tells her she doesn't really want to hurt him.

Willow says he doesn't know how hard this is for her. She loves him so much, and she'd rather see him dead than with that bitch.

This is the turn that comes from both Xander's actions casting the love spell and from that reversal at the Midpoint where he hurt Willow so badly. And now the shift is that these women and girls want to kill Xander and Cordelia. Harmony and the other girls now exit the school. Xander and Cordelia get away while the two groups of women and girls fight each other.

The nice thing about this turn is it doesn't just shift the story, it raises the stakes. Because now we are talking about mortal danger.

Differences From Teacher's Pet

I can't help contrasting this episode with Teacher's Pet. That was the one with the praying mantis from Season One. We didn't spend a lot of time in Xander's point of view, but I struggled to figure out whether Xander or Buffy was the protagonist.

Here, it's much clearer.

A protagonist should have a goal and be actively pursuing that goal throughout the episode, be the main viewpoint character, and have the most at stake.

Xander As Protagonist – The Goal

In this episode, Xander is the only one actively pursuing a goal throughout the episode. His first goal is to advance his relationship with Cordelia. Then we build on that and turn it a bit because it's to get revenge. And then it is to protect himself and Cordelia, which grew out of those first goals.

Buffy, in contrast, is in reaction mode through the entire episode. Reacting to Angel's roses, to what Giles tells her, and then to the love spell by coming on to Xander. And now she's been turned into a rat.

Cordelia initially reacts to her friends' disapproval, and then to the fallout of the love spell. So while as a character, Cordelia will experience the most growth, she is not the protagonist.

Xander As Protagonist – Point Of View And The Stakes

Xander also is our main point of view character. He gets the most screen time. We mainly see through his eyes, though we do see quite a bit through Cordelia's eyes as well.

Finally, Xander has the most at stake. Yes, both he and

Cordelia are in danger of being killed. But Xander also has extreme emotional stakes.

We see how devastated he is when Giles expresses such disappointment, such anger, that he can't even look at Xander. While we haven't learned a huge amount about Xander's home life, we know that it is not good. And we see in this moment how much Giles means to him. How crushed he is by Giles disappointment.

Xander also endangered his friendship with Willow. They've known each other forever, and now he has devastated her. And he put Buffy in jeopardy. Also, he lost Cordelia, or he thinks he has. Things are just awful. Everything is at stake for Xander. So he is clearly the protagonist here, unlike in Teacher's Pet.

Chasing And Running

The scene switches to the school basement where the Buffy rat runs down the stairs. Oz follows with a flashlight. We see the rat encounter a cat.

We switch back to Cordelia and Xander running down the street. Cordelia asks what's going on and "Who died and made you Elvis?" They see Buffy's house. Xander says he'll explain later, but they should get inside.

At first, Joyce is very concerned about the situation. She tells Cordelia to go upstairs and get some bandages and says Xander should sit down and tell her all about it. He sits at the kitchen table. Joyce says she'll get him something to drink. Does he prefer cold or hot?

She starts rubbing his shoulders. He drops his head on the table.

Cordelia Does Care

Cordelia returns and, again through some humor, the plot advances. Plus we get more insight into Cordelia. She pulls Joyce off of Xander, pushes Joyce out the back door, and slams the door.

Cordelia: And keep your Mom-aged mitts off my boyfriend. Former.

Such a nice example of using humor to convey emotional vulnerability here. She then asks Xander if everyone has gone insane. And he says why is it so hard for her to believe other women find him attractive?

We get great quotes here:

Cordelia: The only way you could get girls to want you would be witchcraft.

Xander: That is such a – well, yeah, okay, good point.

More Danger

Joyce breaks the window in the back door to try to get back in. Cordelia and Xander run up to Buffy's room. Again, a nice mix of humor and escalating the plot. Xander says "we're safer up here," and Angel bursts through the window and grabs Xander and yanks him out.

We have a quick scene switch to the Buffy rat in basement as she noses around a trap.

Then we are back with Xander. Angel throws him on the ground. He wants to know where Buffy is, but then he says this will work. He wanted to do something special for Buffy for Valentine's Day. As he's about to kill Xander, someone pulls Angel off and throws him aside. We think it's Buffy. And Xander says, "Buffy?"

But no, it's Drusilla in vamp face. She, too, is enamored of Xander and won't let Angel harm him. She tells Angel that she finally found a real man. Angel says maybe he really did drive her crazy.

Juggling Many Storylines

Sometimes if we have that many different plots and subplots going in a story, it can be too much. It can end up being convoluted or jumbled. But here they mesh so nicely.

Cordelia's inner conflict about wanting to be popular and her external conflict with her friends both thwart Xander, leading to the very thing he fears, which is rejection. Xander then turns to Amy, who is engaging in witchcraft. The spell backfires. This backfire in turn forces Cordelia to confront her conflicting desires and the external conflict between her and her friends.

Also, Angel's threat, which I see as a subplot mainly there to remind us of the danger he poses, also intertwines with the main plot. It's used for humor and a bit of comic relief in Xander's story.

As so often with the writers on the show, I am amazed at how they bring together moving parts and make it look so easy and so natural.

Xander, Dru, And Angel

Drusilla is focused on Xander and asks how he feels about eternal life.

Xander: We couldn't just start with coffee, a movie, maybe?

He's looking very frightened. We are 37.5 minutes in, moving toward our climax where opposing forces will converge, and their conflicts resolve in a dramatic way.

What I like about the scene with Xander, Drusilla, and Angel is that when I first watched it, I'm pretty sure I felt real concern for Xander.

I wasn't too worried about the Buffy rat. We're clearly not going to kill Buffy off at this point. But we saw Jessie in the first episode turned into a vampire and dusted. Maybe the show is going to turn Xander into a vampire.

After all, Angel had this major turn. And the whole season has been about You're Not Who I Thought You Were. It still probably seemed unlikely to me that this would happen, but there was just enough uncertainty there to enjoy the humor and yet feel concerned.

The Angry Mob Helps Xander

Drusilla does start to bite Xander, but the angry mob has

found him. They rush to him, knocking him over, but also shoving Drusilla aside.

Cordelia runs out of the house. She pushes the girls away and drags Xander inside. The mob follows them. Drusilla tries to, but an invisible barrier repels her. Angel, who is over behind a tree, says, "Sorry Dru. I guess you're not invited."

Joyce joins the mob. Many of them have weapons. Cordelia and Xander run into the basement

We're about 38 minutes in.

A Tale Of Two Basements In Bewitched, Bothered & Bewildered

Now we switch quickly to the basement of the school. Oz is saying "Here, Buffy, Here, Buffy." Then we're with Giles and Amy in a lab with a potion.

Then we are back in the Summers' basement. Xander asks Cordelia for a nail and nails the door shut. And this is so nice. Because remember their first kiss was in this basement after they barricaded the door against the bug man (or the worm man).

Cordelia: If we die in here, I'm going to kick your ass.

Xander says none of this would've happened if she hadn't broken up with him. But she's so desperate for popularity. And she fires back and says he embraced the black arts just to get girls to like him.

He tells her that her hide's so thick not even magic can penetrate it.

A Big Change

This changes things because Cordelia stops yelling. And she touches his arm and says, "You mean the spell is for me?" She's clearly touched by this.

Now that we have this lovely moment, a giant knife slices through the door and they run down the stairs. They're backed into a corner. Above them is one of those small basement windows. More people break through the window.

The quick cuts back and forth through the various scenes really helps get that feel of escalating tension and conflict as it all comes together. It also is wrapping up all our different storylines because now we are back in the lab, with Giles and Amy.

Amy is saying a spell about Hecate, telling her to withdraw. There's a small explosion.

Back in the school basement, Oz closes in on the rat. It's behind some stacked boxes. And we get flashing lights and Oz says, "Buffy." Buffy's head pops up over the boxes.

Willow, Joyce, and the other girls break through the door.

Remember, there were two spells Amy did. There was the spell about Hecate to turn Buffy into a rat. But that was after the love spell.

The Climax And Giles' Choice

I find it interesting that Giles had Amy reverse the Hecate spell first and save Buffy. Of course, he doesn't know how much things have escalated. He didn't see Willow with the ax or the mob. But he is the one who warned us about love spells.

I guess you can argue that getting your Slayer back would be the most important thing, even aside from the personal relationship between Giles and Buffy.

In that basement all the girls are closing in, weapons raised. Back in the laboratory Giles adds powder to the potion and says words about Diana.

We flash quickly to all the women and girls with the weapons. Xander and Cordelia cowering. Giles drops the necklace into the potion.

Lots of flashing lights in the lab and in the basement. All the women and girls suddenly stop and start to back away.

Falling Action

Now we're in the Falling Action, which is where we tie up the loose ends. The women and girls are all confused. They don't know what's happening.

In the school basement Buffy crosses her arms over herself. We only see shoulders up because she is behind the boxes.

Buffy: I seem to be having a slight case of nudity here.

Oz: But you're not a rat. Call it an upside.

In the other basement, Joyce asks what happened.

Cordelia: Boy that was the best scavenger hunt ever.

And we cut immediately to the school hallway the next day.

Buffy: Scavenger hunt?

She's walking with Xander and she asks if that's the best he could do. Xander says her mom seemed to buy it. Buffy tells him Joyce was so wigged at hitting on one of Buffy's friends that she's repressing.

Xander says Willow's not talking to him. Buffy tells him that it was worse for Willow than anyone because Willow loved him before he did the spell. She thinks it's going to be a while before Willow forgives him.

Character Growth For Cordelia

Cordelia is walking in the hall with Harmony. They're chatting away, just like they used to, talking about the dance. Everything seems fine until they run into Xander. Harmony yells at him for getting in the way and says something mean, then turns back to Cordelia to pick up their conversation.

Cordelia: Do you know what you are, Harmony? You're a sheep.

Harmony: I'm not a sheep.

But Cordelia says all Harmony ever does is what everyone else does, just so she can say she did it first.

Cordelia: Here. I am scrambling for your approval when I'm way cooler than you.

Cordelia goes on to say she'll do whatever she wants to do so, wear whatever she wants. And then:

Cordelia: And you know what? I'll date whoever the hell I want to date, no matter how lame he is.

She walks away with Xander, arm in arm.

Cordelia then gasps and asks what she did. Xander tells her it's okay, to just keep walking. And if it makes her feel better, whenever they're around her friends they can fight a lot. She says, "You promise?" And Xander says they can pretty much count on it.

So this is what I mean about Cordelia having the most character growth here.

Buffy has been part of this kind of humorous side plot, and she's learned a little more about Angel, but there's no real growth for her.

Xander probably learned not to cast love spells. I'm not sure that he has grown much personally, though.

But Cordelia had a real transformation. She realized some things about popularity. About who is a leader and who is not and why. Also about being who she is. And that her strength is being willing to say what she thinks and do what she wants. She is going to continue to do that even if her popular friends disapprove.

It also says something about the strength of her feelings for Xander, but I do think it is more about her internal growth.

A Strong Story

As I mentioned at the outset, this seems like such an almost light, one-off episode. It's fun. Whenever I'm about to rewatch, I always think, "Oh yeah, that's the love spell episode." And I almost don't want to rewatch it because as I remember it as not going anywhere. It's kind of fluffy, and we don't have a lot about Buffy in it.

Then I watch it and I remember how much happens there. How much we set up for what's coming next.

Spoilers and Foreshadowing

Buffy And Jenny

We see a very subtle thawing of Buffy's anger towards Jenny. Or maybe not her anger but her feelings about not being able to be around Jenny or deal with Giles and Jenny together. She stares at the floor when Jenny comes out. Yet afterwards she asks Giles how he is. She is concerned for him.

Giles And Buffy

We also have more strengthening of the Buffy-Giles bond. We see how concerned he is when she is in danger. He is so angry at Xander. He already thinks Xander is foolish. But when Buffy becomes a rat, Giles says, "Get out of my sight."

And as I mentioned, he reverses the spell about Hecate, or has Amy reverse it, first.

Amy Doing Spells

Amy's storyline also advances. Initially, in The Witch, she seemed like a one-off character, or at least one who might only have a few cameos later.

Now we see her doing spells. This foreshadows Gingerbread next season. That's when Joyce and the other parents will turn on their children, particularly the ones who are involved in the occult.

That puts Amy in danger, along with Willow and Buffy. This episode shows that while Amy can do spells, she hasn't perfected it. So we won't be so surprised when things go terribly wrong for her in Gingerbread. Or I guess in the aftermath of Gingerbread, when for several seasons no one can figure out how to undo a spell where she turns herself into a rat.

The Dangers Of Magic

This episode also foreshadows the larger problem with using spells to advance your own personal interests. That is key to Willow's character arc through the series. Initially, Willow's focus is doing witchcraft to help fight the forces of evil. That is why she learns it and pursues it. And we will see her take a major step forward in this season.

But we will later see her turn to magic more and more to avoid dealing with her feelings. And eventually to try to change other people with tragic consequences.

All of that is foreshadowed here when we see Amy use witchcraft to help her grades. No immediate consequence from that. But then Xander uses it to blackmail her into a doing a love spell for him. Amy is aware of this danger and warns him, but she does it anyway, not wanting her previous spell revealed.

Xander is trying to harm or change Cordelia. A love spell would do that regardless, even if a person had pure intent. In fact, Giles tells us how dangerous any love spell is.

That part of the episode also sets up Giles as the one who will point out that if you use magic, it must be done responsibly. And that will become a conflict between Willow and Giles.

Reminding Us Of The Rules Of Buffy The Vampire Slayer's World

This episode also included a couple quick, maybe not foreshadowings but reminders about when vampires can enter.

We see Drusilla barred. The house literally sets up an invisible wall against her. But Angel, who has been invited in, and has been inside many times, is able to reach through the window and grab Xander.

Angel Danger

That moment foreshadows the danger Angel poses. Also, there's a hint of danger to Joyce because she's the one who goes to the back door and gets the roses. And there is what Giles tells us about brutal displays of affection. We will see that play out in the next episode. We even have this side reference to nailing a puppy to a tree, and next episode Angel kills Willow's goldfish.

These moments and lines foreshadow that Angel will do these things to devastate people emotionally. He will go beyond killing people. He makes an art form of tormenting people, including through gestures like the roses. Things that will make the person, the victim, fearful.

Xander Foreshadowing

We also have foreshadowing of Cordelia's and Xander's relationship never being quite solid. Though it will last for some time, there are these fissures, fault lines, there. And there's the hint that Cordelia really is more invested than Xander is in the relationship.

Xander has mixed feelings. He wants to advance the relationship. Yet he says all these negative things about Cordelia. This also foreshadows his relationship with Anya. Through much of the series, like Cordelia, Anya will seem more invested than Xander. And he will likewise say these critical things about her.

This episode also foreshadows that Willow's deep feelings for Xander have not completely gone away. It sets up some of the triangle issues in Season Three.

Looking Ahead To Passion

Finally, Giles's quote about it's not love, its obsession, foreshadows Passion. I don't think I noticed this on any prior watch, but it signals the theme. That issue of what passion is or means. And the difference between love and obsession (passion).

So I love that the writers worked this in. That the Valentines episode, the love spell episode, brought us right into Passion.

Questions For Your Writing

- Do you foreshadow major developments in your story during earlier scenes?
- How does your plot relate to the themes in your story?

- Does needed exposition come out through genuine conflict?
- Which one of your characters grows the most?
- If your characters don't grow, can you add conflict or plot turns that require one of them to change?
- Are there subplots in your novel? Do they intersect the main plot or stand alone?

Next: Passion

NEXT WE'LL TALK about Passion, including whether Angel or Buffy is the protagonist, the use of voiceover, and actions that show emotions.

CHAPTER 5
PASSION (S2 E17)

THIS CHAPTER TALKS ABOUT PASSION, Season Two Episode Seventeen, where Angelus steps up his harassment of Buffy. Written by Ty King and directed by Michael Gershman.

In particular, we'll look at:

- Whether the protagonist is Angel or Buffy and why;
- More than one major reversal near the Midpoint;
- Shifts in actions and tone that convey intense emotion; and
- Using dramatic irony to ratchet up the audience's experience.

Okay, let's dive into the Hellmouth.

———

THIS EPISODE RAISES questions about who the protagonist is. And it shows two plots, or the same plot from two different points of view, weaving together. That's something that is difficult to do, and it's done well in this episode, despite that some of the plot turns I usually look for are not quite as clear.

Yet there are significant turns that keep the story moving and engaging.

Opening Conflict In Passion

We begin with intense conflict. Buffy and Xander are dancing at the Bronze. That's not the intense conflict – they're having fun. But Angel watches from a distance. We know there is danger here for Buffy.

The voiceover is about passion. Angel tells us it lies in all of us. "Waiting, unwanted, it will stir, open its jaws and howl."

We see Buffy, Willow, Xander, and Cordelia leave the Bronze. But we're not hearing them. We only hear music, and Angel in the shadows behind them bites and kills a woman.

Angel In Buffy's House

We switch to an outside view of Buffy's bedroom, looking through her window. Buffy peers out, looking troubled.

Angel comes in during the night. He strokes her hair.

Voiceover by Angel: Passion rules us all and we obey. What other choice do we have?

And we go to Credits. That was 2 minutes 29 seconds in.

In the morning Buffy wakes up. She finds an envelope and inside it is a charcoal drawing of her sleeping.

Buffy Seeks Help

At the library, Buffy tells Giles. When Cordelia asks how Angel could come in, Giles explains to everyone that once they are invited vampires can come in any time. They don't need an invitation each time.

Cordelia panics. She invited Angel into her car once, and now he can come in anytime. We get some humor here.

Xander: Yep, you're doomed to giving him and his vamp pals a lift whenever they feel like it. And those guys never chip in for gas.

This is the first example of Cordelia and Xander being

comic relief. Cordelia adds humor in the fashion we've become used to, where she is very self-focused and sometimes misses the emotions of others. And that contrasts to her later response toward the end of the episode.

The Story Spark In Passion

Buffy says there must be a spell to reverse that invitation. A no shoes, no pulse, no service kind of thing.

All of these moments lead up to right around 4 minutes 30 seconds, when Giles will identify what's happening. This is where we usually see our Story Spark or Inciting Incident – about 10% into a story. It sets off our main plot. Here, as Giles will say in a moment, it is that Angel is stepping up his harassment of Buffy.

If I needed to pick a particular instant in the episode that starts it all, it is Buffy finding that charcoal drawing Angel left for her. His point was to let her know that he has done it.

When Giles tells them Angel is stepping up his harassment, Cordelia is first to respond.

Cordelia: What, by leaving a drawing? Why doesn't he just slit her throat or kill her while she sleeps or cut her heart out?

Everyone gives her a look.

Cordelia: What? I'm trying to help.

Giles says Yes and then goes on to say these are tactics to throw the opponent off her game, provoke her into making a mistake.

Xander: The Na-Na-Na-Na-Na-Na approach to battle.

Giles: Yes, Xander, once more you've managed to boil a complex thought down to its simplest possible form.

He then advises Buffy that it's best to ignore this provocation. But she's worried because of what Angel told her about how he went after Drusilla's family when he was obsessed with her. And she says she needs to tell her mom something.

Giles warns her against telling the truth, saying it would be too dangerous for Buffy to reveal her identity. But he reassures her he'll find a spell to keep Angel out. In the meantime, he says to keep a level head, don't let Angel get to her.

Buffy: So basically ignore him and maybe he'll go away.

Giles: Yes.

Xander then points out that he didn't scold Buffy about oversimplifying and says, "Watcher's Pet."

Jenny And Willow

Now we see Jenny at the end of her computer class. She asks Willow if she can cover class for a few minutes tomorrow if Jenny is late. She has something to take care of. Willow is super excited about this. And then immediately starts to worry about what if the students don't recognize her authority.

Buffy and Giles come to the door, and Willow apologizes for talking to Jenny.

Willow: Sorry, I have to talk to her. She's a teacher and teachers have to be respected, even if they're only filling in....

She rambles on about that, showing more of her anxiety. I like that we get this moment. It's characterization for Willow. It also shows the tension in there. That Willow and her other friends still really like Jenny as a teacher. It's a difficult position.

Jenny's Planning Something

Also, Jenny's comment about needing to go and do something – we'll see later it is her going to the Magic Shop. So it's a nice way to bring Jenny into this episode and foreshadow her role in a way that we don't realize will be key to the story.

Giles stays back to talk to Jenny after the others leave. He tells her about Angel being in Buffy's bedroom and says he needs a spell. She gives him a book that might help. She's been reading up since Angel turned.

Jenny: I know you feel betrayed.

Giles: Yes, well, that's one of the unpleasant side effects of betrayal.

We get some of the best Giles lines throughout this episode. Both heart rending like this one and funny like his earlier ones.

I think this is because, well, one, the writers are amazing at dialogue. But also, while this is Buffy's story and Angel's story, it is also Giles' story.

So we get some of our best Giles here, which makes us feel all the more for him.

Jenny And Giles In Love

Jenny says she was raised by the people that Angel hurt most. Her duty to them was the first thing she learned. And she didn't know what would happen. She didn't know she'd fall in love with Giles.

Giles is surprised. The Jenny-Giles theme music plays. And she says that just came out but she doesn't want to take it back. She wants to make this all up to him. Giles says he understands but he's not the one she needs to make it up to.

Buffy Warns Joyce

At dinner, Joyce asks Buffy what's wrong and urges her to talk.

Joyce: You can tell me anything. I've read all the parenting books.

And I love that we get this additional reference to Joyce. Before she talked about parenting tapes. Now we hear she's reading books.

So Buffy asks if she remembers Angel, and Joyce says, "oh, that college boy that was tutoring you." Which is a reference to the episode Angel in Season One. Another one where we had intertwining Buffy and Angel plots.

Buffy tries to explain it. She says they were dating, and now they're not.

Joyce: Don't tell me. He's changed. He's not the same guy you fell for.

And Buffy says yes, that he's sending her notes and she doesn't want to see him. If he shows up she'll talk to him. But don't invite him in. So she is anticipating that they will soon have a spell to keep Angel out, but also wants to cue her mom that Angel could be dangerous.

The One-Quarter Twist In Passion

We are coming to our One-Quarter Twist. This comes from outside the protagonist and spins the story in a new direction.

At 11 minutes 5 seconds in, Willow and Buffy are on the phone. We're seeing Willow in her room. She says she agrees with Giles, "don't let Angel get to you." Then at 12 minutes she sees an envelope on her bed.

Back in Lie To Me, the episode about Buffy's friend Ford, Willow invited Angel into her room. So he can come in. And he has.

Willow opens the envelope and finds her goldfish dead inside strung together on a fishing line. This is a little past one quarter, but I see it as that first major twist. Because Angel is doing what Buffy feared. He is escalating the harassment by going after people Buffy loves.

In our next scene. Willow and Buffy are in Buffy's bedroom with garlic hung all around them. (One of the few references we get to the traditional idea that garlic repels vampires.)

And Buffy says it's so strange. When things like this happen her first thought is to run to Angel.

I think this is part of why the show works so well. Most of us have felt this way at some time. You have someone you love who is in your life, who you turned to. And something happens. A break up. And it's terrible, and yet your first thought is to go to that person for comfort, for help, and you realize all over again that you can't. That the person is gone.

All Angel Thinks About

Buffy also apologizes about the goldfish. Willow says she's okay with it, but goes on:

Willow: Though for the first time I'm glad my parents didn't let me have a puppy.

That's a call back to last week when we heard Giles start to tell Buffy what Angel did to a puppy. Willow points out that one thing hasn't changed. Buffy is still the only thing Angel thinks about.

Drusilla Brings Spike A Puppy

Continuing our puppy theme, which is sort of interesting, Drusilla brings Spike a puppy. She's trying to get him to eat it. And she does almost like a little airplane thing with it like what parents do with toddlers.

Spike, not surprisingly, doesn't love this. He says he won't have her feeding him like a child. And Angel says why not? She already bathes him and dresses him and carries him around because he still in that wheelchair. Angel implies he's having sex with Dru in Spike's place.

Drusilla loves being fought over, but suddenly she seems to be in terrible pain. She says the air, it worries, because an old enemy is seeking help.

Jenny Visits The Magic Shop

Jenny walks into the Magic Shop. The proprietor offers her a love potion or voodoo doll.

Jenny: I need an Orb of Thesulah.

Proprietor: Oh, you're in the trade.

He apologizes for giving her the pitch he usually does for tourists. And talks about how Ouija boards and love potions and revenge spells, especially around Valentine's Day, pay the rent.

The proprietor gives her the orb and says it's a spirit vault for rituals of the undead. He also sold a couple as New Age paperweights. And he tells her the transliteration annals are lost and the surviving text is gibberish without them and goes on, "I mentioned it because we have a strict no refund policy," which at least gives us some plot or character reason for this exchange of info.

Jenny says that's okay, she's working on a computer program to translate. He asks what she's planning on doing when she gets that done. She says it's a present for a friend – his soul.

And we cut to commercial. Great hook.

At School Again

Outside the school, Willow is upset to see Jenny and says something like "five hours of lesson preparation out the window."

Buffy follows Jenny and wants to talk to her. She really struggles with letting Jenny off the hook.

Buffy: I know you feel badly, and I wanted to say – good, keep it up.

Jenny: Don't worry I will.

Jenny starts to walk on.

Buffy: Wait. He misses you.

She goes on to tell Jenny that Giles doesn't say it, but she knows he's lonely, and she doesn't want him to be lonely. She doesn't want anyone to be.

Jenny: If I can make it up to you –

Buffy: We're good. Let's leave it.

Reversing The Invitation

In the next scene, Giles tells Buffy and her friends that he's found a spell to reverse the invitation.

Cordelia: Thank God. I had to switch cars with my grandmother.

Another interesting view into Cordelia's world.

We're then at Willow's bedroom. She nails a cross on the wall and says how will she explain this to her dad. Ira Rosenberg's only daughter nailing crucifixes to the wall.

(I can't help mentioning it is not a crucifix. Many many years of going to Catholic mass and CCD – Catholic education for public school kids – taught me a crucifix includes the figure of Christ's body hanging on the cross. If the cross doesn't include that it's just a cross, not a crucifix. Though perhaps Willow has no reason to know that.)

Willow also says she has to go to Xander's just to watch Charlie Brown Christmas. But it's worth it when he does the Snoopy dance.

Cordelia looks at the fish tank.

Cordelia: Do you know, there are no fish in here?

Another example of being a little tone deaf on Cordelia's part. Though, to be fair, she might not have known about Willow's fish. She then finds an envelope on the bed. Inside is a charcoal drawing of Joyce asleep.

Peanuts And Parents

I'm surprised that Buffy didn't protect her house first. They mentioned they already did Cordelia's car and now they're in Willow's bedroom.

I didn't notice that before because I love the episode. The dialogue, the humor about the Snoopy dance, the dramatic moment of the drawing. So I didn't notice that it kind of doesn't fit Buffy's character to go to her house to protect her mother last. On the other hand, maybe it fits because as teenagers their world is mainly about school and friends and their daily lives, with less thought about parents.

In fact, the reference to Peanuts and the Charlie Brown Christmas is interesting. Because in Peanuts the adults are all just "whah whah whah" voices. And that is largely true in Buffy's world. Other than Giles, because he's her Watcher, and occasionally Joyce.

We switch to Buffy's house. And the answer of why she doesn't do it sooner is we want this dramatic scene. We wanted to deal with the fact that she finds this envelope, and that Angel is anticipating where she will go. He left the envelope for her at Willow's, which makes his psychological warfare very effective.

Nearing The Midpoint Of Passion

We are coming to the Midpoint of the episode. Angel is waiting outside, right at the front door. Joyce pulls up from the grocery store, gets out. And the way I see it, to the extent Angel is the protagonist, we'll now see a Midpoint Commitment for him.

Usually at the Midpoint, we have the protagonist throwing caution to the wind, committing to the quest, or suffering a major reversal.

Normally we see him pop into Buffy's world the way he did when he confronted Teresa. More of a blip. He lives mainly with Drusilla and Spike and in the shadows. Leaving envelopes, coming in at night.

But here he is confronting Joyce, having this conversation with her so out in the open. And he is going after the one person, other than Giles, who is most key to Buffy. So he commits.

Reversal For Buffy

This point in the episode is also a major reversal for Buffy as our protagonist because Angel as Angelus is interacting with her mother. The one person close to her who doesn't know what's really going on and whom she loves so much.

Angel plays the stalker boyfriend perfectly. He says, "Mrs. Summers, I need to talk to you." And he tells her he needs to be with Buffy, and she has to intervene to help him.

Joyce is terrific in this. She's very clear with Angel. Very firm.

Joyce: I'm telling you leave her alone. You're scaring her. You need to back off.

And it's also nice because we don't often get to see Joyce as a character being able to protect Buffy. Usually Buffy, whether her mom knows it or not, is protecting Joyce and protecting everyone else.

Joyce fumbles for her keys, and oranges fall out of the grocery bag. Angel helps her pick them up.

We are 21 minutes 47 seconds in, so right about at that episode Midpoint.

And Angel tells Joyce she doesn't understand.

Angel: I'll die without Buffy. She'll die without me.
Joyce: Are you threatening her?
And Joyce says she's calling the police.
Angel: I haven't been able to sleep since the night we made love.

So another significant reversal for Buffy – that now her mother will know this. It leads to Buffy's commitment.

Buffy Commits To The Quest

At 22.5 minutes in the door opens. Buffy and Willow are chanting in Latin. Then Buffy says to Angel, "Sorry, Angel, I changed the locks," and slams the door.

So this isn't quite the throwing of caution to the wind that we sometimes see for the protagonist. But it is in an emotional and subtle sense because this is the most directly that Buffy has shown Joyce this part of her world. They are doing a spell in front of Joyce. It also definitively shuts Angel out of Buffy's heart and her life.

Hope For Giles And Jenny

We switch to Giles in Jenny's classroom. She says she's working late tonight on a special project. And she tells him she spoke to Buffy, and Buffy said he missed her. Giles says something like, "Well, she's a meddlesome girl."

Jenny tells him she might have some news, she needs to finish up, and could she see him later. He says she can stop by his home. We get the Jenny and Giles theme music, and he looks so happy and leaves.

Dark Forces

We switch to Drusilla at magic shop. She's holding the puppy, which she has named Sunshine, and speaks to the proprietor.

Drusilla: Miss Sunshine wants to know what you and the mean teacher talked about.

Drusilla learning about Jenny's spell is another reversal for

Buffy and for everyone. So while there isn't just one clear reversal or commitment here, instead we see a series of them.

Jenny is now in her classroom. It's dark. (There is apparently no budget for after-hours lights at Sunnydale High.) And this is another major reversal that will drive the rest of the story.

Because Jenny is very happy. She clicks the keys and says to herself, "That's it, it's gonna work," and she saves to one of these small plastic disk.

(I forget what they were called, but they were a big advancement at the time because before that we had floppy disks that were bigger, flimsier, and stored less data.)

Anyway, she saves to that disk and pops it out. And she prints on one of these old dot matrix printers that had this rolling paper that went through the printer. They made this very distinctive noise. As it is printing Angel comes into the classroom.

Angel Stops The Spell

Jenny jumps to her feet. She says something about how did he get in. And he recites the Latin inscription over the door, which I cannot pronounce. I think Jenny translates it as "enter all ye who seek knowledge."

Angel: What can I say? I'm a knowledge seeker.

Although my guess is it's a public place. He could come in.

Jenny: I can help you.

Angel: Yeah, I know. You can restore my soul.

He picks up the Orb of Thesulah and says you know what he hates about these things? And he flings it at the wall and it breaks. He says, "They're so fragile."

Angel also throws the computer to the ground and it catches fire and burns. (Even back then computers were not so badly designed that they would catch fire if they broke, at least as far as I know. But we'll go with it.) He burns the pages of the spell over the flames. Jenny is trying to say she can cure him.

Angel: No thanks. Been there, done that. Déjà vu just isn't what it used to be.

What TV Can Get Away With

Television shows have more leeway for things like computers bursting into flames than novels do. Partly because in a novel, as we're reading we think more. On a TV show, like this one especially, action is going very fast. The writers can play with reality a bit more and be less true to it because not too many people will pause and say, "Wait – can that computer really burst into flames?"

So I envy TV and movie writers for that.

Why Angel Doesn't Bite Jenny

Jenny tries to run. She goes out in the hallway. Angel plays cat and mouse with her. He lets her feel like she might be getting away eventually. At the top of the stairs, though, he blocks her way, grabs her, twists her neck, and kills her. I was so sure when I first watched that she wasn't really going to die, but she does.

In the interview on the DVD, Joss Whedon said they have Angel in vamp face when he kills Jenny, even though he doesn't need to be because he's not biting her. But they felt that if he had on his human face no one would ever want to see Buffy kissing that face again.

He also said Angel doesn't bite Jenny for two reasons. One, they didn't want anyone thinking she might come back as a vampire. But it was also an insult to break her neck. Like he wasn't even bothering to feed on her.

I saw it as he's doing it purely for sport. Which I suppose is the same thing

The Pain Escalates In Passion

From here on, we have this emotional escalation much like we saw in Nightmares. (The one with all the people at the school when their nightmares come true.) There, we had the scene with Buffy and her dad where every sentence was just that much more awful than the last one. And you didn't think it could get any worse.

Similarly, in Innocence, the Buffy and Angel scene in his bedroom when she doesn't know he turned yet, Angel is awful to Buffy. And you keep thinking the writers can't make this anymore terrible for her, and they do.

So here we don't see it in one scene, we see it throughout the episode. The writers keep ratcheting up the tragedy. The awfulness and the pain.

Giles At Buffy's House

Next we see the Giles knocking on Buffy's door. Willow lets him in. And we realize that Giles doesn't know yet about Jenny. He's come by to see how the spell went.

The next couple scenes are wonderful in themselves. Added to the tension and the emotional pain is that as viewers we know Angel killed Jenny. We're already feeling the loss and feeling for Giles, though he is completely unaware right now. Everyone is.

That's dramatic irony – where the audience knows something the characters do not. And it adds to the weight of the scene and keeps us even more engaged.

Willow tells Giles the ritual went fine but…. And she tells him that Angel showed up and told Buffy's mom that he and Buffy "well, you know that they had – you do know right?"

Giles says yes, and she says she wasn't sure, him being a librarian and all.

Giles: No, thank you, I got it.

Joyce and Buffy are upstairs talking, and Giles asks if maybe he should intervene on Buffy's behalf with her mom.

Willow: Sure. Like what would you say?

Giles: You will tell Buffy I dropped by?

And he leaves.

Joyce Worries As Buffy Explains

We switch to Buffy and Joyce. Buffy is trying to explain the spell. She says Angel's really superstitious and that will help keep him away.

Joyce asks if Angel was her first, and then says maybe she doesn't want to know. But Buffy says yes, the first -- the only. Joyce is angry at Buffy, saying Angel's older, too old. Also obviously not very stable. And she thought Buffy would use better judgment.

Buffy tries to explain and Joyce doesn't let her. She says "you had sex with a boy you didn't even tell me you were dating." Buffy says she can't tell her everything. And Joyce says, "How about anything?"

Joyce is so angry. Yet we'll learn that Joyce and Buffy apparently have not talked about sex before. Buffy's seventeen, so it seems Joyce is blaming Buffy for her own failure to open these conversations.

But she goes on:

Joyce: You can shut me out. I'm pretty much used to it. But don't ever expect me to stop caring about you. I never will.

And she tells Buffy she loves her more than anything in the world. Joyce then says that's Buffy's cue to roll her eyes, and Buffy says no, she's not grossed out. She's not rolling her eyes. And they have this really nice moment:

Joyce: I guess that was the talk.

Buffy: How'd it go?

Joyce: I don't know. It was my first.

I do love this moment between them.

A Complicated Relationship

I think the show does a great job of showing the complexities of being a parent. We've seen that Joyce is trying, and yet here's an example where it initially seems like she's not doing a great job. And yet she gets important part out. How much she loves Buffy. And we see that's where this anger comes from. A nice use of conflict bringing out character and bringing out their relationship.

This idea of this being the first "talk" is another example -- in a novel it would be more challenging. Because in a novel, we get the characters' interior thoughts. And as the author you would need to, though maybe not at length, deal with why Joyce and Buffy never talked about this before.

But the show moves quickly. So we don't really spend time on thinking, "Hey, Buffy's seventeen. Wouldn't Joyce have had this conversation earlier?"

What The Audience Brings To Fiction

We all bring something different to fiction. That question didn't occur to me when I first saw the episode because I grew up with a mom who was not comfortable talking about those kinds of things.

But Joyce has been built as a character who is very forthright. As someone who I don't see would be uncomfortable with that. So I think there is a little bit of a disconnect there between the idea that the two of them haven't talked about sex before and who Joyce has been built to be. But we as the audience more or less whistle past it because we love the characters and the emotion.

And we're waiting to find out what happens with Giles and Jenny.

Angel Set The Scene For Giles

We switch to Giles's apartment. This whole scene is all the more heartbreaking because of the dramatic irony. Here, we know what Giles is going to learn.

He enters the apartment. There's beautiful, sweeping music playing. Classical music. He finds a bottle of champagne on ice. And a single red rose with a note that says "Upstairs."

Giles smiles, takes off his glasses, smooths his hair. These gestures show us so much about Giles's anticipation. His happiness. On the stairs there are lit candles and rose petals leading up.

And this is just killing us because we know what's coming.

The Three-Quarter Turn In Passion: Giles Sees Jenny

Giles sees Jenny in bed. At first he thinks she's waiting for him. And then at 33 minutes 5 seconds in he realizes her neck is bent wrong. He drops the champagne bottle and glasses. The music crescendos as glass shatters at his feet.

This is the third major plot turn. That is the Three-Quarter Turn. It usually comes out of the Midpoint Commitment and Reversal in a well-structured story, and it's generally about three quarters through an episode or book. (Which is why I call it that.)

Here, it is not quite as clear if it comes out of the Reversal. If we see the major reversal at the Midpoint as coming a little later, when Drusilla learns about Jenny's plan, then this clearly arises from it. If we see the reversal and commitment as Angelus revealing himself to Joyce and confronting her, putting her directly in danger, and telling Joyce about he and Buffy making love, then it's not quite so clear.

Although it is the overall escalation of his harassment of Buffy by killing her friends.

We pan back from Giles' face. Now he is in the forefront as the police process the scene behind him. A detective says he needs Giles to answer some questions.

The Ecstasy Of Grief

In Angel's viewpoint again, from outside the Summers's house on the first floor, we look through the window into the living room area.

Willow and Buffy are together. They look relatively happy. And we get this voiceover:

Voiceover by Angel: Passion is the source of our finest moments. The joy of love, the clarity of hatred, and the ecstasy of grief.

The phone rings inside. From outside, through that window, we watch Buffy answer. We see her face as she listens. She hands the phone to Willow. And Buffy slides down to the floor. Her back is against the wall, and she slides down and sits on the floor.

We now hear Willow the way you might through that window. We hear just that she says No and sobs. Her whole body shows her grief.

Joyce comes in and goes to Willow.

It's set up so that maybe she doesn't quite register Buffy there on the floor. And she's holding Willow and trying to comfort her.

With any other writer, I feel like this would be the climax of the episode. The apex of the grief and the pain that Angel caused. But it's not. Because we're just going to keep ratcheting up the emotional pain and the stakes here.

So about 36 minutes in, we're outside. Xander and Cordelia drive up in her car. Xander gets out of the passenger side and says Giles is gone from the police station.

Underscoring The Characters' Pain

Buffy asks Cordelia will she drive them to Giles' house. And Cordelia says, "Of course."

This is that moment I feel has such significance. It's so minor, but Cordelia is muted. "Of course." No comments, no observations, no funny lines. None of that. Just "of course."

That change in tone underscores our emotional pain and the tragedy here.

At Giles' apartment, Giles is alone. And he takes a large bag of weapons and leaves.

We close up on a charcoal drawing of Jenny. That drawing wasn't there before Giles came back. So we know Angel actually went back to place that drawing for Giles and Buffy to find later.

And we cut to commercial.

Xander Says I Told You So

Back to Giles's apartment. Xander sees the champagne bucket, and he thinks Giles had a big night planned. But Buffy says Giles didn't set this up, Angel did. And she shows Xander the drawing. Buffy says Giles has gone to kill Angel.

Xander now – and this totally fits his character, but it doesn't make me like him – he says it's about time somebody tried to kill Angel. He gets a little push back and he says he hated Angel before everyone else jumped on the bandwagon and he thinks he deserves kudos for not saying I told you so sooner.

I understand his point, but he's kind of awful here.

Buffy says, "I agree." But she says there's one problem with Giles and a revenge scenario. It's going to get him killed.

Spike's Not Happy

At the factory, Spike also is not happy.

Spike: Are you insane? We're supposed to kill the bitch. Not leave gag gifts in her friends' beds.

Drusilla: But the teacher was going to restore Angel's soul.

Now Spike, I love this, says something like who cares, he finds himself preferring the Buffy-whipped Angel. This one's not playing with full deck.

Spike: His little pranks will only leave us with one incredibly brassed off Slayer.

Angel says don't worry, he has it all under control. And a flaming arrow flies in and hits him in the shoulder.

Protagonists And Goals

We're moving into the Climax of the episode. But first, I want to revisit the question I asked at the beginning: Who is the protagonist?

The protagonist should (a) have a goal; (b) actively pursue the goal; (c) be the main point of view character; and (d) have the most at stake.

Angel has a goal here: to harass Buffy. And he actively pursues that goal. We could argue that he is the most active in this episode. Buffy in many ways is reacting.

But she does have a goal as well. And it is from that Inciting

Incident or Story Spark on: to protect her family and friends. And she also actively pursues it. It's just not a violent goal like Angel's. But she is telling her mom things to try to put her mom on guard. She has Giles looking for a spell. She does the spells.

So they both actively pursue a goal.

Protagonists And Point Of View

We do get Angel's point of view often. We start in his point of view. And we get key scenes in a way that we normally don't – literally looking through windows at Buffy. We already hear Angel's ongoing commentary about passion. Which is ominous and conveys a theme for the episode. (And, as I'll talk about in Spoilers, for the rest of the season and some of next season.)

But we also see Buffy's point of view as much if not more. What she's going through. How she is trying to stop him. Her experiences with Joyce.

And we will end in her point of view directly when she's at Jenny's grave. And then, in a way, through Willow. We're definitely seeing that part not literally through Buffy's eyes, but we are in sympathy with Buffy and Willow and the others at that point.

So point of view could go either way, though it is very strong for Angel.

Protagonists And Stakes

Finally, the protagonist should have the most at stake. And that's why I think Buffy is the protagonist here. Because she has at stake her friends, Willow, her mom, and Giles, as we'll see in a moment. And that is the highest stakes for Buffy.

Her life is always on the line. But Angel poses direct threats to the people she cares about the most, while Angel doesn't really have anything at stake. If this strategy doesn't devastate Buffy, he will try another. He doesn't have the high stakes here.

So ultimately I think that Buffy is the protagonist.

Intertwining Plots In Passion

But it is really interesting because we have two intertwining plots that are very strong. It reminds me of the episode Angel where I saw the plot that belonged to the Master. He was the antagonist to Buffy but the protagonist of his own story, of the main plot from his point of view. And in that same episode, Buffy and Angel each had their own subplots about their relationship and what else was happening.

Here, I think we see the main plot, but we see it from these two perspectives that come together really well at the Climax.

The Climax Begins

At about 39 minutes in, the factory is on fire. Giles lights a torch and swings at Angel and beats him with it.

Angel is quipping, though. More irritated than in peril, though there is some danger to him. Drusilla starts to go to help him, and Spike pulls her back.

Spike: No fair going in unless he tags you first.

I think this works so well because we have seen this Angel and Spike conflict building. And I think Spike is like, yeah, whatever. I'm just as happy to see Angel go down here.

Also, we have set up that Drusilla, despite her loving that Angel and Spike fight over her, does care for Spike. She is very concerned for him. So I find it believable that she stays back even though clearly Spike can't hold her back. She's far more physically powerful. But she agrees, and they stay out of the fight.

The fight escalates. Giles actually knocks Angel down but then Angel stands, grabs Giles by the neck, and lifts him up.

Angel: All right you've had your fun, but you know what it's time for now?

Buffy: My fun.

Buffy comes from behind him and starts kicking him. I like this so much because we almost think Giles might be getting the better of Angel, and we realize Angel's just playing with him. And I like that because, yeah, Giles is a good fighter. He's very smart. But Angel is so strong and so smart, or maybe so cunning, you couldn't buy that Giles could get the better of him for very long.

Going For The Kill

Buffy fights Angel, and she is getting the better of him there, going up to the next level onto this catwalk. We can see a difference in her fighting from in Innocence. That's the episode where Angel turned, where she's fighting him but she's not quite going in for the kill. She finds she can't kill him.

Here, though, she is going for the kill. But Angel starts laughing despite that she's about to overpower him.

Angel: You going to let your old man just burn?

Buffy looks down. The fire has gotten out of control. Giles is on the floor and she needs to save him. She leaps down and drags him out. And this is where our emotions become more intense, which I would not have thought was possible.

Giles is yelling at Buffy. Saying why did she come there? It's not her fight. He really wanted to get the better of Angel. And in his fury and hurt and grief he doesn't see that he was going to die. Or he doesn't care.

And Buffy punches him and knocks him to the ground.

Buffy: Are you trying to get yourself killed?

And she just starts sobbing and hugs him and holds him:

Buffy: You can't leave me. I can't do this alone.

Climax Or Falling Action?

We have not seen Buffy fall apart. We've seen her very emotional since Angel turned. That moment in the car with Giles, and with Joyce later. But it was muted, the kind of pain we see in her expression, but we didn't see her sobbing and breaking down. And here she does. And it is so very moving. So that was our climax.

That is why I see saving Giles as the Climax, not the Falling Action.

In the Falling Action, we tie up the loose ends. I don't think that was tying up a loose end. I think that was the Climax of the episode.

Falling Action In Passion

In the Falling Action, we hear Angel's voiceover. He is talking about passion again, and he says it hurts more than we can bear. And we see Giles pulling the police tape off his door and going into his empty apartment.

Angel: If we could live without passion, maybe we'd know some kind of peace. But we would be hollow. Without passion, we'd be truly dead.

We then switch to the graveyard. As Angel is saying "we'd be truly dead," Giles and Buffy stand at Jenny's grave. There's music in the background.

Buffy: I'm sorry I couldn't kill him for you, for her, when I had the chance. I wasn't ready. I think I finally am.

Over Buffy's last sentence, the scene switches to Willow walking into Jenny's classroom. She tells the class that she's filling in until the new computer teacher arrives. (Something that could only happen in Sunnydale where we have a student taking over.)

We continue with Buffy's voiceover then. She says she can't hold onto the past, Angel's gone, and nothing's ever going to bring him back.

This is as Willow puts her books down on the desk. And she knocks something to the floor. We see it's that plastic disc with the spell on it. And it falls into the space between the desk and cabinet. So more emotional pain at the very end because the key to restoring Angel's soul still exists, but none of them know it.

And the episode's finished. So it is a great hook as well for the rest of the season.

The Point Of Jenny's Death

In the DVD interview, Joss Whedon said this episode is Angel's first real offensive against Buffy. And that they specifically put the death of Jenny at a pivotal moment in this story arc for the season. Because Angel needed to kill someone to tell the audience that not everyone is safe. That someone integral to the show, whose death is final and scary, can be ripped away from us.

And he said it is also there to show that Angel is not just a little evil. He's not just grouchy. He is Buffy's enemy. And the episode is there to make Buffy realize that she has to kill him and get him out of her life.

Whedon said he wanted it to be as hard for the audience as possible. His goal was for us to know that redeeming Angel and getting him back would be difficult or impossible, and so fraught with consequences that the audience wouldn't be sure they wanted him back.

I think that this episode achieves all of that.

Spoilers and Foreshadowing

THE SERIES BIBLE

I'll start with a fun spoiler -- Willow mentioning the Snoopy dance. I so love this because it comes back in Season Five, The Replacement, where we have two Xanders. One of them proves he is Xander by actually doing the Snoopy dance. This is less foreshadowing and more the idea of really tracking the back story you create for your characters.

To do that a lot of authors, and I'm sure screenwriters, keep what's called a Series Bible. There, you make notes of this kind of information. So that you don't have to go back and look through previous episodes or books. That way it's easy to remind yourself that hey, Willow goes to Xander's for the Charlie Brown Christmas special and Xander does a Snoopy dance.

Foreshadowing What Joyce Learns

I found the Joyce scene with Angel outside the house so striking because in the season finale, at that very same spot, Joyce will encounter Spike and Buffy. And Buffy will try to cover and explain why Spike is there. It's a great scene. Then a vampire approaches. And Buffy dusts him in front of Joyce.

It's the first time Joyce sees that Buffy is the Slayer. And Buffy has to explain it to her. I love that we have that kind of resonance with Joyce being forced, or Buffy being forced, to tell her mother more about her real identity. And it happens at the same place Angel told Joyce about him and Buffy making love, something else Buffy kept from her mother. I think that can't be an accident.

What Does The Disk Mean?

The computer disk falling in between the desk and cabinet is so interesting. On the one hand, it could be an obvious foreshadowing for the audience. Hey, the spell is still here. Probably this is going to be important. Maybe Angel will get his soul back.

But given the way the show was written, it could also just be Joss Whedon twisting the knife. Saying yeah, it's right there, and they're never going to know it.

So you don't really know for sure when you first see the episode. But it does set up the finale where Willow finds the disk and realizes that they could potentially bring Angel back. Because we also find out that she's been experimenting with Jenny's spells.

The Voiceover

Overall, the voiceover on Passion carries the theme of the episode. Which is what Giles talked about in Bewitched, Bothered and Bewildered: This idea of love versus obsession. And Angel is talking about the same thing. Passion, obsession. What it drives us to do.

Just as it drives Xander to say his I Told You So.

In the rest of the season, we will see that play out with all the characters. Cordelia and Xander have these really strong feelings that they should not bring Angel back. Which is driven by their emotions. Likewise, Buffy deciding that Willow should try raises questions. How much is a logical thing for Buffy, because that would stop Angel from all this killing, and how much is it that she wants him back?

And Willow's love for Buffy and friendship so strong that she will do whatever Buffy wants. But she also thinks it's the right choice. So there is just so much going on there.

Passion also foreshadows Season Three and all those high emotions when Buffy knows Angel is back and doesn't tell everyone. Everything that happens here informs that. How can she tell them that he's back, especially when we see at the end of the season he'll torture Giles? And then passion drives everyone's anger toward Buffy for sheltering Angel.

Audience Uncertainty

And then there's Joss Whedon's comment that he wanted the audience unsure if they wanted Angel back. If they wanted his soul restored. And that is all foreshadowed here because we know Angel's soul can be lost and because he killed Jenny, we feel those dire consequences. So it is a very real fear, grounded in reality, of what could happen.

So we are on the sides of all the characters. Of Buffy wanting to restore the soul. Of the others who think it's a terrible idea.

Easter Egg

I will end with one last foreshadowing that, the more I think sort of it, is more like an Easter egg for those fans who really paid attention. It would be more obvious now if you are binge-watching Buffy. But at the time the episodes could often be quite spread out, so you might not see it.

I don't recall how much time there was between Passion and the finale. But it was probably at least six weeks. Here, the proprietor of the Magic Shop talked about the Orb of Thesulah and said he sold some as New Age paperweights. Kind of scoffing at these people who don't really know the trade. And we'll see when Willow says they need an Orb of Thesulah in the finale, Giles goes in his office and brings one out. He says he's been using it as a paperweight.

That's a fun thing for the fans back then when you couldn't binge watch.

Questions For Your Writing

- Is it clear which character is your protagonist? If not, how can you adjust your plot and point of view to make it clear?
- Does your protagonist suffer a major reversal at the Midpoint of your novel, commit to the quest, or both? If not, can you add a reversal or commitment?
- What do your characters do when they are angry? Sad? Afraid? How does that vary from one character to another?
- Can you use a shift in a character's speaking style or tone to convey strong emotion?
- Are there any spots in your story where you can use dramatic irony to increase tension for the audience?

Next: Killed By Death

NEXT WE'LL TALK about Killed By Death, where Buffy's in the hospital and Cordelia defines tact as just not saying true things. The chapter covers flashbacks, pace, and unclear plot turns.

CHAPTER 6
KILLED BY DEATH (S2 E18)

THIS CHAPTER TALKS about Killed By Death, Season Two Episode Eighteen, where the flu puts Buffy in the hospital and she encounters a demon. Written by Rob DesHotel and Dean Vitali and directed by Darren Serafini.

In particular, we'll look at:

- Why the pace of this episode feels slower than usual;
- Whether the flashbacks are necessary;
- Fuzzy major plot turns; and
- Very subtle advances in the Season Two series arc.

Okay, let's dive into the Hellmouth.

OPENING **Conflict**

We start with conflict as Buffy climbs over a stone wall into the graveyard, coughing as she does. She stumbles when she lands on the ground and puts her hand to her head, clearly feeling ill but struggling to patrol anyway. She moves around a tombstone and almost stakes Xander.

Xander: Damn Buffy. My whole life flashed before my eyes. I gotta get me a life.

Cordelia and Willow are with him. Willow scolds Buffy for being out patrolling when she is so sick.

Cordelia: Half the school is out with the flu and we're all concerned about how gross you look.

Buffy says she needs to patrol. She's not going to let Angel kill even one more person. From behind her:

Angel: Oh, come on, just one more.

He runs for Cordelia and knocks her down. Buffy pulls him off of Cordelia. They fight. She is struggling, but she does get some good punches and kicks in. Angel, though, says her being off her game kind of takes the fun out of it. Then he hits her really hard.

Angel: Nope, still fun.

The Fight Goes On

The others join in and help fend Angel off. Buffy is angry at them, insisting she is fine and then she collapses and we go to credits.

When we get back, Willow, Xander, and Cordelia are bringing Buffy to the emergency room. The doctors whisk her away after saying she has a high-grade fever and possible fractures. Willow tells Xander to call Giles and tell him what happened.

Willow (to Cordelia): Call Buffy's mom and tell her – not what happened. Just get her here.

In the next scene, Giles paces and cleans his glasses as they wait in the emergency room waiting area. Joyce appears, very worried. The doctor comes out and says that Buffy has stabilized, but the doctor wants to keep her here a few days to heal.

Story Spark In Killed By Death

The doctors says that around 5 minutes in. The episodes are

about 42 to 44 minutes long. Usually, we see our Story Spark or Inciting Incident a little before this. It comes about 10% through any story and sets the main plot in motion. Here, the main plot will be Buffy defeating a monster that is killing children in the hospital. So the fact that she now must stay in the hospital is what sets that plot moving.

Everyone walks along with Buffy's gurney as she's being wheeled to a room. She gets agitated when she hears she has to stay in the hospital. She's a bit delusional from the fever, which is a good thing because she starts raving about getting the vampires. Giles reassures her, saying, "I'll take care of those vampires." And then he tells Joyce it's best to humor her.

The hospital hallway, like so many places in Sunnydale, is dimly lit. We will see a lot of dark rooms and hallways in this episode.

Back Story, Lack Of Conflict, And Flashbacks

Xander is really shaken by seeing Buffy scared. He's never seen that before. Joyce explains that when Buffy was a little girl her cousin Celia (whom we've never heard about before) died in the hospital. Buffy was alone with her when it happened.

This tells us almost everything we need to know about this back story. And in my view, it makes the later flashbacks for the most part unnecessary.

This dialogue also stands out to me because usually the show is so good at getting exposition in through conflict that's compelling and interesting by itself. Here we have a little bit of conflict because Xander is shaken. Then of course Joyce is worried about Buffy. But it's not a conflict between Joyce and Xander. So it feels more like just handing us information. It's very quick, though, so I think it generally works.

Backfilling

This mention of Celia is an example of how sometimes you need to backfill back story. Back story that maybe you didn't think about in advance as you were setting up your story.

Particularly if it's part of a series, whether TV or novels or movies. So you just add in some back story when you need it.

Generally, an audience or readers will go with that as long as you're not contradicting anything from the past. It helps, though, if you can tie that new back story to something that we've heard about before. Here, for example, if we already knew there was some sort of tragedy in Buffy's family's past but not what, the Celia back story would feel more believable.

As it is, this is such a big thing. We find out later Buffy was about ten years old. To have watched a cousin of your age die when you were ten is so traumatic. It seems like something that Buffy might have alluded to somewhere along the way. Especially because being the Slayer is so much about death and saving people.

So this addition to her back story feels clunky to me. And because the show is so overall well written, when you get these moments that aren't quite as elegant it sticks out.

Does Joyce Wonder Why Giles Is There?

Joyce says she needs to go call Buffy's dad. Giles takes her to show her where the phone is. (This is before cell phones were common.) Joyce tells Giles she really appreciates how he looks out for Buffy.

I think it's not an accident that she says this as she's going to call Buffy's dad, who we have not seen since the pilot of Season Two when he brought Buffy back from spending the summer with him.

I'm not even sure he's been mentioned since then. And I think this linking of him, though fairly subtle, helps us believe that Joyce is grateful for Giles's presence in Buffy's life. (As opposed to wondering why the high school librarian is at the hospital before she is when her daughter is brought to the emergency room?)

Joyce And Giles Bond

Joyce also tells Giles she was sorry to hear about Miss

Calendar. That Buffy told her the two of them were close. I really like this moment. As in the previous one, we get exposition, but this feels more genuine.

For one thing, Joyce is feeling awkward. She says, "I don't know if I should say anything, but Buffy told me." And she tells him Buffy's been so down since it happened and Buffy never gets sick. So we know this probably is part of what has made Buffy vulnerable.

And even though Joyce is giving us information here, I like the little bit of tension. Her sort of uncertainty. Should she raise this with Giles at all? And his response, which is that he appreciates Joyce's words.

Reminders In Killed By Death

This mention of Jenny also reminds our audience why Buffy is so concerned about missing even one day of patrolling and allowing Angel to kill one more person.

These types of reminders are helpful when you're telling a longer story. In a short story you don't need it. But in a novel, if you haven't visited with certain characters in quite a while, or something happened very early in the novel (maybe in a prologue) and you're halfway through and it hasn't been referenced, it's good to throw in something to help the reader remember.

I feel like that is what the show was doing here, plus showing this developing relationship between Joyce and Giles.

Freddy Kruger-like Killer

We switch to Willow and Xander who are worrying that Angel could attack Buffy while she's in the hospital because it's a public building. So he can come in any time.

Then it's nighttime. We already raised this issue of Buffy's added vulnerability. She is sleeping hooked to an IV drip. Her arm is in a splint. She opens her eyes and a little boy pauses in her doorway. He looks at her, then walks on. A man follows.

He has long curly hair, a hooked nose, and a bowler hat.

And he looks a lot like Freddy Kruger from the Nightmare on Elm Street series. (Which I have never seen. Seems kind of amazing, given that I do enjoy Buffy so much and horror. But I've not watched that series.)

First Flashback

Buffy gets out of bed and starts walking. The hall spins a bit and the colors fade. So now we're in a black-and-white scene. We see little girl walking through the hospital hallway and into a room with a curtained bed. This is the first of the flashbacks. I'm not sure it adds anything.

We already know that Buffy as a little girl was in the hospital and saw her cousin die. It might've been more interesting if we hadn't gotten that exposition from Joyce. Because now we would see this scene and we wouldn't know for sure that was Buffy as a little girl.

In fact, we might think it was part of current strange happenings at the hospital. That could add some mystery and give us as an audience something to figure out. A way to be more engaged with the story.

Moving Toward A One-Quarter Twist (Or Two)

Next, we see Buffy in her hospital bed again. The time clock is the same as it was before she saw the little boy. So we know at one point or another in this she has been dreaming.

We're about 10 minutes 5 seconds into the story, nearing the one quarter mark in terms of timing. Usually around here we will see the first major plot turn that comes from outside the protagonist and spins the story in a new direction.

Here, Buffy yet again walks the halls. She sees orderlies take a body out from under a sheet. One of them says he hates it when they lose the young ones. At about 12 minutes in, Buffy peers into the room. Two doctors argue about the treatment of the children. The male doctor – who we'll find out later is Dr. Backer – tells the woman doctor to take it up with the board if she doesn't like his methods. She says that she has.

At almost 12 and a half minutes in, a little boy and girl come up behind Buffy. The boy, who we'll learn is named Ryan, says to Buffy, "He comes at night. The grown-ups can't see him." He tells Buffy that he (the monster) was with Tina and then Tina died. Buffy asks who he is and the boys says, "Death."

And we go to a commercial. So that's a great hook into the commercial.

As far as the major plot turn, I think maybe it is that whole sequence. Because this is where we find out that something supernatural may be causing the children's deaths. Or perhaps it's the doctors. But something more than simply a bad flu.

Angel Visits

When we come back from the commercial, Xander is sitting outside Buffy's room. Angel comes through the hallway holding white roses. Xander stands in his way. Angel taunts him, saying Xander couldn't stop him if he wants to go into Buffy's room.

And Xander says maybe not, but there's a security guard over there and cops and orderlies. Together they might be able to stop Angel.

Angel calls Xander Buffy's white knight, and says Xander still loves Buffy. He leans very close and whispers into Xander's ear.

Angel: It must just eat you up that I got there first.

Xander: You're gonna die. And I'm gonna be there.

Angel slaps the white roses against Xander's chest and leaves. Xander lets out a breath, very shaky, and sits. Which shows us how tense and frightened he was in that confrontation.

I don't believe that the orderlies, Xander, and the cops together could stop Angel. But I think he leaves because, one, he wants to terrorize Buffy. He doesn't necessarily want to kill her yet. Also, I feel like what we've seen of him, when he does kill her he wants it to be a very emotional dramatic moment for her. Not in the midst of a bunch of chaos with all kinds of people around.

So I buy that Angel would leave.

Superhero Flashback

We are back in black-and-white. Buffy as a little girl is playing superhero with her cousin Celia. After declaring that she is Power Girl, Buffy saves Celia, who is buried under a bunch of pillows.

This flashback doesn't move our story forward. So it is definitely not necessary to the plot. But it is really fun to see little girl Buffy as Power Girl. And it adds to the character development. We learn that Buffy and her cousin had fun together and were close and that Buffy wanted to be a superhero.

It also adds to my view, along with the next part of the flashback, that this might've been a more intriguing episode to watch if we didn't already know Celia's and Buffy's back story. Because next we see Buffy approach the hospital bed where Celia sleeps. If we hadn't already known that Buffy watched Celia die, this could be really engaging.

As it is, this flashback of Buffy going up to Celia's bed just slows down our story.

Buffy Healed Fast

Buffy wakes up. It's morning. She's much more perky. The doctor tells her that her fever went down. She's also surprised to see the swelling on Buffy's wrist is gone. Buffy feels ready to leave the hospital. But the doctor tells her she needs to stay another day to be sure the fever is really gone.

Buffy asks about kids dying, but Giles comes in along with Cordelia, Willow, and Xander. The doctor leaves without answering.

Xander brought balloons. Willow brings Buffy her homework. Which doesn't make Buffy really happy until Willow says that she did the homework for her. Then she steps back and everyone kind of looks at Cordelia, who is empty-handed.

Cordelia: Nobody told me I was supposed to bring a gift. I was out of the loop on gifts.

Giles: It's traditional among – people.

Repeated Exposition

They take Buffy for a walk outside. She tells them about Dr. Backer and his experimental treatments. And that a little girl, Tina, died and Ryan said he saw Death. The others are a bit skeptical that there's anything unusual going on given that the flu is going around and it's really bad.

This scene feels slow. Much of what Buffy tells her friends we already know. It's not typical for Buffy to recap information the audience knows from the very same episode. Yes, we get some of those reminders through conflict, such as the reminder about Jenny. But that's a reminder about what happened in a previous episode.

Tact Girl

There is some conflict in that the others push back against Buffy's theory, leading to some of my favorite dialogue. Cordelia points out Buffy might just be looking for a monster to fight because that's easier than dealing with her feelings about her cousin's death in the hospital.

Giles: Have you ever actually heard of tact?

Cordelia: Tact is just not saying true stuff. I'll pass.

Buffy argues that Ryan is afraid of something. As long as she's forced to stay here, she's going to find out what it is. So the others, though still skeptical, offer to help.

Cordelia and Xander sneak into the records room. They split up to look around. A security guard comes in and confronts Cordelia.

At the library, Giles tells Willow that Cordelia might be tactless but right. Death and disease might be the only things Buffy can't fight. And she might really need a defeatable opponent, especially after what happened to Jenny.

But Willow says on the "we live on the Hellmouth side" the

kids might have seen something real. Giles says sometimes children do see something adults miss – the true selves of adults. Their hidden faces. They start researching Dr. Backer.

Dr. Backer Understands

Cordelia is flirting with the security guard to keep him distracted while Xander keeps looking around. And she gets information.

Cordelia: I bet you see a lot of tragedy, like that little girl who died.

Guard: Dr. Backer understands the truth about children, that sometimes they die.

Xander drops something. The guard is about to go check out the sound but Cordelia, clearly struggling for something to say but making it sound very natural, tells him he has the most perfect nose she's ever seen. He must work out.

Xander sneaks out. Later he's clearly jealous of her flirting. She calls him on a double standard when he says he needs to stay at the hospital to protect Buffy.

Cordelia: Oh, your obsession with protecting Buffy. Have I told you how attractive that's not?

We are now approaching the Midpoint of the episode.

Nearing The Midpoint Of Killed By Death

We're 22 minutes in. This is where we should see a major reversal for our protagonist or a strong commitment by the protagonist or both. Neither feels all that strong here, although we will see a reversal and a commitment later. This is another reason the story doesn't have that much momentum.

Buffy, already looking stronger, walks down another dim hallway and goes to the play area in the children's ward. Ryan is drawing a picture of the scary guy Buffy saw. And Ryan says he'll come again tonight.

At 23 minutes in Buffy says she believes Ryan. They both know there are real monsters, and she's not going to let this one hurt him. Or any of the kids. So this is a commitment on Buffy's part to protect Ryan and the kids.

It's less powerful for me than many Buffy makes because it doesn't feel like throwing caution to the wind, or the full commitment to the quest. Because Buffy – that's what she does. She protects people. So it doesn't feel like a big moment. Or it doesn't feel like something that really propels the story forward.

It feels more like, yeah, that's what Buffy does.

Controversy And Backer

At the library again, Willow finds Dr. Backer's records. He's been sanctioned for risky procedures and controversial treatments.

We go back to a very dark hospital. The doctor is in his office. He's checking test tubes in his refrigerator as he whispers to himself. Then he makes notes in a journal. This is another scene that feels unnecessary given what Willow just told us.

Xander is dozing in the hall outside Buffy's room. Cordelia brings a bag of Krispy Kreme donuts and coffee and sits with him. I like this moment. There's no dialogue, but I feel like there is this shift between the two characters that we see from the way the scene is directed and acted. We get the sense that despite a bit of an argument earlier, Cordelia is there for Xander. She is also concerned about Buffy and understands the need for someone to be there.

A Major Turn

Dr. Backer starts to inject one of the kids when something invisible starts hitting him and slashing him. Ryan watches as Backer's killed. We see it in shadow on the wall. At 26 minutes 30 seconds in, Buffy gets to the door of the children's ward just as Backer is being thrown out of it. The invisible being knocks Buffy out of the way and drags the doctor down the hall.

This seems like a major reversal for Buffy. But it's past the Midpoint where we needed that stronger turn.

Backer's murder also could serve as the next major plot turn. That usually comes about three quarters through the episode and arises out of the protagonist's commitment at the Midpoint, but turns the story in another new direction.

Here, it's a turn because it's the first time Buffy gets a look at the monster, even though it's invisible. She sees part of what the monster does, and it knocks into her. Also, it makes it clear Backer is not the villain.

But it's early for that Three-Quarter Turn. The episode is about 43 minutes long. So we would normally see that around 30-31 minutes, and we do see another turn there. So I don't feel like this moment is it.

What Ryan Sees

The thing that kind of bothers me in this episode is Ryan watched this monster kill a doctor. I know he already saw it kill a little girl. But we didn't see that. We heard about it. Now we have seen this. And it must be so traumatic for Ryan, and there isn't much of an acknowledgment of that. That's what I see as truly the major reversal. Buffy has not been able to protect Ryan from seeing this monster kill the doctor. The doctor who it turns out was trying to help him.

In Buffy's hospital room the next day Giles tells her that Tina's records show that she improved after getting the flu but then deteriorated suddenly. And he and Willow think it's because of Dr. Backer and his questionable methods. But Buffy tells them the monster killed Backer.

More Repeated Exposition

I think the info on Tina's records is new, but otherwise again we have Giles telling Buffy something we know, which is about Dr. Backer's methods. Also Buffy tells Giles what we just saw – that the monster killed Backer. I'm not sure how you would do this scene without that exchange. They both need to convey that information to the other. But avoiding repetition is another thing that usually the show does so well, yet here it's left in.

There is a really nice moment, though, where Buffy shows Giles Ryan's crayon drawing of the monster. Giles looks really troubled. And he takes off his glasses and says, "This is your work?" Buffy shoots him a look and says it's Ryan's.

Joyce Interrupts A Secret Meeting

The group is trying to figure out why the kids see the monster and Buffy doesn't, except for that one time when she was delirious with fever. At that moment Joyce walks in. They all look very serious, and she says she hopes she didn't interrupt a secret meeting.

Cordelia says, "You sure didn't," far too adamantly.

Joyce has good news. The doctor says Buffy can go home. Joyce is understandably puzzled when now Buffy doesn't want to leave when before she'd been so insistent on it. But Buffy claims she doesn't feel quite well again. Joyce says she'll go talk to the doctor.

More Possible Midpoint Commitments

So this is 28 minutes in. This, too, could have been a great Midpoint Commitment for Buffy. Because despite her fear of hospitals and how insistent she was on leaving even when she was delirious, she stays. It shows us how much it means to her to protect these kids. But it comes very late in the episode, almost three-quarters of the way through.

After Joyce leaves, Buffy asks Giles to do some more research and figure out what this monster is.

Buffy: I'll check Backer's office. See if I can find any Post Its that say "why a monster might want me dead."

She asks Willow to come with her because Willow will better know what the medical terms might mean. Xander says he'll stay on sentry duty and that Cordelia should help Giles research.

Giles (looking distressed): Why do I have to have –

He cuts off as Cordelia stares at him, then backpedals and says good thinking, he can use a research assistant. But she is not fooled.

Cordelia: Let's go, Tact Guy.

Filler

At a little after 30 minutes, Willow and Buffy break into Backer's office. Willow finds his notes and says Backer was trying to give the kids controlled doses of the virus and raise their temperatures to burn it out of them. Buffy looks at the test tubes in the refrigerator. This covers everything we saw in that scene with Backer in his office looking at the test tubes and making notes. Which is another reason why the scene feels like filler and slows the episode.

I look for these types of scenes when I revise my novels. Personally, I think it is better to eliminate a scene that covers the same ground for the plot unless there's something of great emotional or character significance in revisiting it.

Cordelia Aggravates Giles

We switch back to the library for another really fun moment. Cordelia is looking through the books across from Giles who is also researching. But she keeps interrupting and asking, "What does this demon do?"

And Giles explains it, and she says what does that one do. And he explains that, looking irritated. The third time she says "what does this one do?" Giles has had it.

Giles: It asks endless questions of those with whom it's supposed to be working so that nothing ever gets done.

Cordelia: Boy, there's a demon for everything.

Giles slams his book shut and walks away from the table. He says he's not sure they'll ever find the monster since it's invisible to adults. This is such a nice moment. One, just for the dialogue. But also because we see Giles's frustration and irritation. Not just in snapping at Cordelia but in his actions: slamming the book, walking away from the table.

I like that he says they may never find this and why, because it shows us that, yes, he is irritated with Cordelia. But what he is really worried and angry about is not getting anywhere. It also tells us it's unusual for them to get nowhere.

Cordelia Finds The Demon At The Three-Quarter Turn

At about 32 minutes in, though, Cordelia says, "Well, it's not in here," and closes her book. Then we see the front cover. It has a drawing of the monster.

By timing, this is the Three-Quarter Turn or three-quarter mark, at least in the story. And in a way it arose out of the Midpoint where Buffy told Ryan she'd protect the kids. And it does turn the story because Cordelia will tell Buffy what the monster is and what it does.

But it doesn't feel like much of a major plot turn because we already knew there was a monster. We already knew it killed the kids and Dr. Backer. And we knew what it looked like. So it doesn't feel like a new direction when Cordelia calls Buffy and starts talking about the monster.

Buffy is confused and says, "Who is this?" Cordelia persists and tells her the monster is called Der Kindestod, and the name means child's death. It feeds on children by sucking the life out of them. And that it's basically looking at the children's ward as an all-you-can-eat kind of thing.

When Giles gets on the phone, he tells her it gorges by sitting on the prey, pinning it down, and it must be horrifying.

One More Flashback

Buffy then flashes back to Celia's death and Celia screaming with her hands up as if to push something off of her. So this flashback does move our story forward a little. Buffy freezes as it hits her that this monster is what killed Celia.

Again, if we hadn't known about Celia's death, this would've been a really neat moment. All those flashbacks we as the audience could have put together and realized that this was why we kept seeing these little girls in the hospital.

I think I would've really enjoyed that. And I'm curious to know whether there was a version of the script where Joyce didn't give that exposition. Maybe someone came back and looked at it and decided that it might be too hard for the audience to put together the pieces.

Buffy's Realization

So we're 34 minutes in and Buffy says, "It killed Celia, and I have to defeat it."

This also could be that Three-Quarter plot turn. It's a tiny bit late, but it does spin the story in the sense of now Buffy has a personal reason to kill the monster.

The reason that also doesn't quite work for me as a turn is because, again, Buffy was still going to go kill the monster. Maybe this makes her more committed to it. That could have worked at the Midpoint, giving Buffy a personal stake in prevailing over this being.

Willow reassures Buffy she'll defeat the monster, but they aren't sure how Buffy can do that when she can't see it. Buffy says she only saw it when she was crazed with fever. Then it hits her. That's why Celia saw it and why Ryan saw it. So it's not about children and adults. It's about who has the fever.

The Three-Quarter Turn In Killed By Death

That moment is a plot turn. In fact, it probably is the best candidate to be the Three-Quarter Turn. Now Buffy knows it's the fever that makes people see the monster, and this propels her actions from this point on.

Buffy could have had this realization back when she first mentioned how she only saw the monster when she had a fever. Then either the doctor or Joyce came in and interrupted. As it is now, this realization doesn't grow out of any earlier plot point or turn. She had the flashback to Celia and realized Celia was probably seeing that monster on her. But for me, that just doesn't feel like enough of a difference that Buffy wouldn't have made that connection to being feverish earlier. The only reason she didn't is we had someone happen to walk in and interrupt her.

Delaying Your Protagonist's Light Bulb Moment

That's an example of simply delaying Buffy's realization for chance reasons. That can work very early on in your story. If it's a tiny hint of an idea, then something derails the protagonist to go do something else, that is very typical in a mystery. It works early on because the protagonist doesn't know enough yet to know what's significant and neither does the reader. So you can weave in these little clues, and it makes sense the protagonist doesn't put the pieces together.

But the fever and seeing the monster, that discussion happened the first time well into the episode. They already knew about the monster, that the kids saw it and Buffy didn't except when she was very ill. So it feels artificial that Buffy's realization was simply delayed. And that makes this turn less dramatic.

But when Buffy does put those pieces together, the rest of the episode is more dramatic and moves more quickly.

Buffy now takes a really significant action. She and Willow go back to Dr. Backer's office. Buffy drinks some of that serum to make herself sick again. Willow asks if she can fight with the fever and Buffy says she'll find out. She starts feeling weak and sick almost immediately.

This too, could've made a nice Midpoint Commitment. It truly is a throwing of caution to the wind. But we would've had half an episode to go with Buffy so sick. And we saw that she could not fight very well with that fever against Angel, and now she's that sick again. We don't do a ton with that because there isn't a lot of episode left.

Buffy and Willow go to the children's ward, and all the kids are gone. And we cut to commercial. Another good hook.

When we come back, we see a quick scene with the kids running through a basement hallway. Buffy is looking at that empty ward and the monster fades into view. He, too, was looking around the ward. He doesn't see any kids.

But he does see Buffy watching him. He laughs and tips his hat to her, then exits through a door labeled Basement Access. He figured out where the kids must've gone.

More Obstacles For The Protagonist

Buffy's doctor comes around the corner as Buffy is trying to get into the children's ward. I guess the door is locked. The doctor sees how ill Buffy is and tries to take her back to her room.

Buffy and Willow break away and run. The doctor calls for Security. In another hallway, guards stop Willow and Buffy. Buffy gives Willow a desperate look. Willow starts brushing at her legs frantically and shouting about frogs as if she's trying to get them off of her.

(In a previous episode, Willow fell asleep in the library and woke up, very startled, talking about tadpoles. When Giles asked about that, she said she had frog fear. It's a nice thing that Willow makes use of that.)

The guards fall for it and surround Willow. Buffy runs off.

I love this froggy moment, and we need barriers in our protagonist's way. It shouldn't be easy for the protagonist to accomplish pretty much anything in a story. There should be obstacles. Yet, I find these scenes with the doctor and the security guards unsatisfying because the antagonist doesn't cause these obstacles.

The monster doesn't send the doctor or the security guards there. (It would seem very unmonsterlike if he did.) It's not supernatural, and the hospital itself is not the villain here, though that could also be an interesting story. Finally, while it's good to have multiple forces push against your protagonist, these obstacles don't feel as strong as the ones we usually see in Buffy. The writers may have done that because Buffy herself is weaker, which makes the guards and the doctor more of a threat. But the scenes lack a real sense of peril.

That being said I do love the teamwork aspect. I love how smart Willow is and how quickly she acts. Then Buffy staggers around the corner and finds Xander. He helps her down to the basement, partly supporting her.

Xander: You don't how to kill this thing.

Buffy: I thought I might try violence.

Xander: Solid call.

The Climax Of Killed By Death

So now we are at our Climax. About 38 minutes 40 seconds in the monster is attacking Ryan. All the kids are screaming. And we will hear kids screaming for pretty much all of the climax. Which is another somewhat unBuffy-like thing. Usually, we don't have all the screaming. To me it feels a bit like the laugh track in the sitcom that's telling us, oh, you should laugh there. And this is saying you should be really afraid.

Here, for whatever reason, I'm not. Maybe because I don't in any way think that this is going to end with the monster killing more kids.

But it is holding Ryan down. Its eyes pop out. They are almost like corkscrews that go down towards Ryan and then clamp onto his forehead. (So I guess that isn't exactly a corkscrew. But both of them look that way spiraling down.) Ryan is crying and screaming and holding up his hands the way Celia did in Buffy's flashback.

Buffy is able to get the monster off of Ryan. But she struggles to fight it because she so sick. Xander herds the kids out of the way, then stays to watch Buffy fight. All he sees is Buffy fighting because the monster is invisible to him.

It gets Buffy. And we are in her point of view again. Its eyes pop out and are spiraling down toward her. And she finally reaches up and snaps its neck.

Falling Action

Xander at first asks if she's okay, and then asks if the monster's dead Because he heard something snap. And Buffy says that would be the monster's neck. Xander's holding her up as they walk out of the basement.

Xander: You're not going to yak on me are you?

We have moved to the Falling Action where the loose ends in the story are tied up. There aren't a lot of loose ends here, but this Falling Action is pretty fun.

Buffy, Willow, and Xander are all in Buffy's bedroom. They're lying on her bed watching TV. Buffy is still recovering, and Joyce brings her sandwiches with the crusts cut off just like Buffy likes. But it turns out it's not quite the right peanut butter. Buffy wants crunchy.

Xander and Willow ask for drink refills and chips. Joyce claims there are no more cheesy chips but Xander tells her there are. They're hidden behind some other things in the cabinet. She says she'll go get them.

Joyce is really good-humored about this. She has a lot of patience with all three of them. When she comes back she tells Buffy that Ryan sent her something. Buffy opens the envelope and inside is a drawing of her killing the monster. Joyce looks rather bemused.

Joyce: Oh, he drew you a picture. How nice.

And that is the end of the episode.

The Monster Of The Week

Killed By Death is the very definition of a Monster Of The Week episode. We've had those before in Buffy, but I feel like usually they have a little bit more in the way of plot or character development.

Here, Angel doesn't really step up his harassment of Buffy, though he does goad Xander at one point. Buffy says that Angel put her in the hospital, but I feel like that is clearly not the case. She's in the hospital because of the flu. It seems pretty obvious she would've collapsed anyway. She was so sick I think fighting any vampire or demon would've put her in the hospital.

This episode does in some very small subtle ways advance our plot and foreshadow the season. So I will talk about that in Spoilers.

Movie Connections

The IMDB Movie Connections page says Joss Whedon modeled the monster after Freddy Krueger, Nosferatu, and the bogeyman. It also mentions that a line of dialogue references the most famous scene in The Invisible Man when Xander acknowledges that he won't be much help in a fight against the monster because he can't see it. He adds: "If I see a floating pipe and a smoking jacket, he's dropped."

There's also a reference to the 1957 movie The Seventh Seal. Curiously, while I didn't see the Nightmare On Elm Street movies, I did see The Seventh Seal. (The University of Chicago ran it as part of either a class or a film festival that was open to the public.)

It's about a character grappling with Death with capital D. And the protagonist plays chess with Death. Xander has a line in Killed By Death where he refers to Death and says, "If he asks you to play chess, don't even do it, the guy's like a whiz."

Spoilers and Foreshadowing

XANDER-ANGEL ISSUES

When Xander says to Angel, "You're gonna die. And I'm gonna be there," I can't help feeling that this moment might be part of why in the Season Two finale Xander chooses not to tell Buffy that Willow is doing the spell to give Angel back his soul. Buffy has the sword. She is about to go into battle with Angel. And Xander almost tells her about Willow doing the spell.

Then he doesn't and instead says, "Kick his ass." Or, rather, tells her that's what Willow said. Which is worse.

This interchange with Angel in Killed By Death might explain that. Xander really wants her to kill Angel, and he wants to be there. However, I do think Xander has other and better motives, and I'll talk about that when we get to the episode.

Joyce Appreciates Giles

Another moment here that I never noticed before in terms of foreshadowing:

That moment when Joyce tells Giles how much she appreciates him looking out for Buffy. And maybe it's less foreshadowing and more that it adds a layer to the Season Three pilot when Joyce expresses anger at Giles. And says she blames him for Buffy running away because he had all this influence on Buffy's life, and he knew about this whole part of her life being a Slayer, and he did not tell Joyce about it.

Ryan's Drawing

Joyce seeing that drawing Ryan sends at the end of the episode is one of those subtle moments I feel does advance our season plot. In the drawing, Buffy's foot is on the monster. And she clearly killed it. I think that contributes a bit to our finale of the season when Joyce sees Buffy dust a vampire right in front of her.

We were told in the beginning, and we've seen over and over, that even when people in Sunnydale see a vampire attack someone, or see Buffy kill a vampire, they find a way to rationalize it. And we know that's what Joyce has been doing.

But Joyce's ability to deny what's in front of her gradually gets whittled away as we go through the season. Joyce must be asking somewhere in her mind why this little kid would draw this. So that when she does finally see Buffy dust a vampire, this drawing has opened her mind a bit. And instead of rationalizing it away, she's finally willing to listen when Buffy tells her she's a Vampire Slayer and what that is.

Joyce still definitely has trouble with it and pushes back against it. But it makes it much more believable that she doesn't do the rationalizing and forgetting thing.

Angel's Heart's Not In The Fight

Finally, when Buffy and Angel fight in the graveyard, it foreshadows the fight that they'll have in Part One of Becoming, where Angel doesn't seem to be giving it his all. Buffy is a bit slow to realize that and definitely slow to grasp the reason for it.

And I feel like this scene at the beginning of this episode lays the groundwork for that. Because Angel probably could have killed Buffy when she had the flu. Yes, the others also gang up on him and hold out crosses. But if he wanted to end it there, it seems pretty certain that Angel could have done it. All he needed to do was back off and wait a few moments until Buffy collapsed. But he didn't. Because Angel isn't ready to kill Buffy yet.

And Buffy I think absorbs this. So when she is fighting Angel the first time in the finale it's much more believable that it takes her a bit to realize that there is another reason that he is stalling.

Questions For Your Writing

- Do your characters give each other information that your audience already knows? If so, can you edit the scene to avoid the repetition?
- If you use flashbacks, do they move your main plot or a subplot forward? Are they necessary for character development or exposition or can you

replace them with a sentence or two of narration or dialogue?
- Are your plot turns clear?

Next: I Only Have Eyes For You

NEXT WE'LL TALK about I Only Have Eyes For You, the episode where both Angel and Buffy are taken over by ghosts. The chapter includes plot turns in key subplots and what happens when the magic makes no sense.

CHAPTER 7

I ONLY HAVE EYES FOR YOU (S2 E19)

THIS CHAPTER TALKS about I Only Have Eyes For You, Season Two Episode, Nineteen, where ghosts take over Buffy and Angel. Written by Marti Noxon and directed by James Whitmore, Jr.

In particular, we'll look at:

- Conflict that conveys exposition;
- Scary moments that don't ring true;
- Midpoint questions and multiple major turns late in the story;
- A subtle subplot; and
- How vulnerability helps the audience feel for characters.

Okay, let's dive into the Hellmouth.

———

OPENING **Conflict**

The opening conflict in I Only Have Eyes For You shows Buffy standing alone at the Bronze on the upper level. She's leaning on the railing and looking down. The moment is echoed in a way in the climax of the episode.

Here, another student walks up to her. We have not seen him before. Below, a band plays. The young woman vocalist is singing a song about language as an annoying necessity. Which fits because language becomes key to this entire story.

The student tells Buffy he was in her Algebra class. She doesn't remember him, but she tries to. He asks if she's going to the dance tomorrow. And she says, "Oh, the Sadie Hawkins Dance where the girls are supposed to ask the boys." He says right, and he thought if she wasn't going already maybe she could ask him.

Buffy stutters and stumbles. He immediately backs off. Buffy apologizes and tells him he seems like a great guy but:

Buffy: I'm not seeing anybody. Ever again actually.

He says that's too bad and leaves, and Buffy looks sad.

She goes down to the first floor where Willow asks if she's bailing. Buffy says she'll go to the library, patrol if Giles think she should, and then hit the sack. Willow says Buffy's been doing that a lot lately, adding, "You've kind of been all work and no play Buffy."

When Buffy says she came to the Bronze tonight, so she does have fun, Willow responds:

Willow: You came. You saw. You rejected.

Excellent Exposition In I Only Have Eyes For You

Buffy doesn't think she's in date mode. Willow suggests that maybe she's thinking too much. Maybe she needs to be impulsive. And Buffy responds by saying remember her last boyfriend?

Buffy: I slept with him. He lost his soul. Now my boyfriend's gone forever and the demon that wears his face is killing my friends. The next impulsive decision I make will involve my choice of dentures.

This entire scene is such a great example of getting exposition in through conflict. Even the background of the Sadie Hawkins Dance where the girls ask the boys slips in there really naturally during the humor and awkwardness of the scene where the boy asks Buffy out.

Buffy's dialogue summing up what happened with Angel gives us a ton of information. But unlike in Killed By Death, discussed in the last chapter, where the exposition was simply the characters passing information back and forth, here it comes out in a compelling way.

One, it's part of a conflict. Willow is saying, hey relax, have some fun, be impulsive. And Buffy tells Willow exactly why she fears being impulsive. The dialogue also uses that rhythm and style of the language of the show that fans just enjoy listening to. And Buffy's explanatory line ends with humor (about the dentures).

All of that makes the dialogue fun despite that it conveys lots of information. It prepares us for what's coming in the episode and quickly reminds us what happened earlier in the season. And sets up a major conflict, which will be key to this episode as well.

The First Couple Fights

We switch to the school to a young couple fighting. Two teenagers. She's breaking up with him.

Boy: A person doesn't just wake up one morning and stop loving someone. Love is forever.

He pulls a gun on his girlfriend and we go to credits. This is a great hook.

Story Spark In I Only Have Eyes For You

That hook could also be the Story Spark in a different episode. The Story Spark or Inciting Incident gets our main plot moving. But we will find out that the gun and this particular fight isn't exactly what this story is about.

We return at 4 minutes 48 seconds in. The boy says he's not afraid to use the gun.

Boy: Don't walk away from me, bitch.

Buffy sees the two of them. She runs in and tackles the guy. At a little over 5 minutes into the episode, the gun flies away, and as it skids across the floor it disappears. The Story Spark usually comes about 10% into the story. So here that's 4 minutes 40 seconds.

So 5 minutes, 20 seconds in, when the gun disappears, is a little late, but close. And I see this as the Story Spark – that attempt to shoot and the gun disappearing – because it is what sets off the supernatural conflict here. Otherwise, it would've been a story about Buffy stopping a guy from killing his girlfriend, and the story pretty much would be over.

Principal Snyder Suspects Buffy

In the next scene, Buffy sits in Principal Snyder's office. She tells him she stopped the boy from killing his girlfriend. The janitor saw it, too. But Snyder says people can be coerced, and he is going to look at all the pieces of this puzzle carefully and rationally until he can see how it's all Buffy's fault.

This is another reference to fault or responsibility. We already had Buffy expressing her feelings of responsibility and guilt about what Angel has done. Now Snyder is telling her this incident is all her fault. But Snyder gets called away to deal with a vegan boy who chained himself to the vending machine again. He tells Buffy to wait for him.

While she waits, a 1955 Sunnydale High yearbook slides off the shelf. Buffy takes a quick look and replaces it.

Jenny Calendar Remembered

Willow is teaching Jenny's computer class. She tells a joke toward the end and is very pleased when the students laugh. Giles stops by as that's happening to see how the class is going. And he tells her she looks like she's doing fine.

Willow says she found good lesson plans on Miss Calendar's computer. (Which I thought burned in Passion, but perhaps that was a different one. Perhaps it was only the printer.) The line is here to let us know why Willow is teaching a class and that Miss Calendar is gone.

She also tells Giles she found files on paganism and magic on the computer and they're really interesting. And she gives him a rose quartz she found in Miss Calendar's drawer and says it has healing powers. She thinks Jenny might've wanted Giles to have it. Giles looks touched and thanks her, saying it's very thoughtful. The Jenny and Giles theme music plays.

Buffy's First Vision

We switch to Buffy in class looking bored. The teacher is talking about the stock market and the Great Depression. Buffy shuts her eyes for a moment.

When she opens them she's in a different classroom. A pretty, dark-haired teacher hands a book to student in a varsity jacket. They're alone in the classroom. She calls the student James and asks if he liked the Hemingway book she gave him.

Their hands are touching, just barely. She says the book is based on a true story. He fell in love with his – A door opens, interrupting them.

A Message

Buffy is back in her real classroom. The teacher is still lecturing. He's writing on the chalkboard. The students start to laugh, and he looks in shock at what he wrote: "Don't walk away from me, bitch." In the hallway after, Buffy tells Xander something weird is going on.

Xander: Something weird is going on. Isn't that our school motto?

He opens his locker. An arm shoots out of it and grabs him by the neck and tries to strangle him. Buffy gets the arm off of Xander. It disappears back into the locker but there's nothing there when she looks.

Buffy and Xander go into the library. He is looking a bit disheveled from the experience.

Willow: Xander. What happened? Did Cordelia win another round in the broom closet?

She is so lighthearted when she asks that it shows us Willow really has gotten past her disbelief and anger that Xander is seeing Cordelia.

Buffy and Xander tell Giles what happened. He thinks it's a poltergeist.

One-Quarter Turn In I Only Have Eyes For You

This happens a little more than 11 minutes into the episode. We usually see the first major plot turn around here. It comes from outside the protagonist and spins the story in a new direction.

I feel like this library scene is it because now Buffy knows there's some kind of ghost causing this trouble. She had a hint before because the gun was nowhere to be found. (Part of why Snyder doubted her story.) But this is confirmation.

Buffy: So we have some Bad Boo on our hands.

Giles says it's a spirit struggling to work something out but the spirit can't, so it lashes out. The only way to get rid of it is figure out what those issues are and how to resolve them. Buffy says something like, "Great, now we're Dr. Laura for the deceased." Giles points out they have to figure out first who the ghost is.

Another Couple

The next scene takes place later that night, again in the school hallway. The janitor is mopping. A teacher asks if it's okay to walk through. She calls him George, and then says, "That is your name, right?" And he says yes and it's fine.

It's clear they don't know each other very well. As she walks away, though, he says, "Oh, Ms. Frank." She turns back toward him. He drops the mop and they both start saying the same lines that the girl and the boy who fought did.

George: You can't make me disappear just because you say it's over.

She tells him she just wants him to have a normal life. She persists in saying it's over.

George: Then tell me you don't love me.

Teacher: Is that what you need to hear? I don't.

George: A person doesn't just wake up one day and stop loving someone. Love is forever.

A gun appears in his hand and we cut to commercial.

Guns As Hooks

So this is the second time we have seen the gun right before the commercial. It is a good hook. The repetition makes me wonder if the writers are doing a little bit of an inside joke because this makes me think of Chekov's gun. The idea that if you mention a gun in the first scene, someone needs to use it by the end.

So if you set up something so significant, there needs to be a reason. It's there, and it shouldn't just be a random detail.

Giles Overhears

When we come back, Giles is alone in his office. He hears George and Ms. Frank in the background. He steps out of the office into the main area of the library. A woman whispers, "I need you."

Giles (to himself in a bit of wonder): Jenny.

He walks out to the hall to see what's happening and sees George shoot Ms. Frank. Giles tackles George. The gun flies away and disappears. George asks what's going on and Giles tells him he just shot a woman. As the boy did in the earlier scene, George looks shocked and confused.

Drusilla Dances

The scene changes to a courtyard garden at night. Drusilla dances around, loving it. Angel points out that the jasmine is night blooming. Spike sits on the edge of the garden in his wheelchair.

Spike: It's paradise. Big windows. Lovely gardens. It'll be perfect when we want the sunlight to kill us.

But Angel says if Spike doesn't like it, he can hit the stairs and go home. Or he can take a stand. Throughout the episode Angel will mock Spike for being in the wheelchair.

This is the first of the scenes I mentioned at the outset that seem insignificant, or like they are here just to give us a glimpse of what Angel is doing before he and Buffy cross paths later in the episode. But the scenes turn out to tell their own story, which is what you want in the subplot. And I love the subtlety here. Even on rewatch I had forgotten how the episode ended. And I did not necessarily see the scenes as part of an episode subplot.

I thought they were going only to the season arc.

Spike also says their old place was fine until Angel got it burned down – a reference to the end of Passion. That's where Giles goes after Angel with flaming arrows.

Angel: Life changes. You have to roll with the punches. But I guess you got that covered.

Connecting The Dots

16 minutes 35 seconds in, Giles tells Willow, Buffy, and Xander about the shooting the night before. They agree that it's the same scene Buffy witnessed, including the gun disappearing. Giles says it's Jenny because she died violently in the school and is trapped there and lashing out. Buffy and Willow argue that doesn't fit. Jenny wasn't shot. And Buffy points out that the fights follow a pattern that doesn't fit Jenny's death.

Here we get some wonderful lines from Giles. They sum up the conflicting message that some adults send to children (and that I think we have all heard in the workplace), though usually we don't get this from Giles.

Giles: I appreciate your thoughts on the matter. In fact, I will encourage you to always challenge me when you feel it's appropriate. You should never be cowed by authority. Except of course in this instance where I am clearly right and you are clearly wrong.

Buffy and her friends meet separately in a classroom without Giles, puzzled by his insistence that it's Jenny.

Xander: He's usually investigate-things-from-every-boring-angle guy. Now he's like clinging-to-my-one-lame-idea guy.

Buffy: Giles misses Jenny and he can't think.

Willow searches the Internet and finds out that a student murdered a teacher the night of the Sadie Hawkins Dance. They were having an affair. After he killed her, he committed suicide by shooting himself. She says it happened in -- and Buffy cuts her off and says 1955.

They ask how she knew. Buffy tells them about the yearbook before hearing the names of the two people involved. She finds their photos. Grace Newman, the teacher, and the student, James. And Buffy says he couldn't make her love him so he killed her.

The others feel bad for both James and the teacher. But Buffy only feels bad for Ms. Newman. She says James murdered her and he should pay.

They all agree that probably James, not Ms. Newman, is the ghost causing the shootings and other incidents because it's all so violent. Willow says she's been browsing Miss Calendar's pagan websites and maybe she can figure out how to communicate with James so they can figure out what he wants.

Nearing The Midpoint

Buffy says who cares what James wants? They need to shut him down before some other innocent guy kills someone.

We're at 19 minutes 42 seconds in, so we are nearing the Midpoint of the story. That's where, in a well-structured plot, the protagonist suffers a significant reversal or fully commits to the quest. Or both.

In the lunchroom, Cordelia says she's organizing a boycott. She's appalled that the girls have to ask the boys to the Sadie Hawkins Dance and pay and everything. And she says they have to stop this or things will get really scary.

Which leads into our Midpoint Reversal (to the extent I see one here).

Midpoint Reversal In I Only Have Eyes For You

At 20 minutes 40 seconds in, suddenly snakes are everywhere. The students are screaming. One of the snakes strikes Cordelia's face.

This could be seen as a reversal for Buffy because she didn't stop the spirit from lashing out before this happened. But I'm not sure how well this works as a Midpoint Reversal. For one thing, it doesn't feel that personal to Buffy. And it doesn't really drive her forward in any different way than she was already going.

My other issue with the snakes in the cafeteria also applies to the arm shooting out of the locker. Both of these are pop scares. They give us little jolts and surprise us. But neither incident seems to relate to James when the story resolves. I can't see why he caused either one, while I understand why he causes the fights between people that mimic his experience with Grace.

Giles sort of covered this by telling us the spirit is frustrated and it lashes out. But it still doesn't feel like it fits James's and Grace's story.

Sunnydale Police And Principal Snyder

As is usually the case in Buffy, the snake incident does result in us learning a little more about Sunnydale, which I love. Outside the school, everyone has evacuated. Principal Snyder is talking to an official. I think maybe he's a police chief because we see all these police cars.

And they're talking about what sort of cover story they can come up with. Snyder says maybe he can sell backed up sewers. At that point, someone in the crowd shouts a question at Snyder. And he says without missing a beat:

Snyder: Backed up sewer line. Same thing happened in San Diego last week.

I love watching Snyder cover because he's so good at it. But then he turns to the police chief.

Snyder: We're on a Hellmouth. Sooner or later people are going to figure that out.

The chief is not impressed. He says the City Council was told Snyder could handle this job. If he can't, maybe he'd like to take it up with the mayor. Snyder reassures the chief that he can handle it.

This scene adds to my view that perhaps Snyder is not simply a bad guy, though he could be. But now we know he knows about the Hellmouth. And it's possible he does think that Buffy is somehow responsible for some of the chaos he's trying to manage. Or that she is working on behalf of the Hellmouth, not against it.

It also shows a bit of vulnerability for Snyder. Because he seems afraid about having to talk to the mayor. Or at least nervous. And we don't know – is it about losing his job? Is it because the mayor is intimidating? Or both.

The vulnerability makes him a little more interesting. And we see that he too is under great pressure here. Which makes him a tiny bit relatable.

Midpoint Commitment

At 21 minutes 42 seconds in we do get a Midpoint Commitment. The friends gather at Buffy's house. Willow says they should scrap the plan to communicate with James. It won't work. She's been doing research. And the only way is an exorcism. Buffy agrees.

I see this as the throwing of caution to the wind. Because, as Cordelia will make clear, it's a dangerous approach:

Cordelia: Are you crazy? I saw that movie. Even the priest died.

The way this plays out is part of why I feel this Midpoint is a little bit soft. As a group, yes, they throw caution to the wind. But Willow pushes us there. And Buffy kind of goes along. In a way it's what she wanted to do anyway. She wants to get rid of James, not try to resolve his issues.

Also, we don't see how Willow gets there. And I get that it's not Willow's story. We can't see all her steps. But it feels a little like the plot just needs to get everyone to the school and this is the way we do it. It doesn't feel as organic to the story as most Midpoints in *Buffy* are.

It does the job though.

Willow shows the map of the school and says they need to create a tripod. Buffy will chant at the hotspot Willow located. The other three will chant at other places in the school, forming a triangle around her.

And Buffy does make a choice here. She is the one who says she will go to the hotspot.

They meet that night at the school. Willow has made them each a scapular, which is a cloth necklace with pouches. She put sulfur in there to help ward off evil. They all hold candles they need to light at midnight at their different spots. Once they are all in the school, the doors slam shut around them.

Back To The Trio

We go back to Drusilla, Spike, and Angel outside in the garden again. Angel loves the way Drusilla is dancing around.

Spike: Fortunately no one cares what you like, mate.

Angel suggests that Drusilla very much cares. Then she has a vision and says, "There's a gate. It wants her." She says this is the moment that the Slayer is vulnerable.

And Spike says what difference does it make? Angel's not going to do anything about it anyway.

Angel says the Slayer thing has run its course. He wants to focus elsewhere, and he grabs Drusilla. Spike says, "Is that right?" Angel tells Spike that with him being special-needs boy, Angel figures they can always use an extra pair of hands. And he runs his hands over Drusilla's body.

Distraught Giles

At 25 minutes 15 seconds in, Giles startles Willow in the school hallway. He's there trying to contact Jenny. He smells a pungent odor. Willow tells him it's the scapular. He asks if she used sulfur. She says yes. And he says, "Oh, that's very clever."

And then he tells her to run along in case there any phenomena when he contacts Jenny. Giles doesn't ask why Willow is there at midnight or why she needs the sulfur. All of this shows how distraught Giles is. How deep he is in his grief.

Quick Scene Shifts Keep The Pace Fast

Now the scenes at the school flip between our four characters. This works really well to keep the pace quick. And it raises the tension as each of them gets ready to do their part.

I'll cover highlights rather than cycling through all of the different scene shifts. But hopefully you get the idea if you haven't rewatched recently. Xander enters the snake-filled cafeteria. (Lucky him.) That's where he gets to light his candle and chant. And he says, "Snakealicious."

As Buffy walks the hallways, she hears music. It's the song I Only Have Eyes For You. She sees an old Sadie Hawkins poster and looks through the window in the door to a classroom. Grace and James slow dance inside. The song plays on an old vinyl record player. The camera zooms in on James's face, which becomes decayed.

Cordelia is in the bathroom, which is her spot to chant. She looks at herself in the mirror where the snake bit her. We cut back to her just after seeing James's face decay. Half of Cordelia's face becomes burned and red and she screams.

Willow is at the top of the stairs where Jenny was killed. (I find that very interesting because I would've thought that would be the hotspot but it isn't.) She's about to light her candle. But a vortex opens at Willow's feet and starts pulling her in. She screams for Giles. He runs out. Willow is almost all the way sucked into the void. But he pulls her out, and they both fall down the stairs.

Buffy's Drawn In

We're about 28 minutes 30 seconds in. Buffy stands on one of the outdoor upper walkways. This is what I referred to when I said we started with her on that upper balcony in the Bronze, leaning on the railing. Now we come back to similar imagery. She puts on her scapular and sees a flash of James shooting Grace Newman, then putting the record on the record player in the classroom.

We see his decaying face again. He yells, "Get out."

A Quiet Moment

Cordelia's face returns to normal. She takes a deep breath. Giles asks Willow if she's all right.

Willow: Giles, Jenny could never be this mean.

He says he knows. And he sits on the stair next to her and says it's not Jenny.

A clock starts striking. Its gong reverberates through the school. Willow and Giles go to the top of the stairs. Cordelia lights her candle. Buffy starts to. Willow struggles to get hers lit, and finally does.

Willow: I shall confront and expel all evil.

Cordelia: I shall totally confront and expel all evil.

Xander is sitting cross-legged on the lunch room table, lit candle in front of him, snakes around him. I really like this Xander moment. He shows great bravery in doing this. And he seems so calm.

Xander: Out of marrow and bone –

Buffy (with her lit candle): — out of house and home....

Buffy continues the chant. When she's done, there is silence. Then all the candles go out.

At nearly 30 minutes in our friends gather in the dim hallway, holding their candles. Momentarily we think it will be okay.

Multiple Major Turns

We're nearing the three-quarter mark in the story. It's where we usually see the last major plot turn. It comes out of the Midpoint and spins the story in yet another new direction. It should grow from the protagonist's actions at the Midpoint or from the reversal she suffered. So it should not feel like something random just thrown in there to spin the story.

This episode is really interesting because there is more than one major turn. Each one does grow out of that Midpoint for the most part, or out of what came right before it.

At 30 minutes in a buzzing sound starts. Everyone looks around. Giles says, "Oh my God." They all run as swarms of wasps appear from all directions. The doors are still shut and locked. Buffy kicks them open so they can run outside. The wasps form around the school. So our friends are standing across the street watching. And it's impossible for anyone to get inside.

This development could be that Three-Quarter Turn. It comes out of their decision to do the exorcism, and it forces them to take a new approach. But we don't know what that approach is yet, and there is a more significant turn to come.

At Buffy's house, Giles says the good news is that none of the girls were shot while they were inside. As they talk, they realize James keeps reliving shooting Grace Newman to try to work out whatever is keeping him in limbo.

Giles: Whatever it is he wants –

Buffy: He wants forgiveness.

Giles stands and says yes, but when James possesses people the scene always plays out the same way. So, Giles says, it's a form of purgatory.

Giles: He's doomed to kill his Miss Newman over and over again and forgiveness is impossible.

Buffy: Good, he doesn't deserve it.

Giles: To forgive is an act of compassion, Buffy. It's not done because people deserve it. It's done because they need.

But Buffy goes into almost a rant:

Buffy: No. James destroyed the one person he loved most in a moment of blind passion. That's not something you forgive. No matter why he did what he did. And no matter if he knows now that it was wrong and selfish and stupid. It's just something he's gonna have to live with.

Xander (quietly): He can't live with it, Buff. He's dead.

Buffy leaves the room. She goes into the kitchen.

Cordelia: Okay. Over identify much?

The next moment also is a major turn. And I think that it is the real Three-Quarter Turn because it spins the story in another new direction. And it is triggered by Buffy's actions.

Three-Quarter Turn In I Only Have Eyes For You

At 33 minutes, 5 seconds in, Buffy finds a 1955 Sadie Hawkins flyer in her pocket. She hears someone whisper, "I need you." She walks to the school, and the swarm of wasps parts to let her in. And we cut to commercial. Another great hook. That might be my favorite one in this episode.

Willow discovers Buffy is gone and sees the flyer. They all go to the school. But they can't get in because of the wasps. Giles says Buffy's under the spirit's thrall and James wants to change what happened.

Willow is worried because it always ends the same and Buffy will get shot. All the characters are assuming that the female ghost will inhabit Buffy and that's what James wants. And she'll be in danger. Which sets up the major twist of the story.

The first time I saw the episode I think I too assumed that Buffy would be Grace. And that Buffy was so angry at James because she identified with Grace. Once you know that James will take over Buffy, looking back at her dialogue, especially that last rant, it does seem clearer why she is so angry at James. Because she's angry at herself. But at this point, Giles says Buffy should be safe because there is no man inside for James to possess. And Willow says, "In theory."

Angel Confronts Buffy

Buffy slowly walks through the hall. Angel appears behind her.

Angel: Fun fact about wasps. They have no taste for the undead.

This is yet another twist that could have served as the Three-Quarter Turn in a different story. Simply the fact that Angel appears there. It is late in the story to be the Three-Quarter Turn, but it is just as major as the one where Buffy chose to go to the school. And that's part of what makes the second half of the story so intriguing.

Buffy has her back to Angel. And she says he is the only person she can talk to. On rewatch I know she's been possessed by the spirit of James at that moment. I don't know that I realized it on first watch. That isn't a line we've heard any of the characters James and Grace inhabit say.

Angel definitely doesn't know any of that.

Angel: Buff, that's really pathetic.

Buffy (spins around to face him): You can't make me disappear just because you say it's over.

This is obviously one of the lines we heard the other couples say. So now we know she's possessed, but it takes a second for it to happen to Angel.

Angel: Actually I can. In fact –

But he pauses. The sound effects and music cue us that a spirit is taking him over. And he continues.

Angel: I just want you to be able to have some kind of normal life. We can never have that.

Grace And James And Angel And Buffy

It's clear James possessed Buffy and Grace possessed Angel. Because Angel's words are what Grace said to James. And she was the one breaking up with him.

Now Angel and Buffy act out the Grace and James lines. We

see how perfectly they fit their relationship before Angel became Angelus.

Buffy says she doesn't give a damn about a normal life. But Angel continues the breakup. And so does Grace because we switch between the present and the past. We see that Grace did not want to break up with James. But she feels she has to. She even says, "It doesn't matter what I feel."

But Angel is the one we see deliver that line.

Buffy: Then tell me you don't love me.

Grace: Is that what you need to hear? Will that help? I don't.

Angel: I don't.

Now we get the most heartbreaking lines. They fit that terrible night when Angel changed. And we see why James is drawn to Buffy.

Buffy: A person doesn't just wake up and stop loving somebody.

Buffy holds the gun. Her hand is shaking.

Buffy (pointing gun): Love is forever.

Grace runs away from James, and he chases her.

Buffy: Don't run away from me, bitch.

Angel stops with his back to Buffy and turns. But it's Grace turning around to James.

Grace: You know you don't want to do this. Now give me the gun.

James: Don't talk to me like I'm some stupid –

And we know he's going to say "child." And this, too, echoes Buffy and Angel before Angel changed. She got angry at him when he treated her like a child.

James is gesturing for emphasis with the gun and it goes off. This is the first time we see that while he threatened Grace, which is terrible, he may not have meant to shoot her.

And I wonder, is this how Buffy feels? As if sleeping with Angel was the equivalent of holding a loaded gun and it went off. This shows us how hard she is on herself. The danger of a loaded weapon, everyone knows this. But Buffy could not have known what would happen to Angel.

Buffy, though, is not willing to let herself off the hook. And I buy that because emotions aren't logical. She can know, and her friends can tell her, that there was no way she could've known. Even Giles can tell her that. But because she's Buffy and she always holds herself to a high standard, and because she loves Angel so much, she feels that she did the equivalent of waving a loaded gun around. It went off, and she killed the person that she loves.

The Climax

We are at the Climax where all these plot elements come together and resolve. James and Grace and Buffy and Angel have run out onto that outside upper walkway.

This is the hot spot where Buffy was chanting. So that's where they are when Grace is shot. Angel falls over the railing. James goes to the music room, but we see Buffy walk into the room.

Grace had been lying on the pavement below, dead. Now we see Angel lying there, blood on him. But he opens his eyes. Another major turn or twist.

In the classroom, Buffy puts the record on. The static from the needle as it starts gives us that feeling of the past. Holding the gun at her side, Buffy looks at herself in the mirror and sees James. She lifts the gun to her head.

But Angel takes the gun away.

Buffy, still inhabited by James says, "Grace." Angel tells her not to do this and she says, "But I killed you."

Angel says it was an accident. It wasn't her fault. And Buffy says, "It was my fault." But Angel tells her that he is the one who should be sorry. It morphs into Grace telling James that "you thought I stopped loving you."

Angel: I loved you with my last breath.

Which takes us back to that moment at the end of

Surprise and the beginning of Innocence. When Angel staggered into the alley and gasped Buffy's name just before he lost his soul.

The music changes. As Buffy and Angel kiss, we also see Grace and James. And then back to Angel and Buffy. A shaft of light beams down on them. There's so much emotion between Buffy and Angel. Then we see sparkling and streaks of light that go up and disappear. And we know the spirits of Grace and James are at peace and gone.

Angel And Buffy Together

Angel and Buffy finish the kiss. They're still holding each other.

Buffy: Angel.

Sarah Michelle Gellar is amazing through all of this playing that dual role of James and Buffy. She really conveys the emotions for both characters in that one word. Her longing and her love. And how, for that quick second, she thinks she has Angel back.

The next instant is also amazing with David Boreanaz. We see this complete shift. There is a millisecond after the kiss when Buffy says, "Angel." And we see him as Angel. His love, and his tenderness, and his feelings for Buffy.

An instant later his body language changes. He stiffens. We hear an intake of breath. He shoves Buffy aside and runs out. And we know Angelus is back. Buffy is left sitting alone on the classroom floor.

The Falling Action – Buffy And Friends

Now we are in the Falling Action. This is where all the loose ends are tied up. We're 41 minutes in.

Willow, Xander and Cordelia walk into the library. They just checked out the school. Willow says everything is normal, no snakes or wasps. Cordelia says the school can open tomorrow.

Xander: Explain to me again how that's a good thing.

Giles goes into his office. Buffy sits there alone, looking pensive.

Buffy: James picked me. I guess I was the one he could relate to. He was so sad.

She goes on to say part of her still doesn't understand why Grace would forgive James.

Giles: Does it matter?

Buffy: No. I guess not.

We switch to the courtyard. Angel (with no shirt on), washes himself in the fountain, rubbing his hands, his arms, over and over.

Spike: You might want to let up. They say when you've drawn blood you've exfoliated.

Angel tells him he doesn't know anything about it.

Angel: I'm the one who was violated.

Drusilla asks what it was -- a demon?

Angel: No, it was love.

This line confirms what we saw: that for those moments he was feeling love for Buffy. He says he needs a really vile kill to wipe this crap out of his system.

Drusilla asks Spike if he wants to come with, but Angel says no. He's sure Spike would be hell on wheels but they don't have much time and they need to travel light. As they leave, he tells Spike to try to have fun without them. Spike sighs, and then smiles.

Spike: Oh, I will.

The music changes. It's similar to what we heard when Buffy lifted the rocket launcher on to her shoulder to fire at The Judge. It's triumphant and tense. The camera pans to Spike's boots. He places one foot and then the other on the ground, stands, and knocks over his wheelchair.

Spike: Sooner than you think.

And the episode ends.

Subtle Subplot

That moment ends our subplot that we didn't really know was happening. Angel and Spike spar throughout the episode, and it seems like it's just part of the season arc of their relationship. It also feels like the scenes are there merely to show why Angel goes to the high school when he does – because Drusilla tells him that there is a window to truly hurt the Slayer.

But it turns out each scene where Angel taunts Spike leads to this moment where Spike has had enough. And we find out that he has been hiding his recovery and his strength all along.

The subplot also builds sympathy for Spike. He already was an intriguing and layered villain. Much more so than the Master, who was fun to watch, but we didn't really connect with him emotionally. Spike, on the other hand, was vulnerable even before he was injured. He wore his heart on his sleeve. And we like him because he has such a great joy in the undead life in a very different way than Angel does.

Angel as Angelus likes being evil. He delights in it. But Spike seems to delight in everything about his continued existence.

Now, though, in that wheelchair we saw him so vulnerable. He's also vulnerable emotionally because of his deep love for Drusilla, while she is more – I guess she loves him, but she's clearly just fine with Angel being part of this dynamic too, and Spike is clearly not.

I also love the differences among these three vampires. All powerful and dangerous in their own ways but very different characters.

The Pluses And Minuses

Overall, this episode is one that I don't usually look forward to re-watching, and then when I do I find so much in it that's amazing.

I think it's because while I love certain moments of the first half (particularly with Willow and Giles when she gives him a rose quartz), the poltergeist incidents don't quite add up. They don't intrigue me that much.

But the second half I love. There is so much there. So much emotion. So many significant plot turns that work. When I think about re-watching, I'm probably remembering the first half and not how much the second half speaks to me.

A quick memory from when the show originally aired – they showed that Buffy and Angel kiss in the trailers to tease the episode. And everyone thought that perhaps Angel was back. So, great marketing.

I wonder whether they created the whole episode with that idea. Or at least whether part of the goal was to have a moment so the audience could see the Angel and Buffy romance, their love, again before the end of the season.

Joss Whedon Talks About I Only Have Eyes For You

In the DVD interview, Joss Whedon talked about how each episode of *Buffy* takes an emotional experience and blooms it into a horror plot. Here, it is Buffy who starts out thinking she can't forgive Angel. And everyone else thinks that's what's going on to. But it turns out in reality she can't forgive herself. Through Grace's and James's story she discovers she can be forgiven and move on. That there is redemption.

Whedon also said he liked the twist of the gender reversal with the ghosts. And he said seeing David Boreanaz play this part is what made him feel confident that David could carry his own show. He liked seeing him play this emotional role without overplaying it. And liked that David was open to playing a female part and didn't shy away from it as a lot of male action stars might.

And it's funny. I hadn't really thought about that David Boreanaz being a male action star in *Buffy*, but that is a fairly good description of Angel and Angelus to this point.

The character doesn't have a wide emotional range. In *Buffy and the Art of Story Season One*, I talked about Angel didn't have that much to do. He mostly showed up and looked gorgeous and was very cryptic.

In Season Two we see a little more of how he was a good partner to Buffy in many ways. We saw some more emotion. But the character of Angel -- he broods. He has a little bit of a lighter side, but he doesn't express a wide range of emotions. And then Angelus this out-and-out evil character. He's not one note, but we don't get to see him play the types of emotions he does when the ghost of Grace takes him over.

Spoilers and Foreshadowing

Season Three

The mentions of the mayor, and Snyder feeling nervous about needing to talk to him, are great ways to foreshadow the mayor being the Season Three Big Bad. The same scene also sows the seeds for the Sunnydale infrastructure and government knowing about the Hellmouth.

This episode also foreshadows Angel breaking up with Buffy toward the end of Season Three. He'll tell her he wants her to have normal life, and it's very much like the Ms. Newman dynamic with James. There are some differences. But it is Angel making that decision for both of them, being the one who initiates the breakup as Ms. Newman does. And Buffy is devastated.

Willow's Spells In Season Two

We also have some major foreshadowing for the end of Season Two. One aspect is fairly subtle and the other is obvious.

Willow twice mentions looking at pagan websites and resources Miss Calendar left. The first is during that scene with Giles in the classroom. It is sort of a throwaway line. But later

Willow does the research and says that they need to do an exorcism, making it more obvious Willow's actively learning spells.

All of it nicely sets up the moment when Willow says she can do the spell to bring Angel's soul back.

Willow's Arc

But the more I thought about the magic references in this episode, I realized they also foreshadow Willow's series arc. Notice how quickly Willow goes to "we need to do an exorcism." Yet what gets rid of James and Grace is what Giles says in the beginning. Helping them resolve their issues. The exorcism does not work.

And it fits with how Willow, over time, starts going to magic to solve emotional issues. Specifically, to big gestures with magic to try to fix things with spells and avoid painful feelings. Which has terrible results. (Although we do get a really fun episode when everyone acts out what Willow wills to happen to them.)

There are so many steps along Willow's arc where she doesn't want to let things play out. She wants to go not just to magic, but to a very significant spell that has dramatic consequences. And sometimes very dark ones.

Spike

The most obvious foreshadowing here concerns Spike. We learn that he's been building his strength, that he is in fact powerful and fed up with Angel. It's clear we're shown this for a reason. It sets up so well that scene when he comes to Buffy to team up with her against Drusilla and Angel. Spike wants to stop the world from ending – and to get Drusilla away from Angel.

Because of what happens in I Only Have Eyes For You, we believe Spike will be perfectly happy if Angel gets killed and sent to Hell. I had forgotten just how well this was woven into the earlier episodes.

Questions For Your Writing

- Does your first scene include conflict? If not, how can you revise it so that it does?
- When your characters share information, is it part of a conflict among them?
- If you use magic or frightening moments, do both fit the story's logic?
- Will the audience understand how the magic works or why the antagonist does scary things?
- Does your protagonist personally suffer a reversal or make a major commitment at the Midpoint? Is it clear why the protagonist takes action or suffers a defeat?
- Can you include more than one major turn or twist in the second half of your story;
- If you read the scenes of your subplot separately from the main plot, is there conflict and resolution?
- In what ways are your characters vulnerable?
- Can you show vulnerability for your antagonist?

Next: Go Fish

NEXT WE'LL TALK about Go Fish, when Buffy will once again show how bad she is at undercover and Xander will wear a speedo. The chapter discusses tone, plot twists, and messages inside of humor.

CHAPTER 8
GO FISH (S2 E20)

THIS CHAPTER TALKS about Go Fish, Season Two Episode Twenty, where Xander joins the swim team to find out who or what is killing its members. Written by Elin Hampton and David Fury and directed by David Semel.

In particular, we'll look at:

- A clear, quick opening conflict.
- How treating disturbing issues as a joke undercuts the episode's lighthearted tone;
- Some of the most fun lines in Buffy to date ("Oh forgive me Your Swimteamlyness");
- An especially fun and interesting twist at the Midpoint; and
- Major plot turns in unusual places that rob the episode of momentum and make it feel uneven.

Okay, let's dive into the Hellmouth.

———

Is Go Fish Fun Or Troubling?

I always remember Go Fish as a light, fun episode that gives the audience a break before the intense two-part Season Two finale. I tend to forget its troubling aspects, which include threatened and actual sexual assault and rape treated lightly and played for jokes.

There's nothing graphic in my breakdown below or in the episode itself, but I'm flagging it in case you, too, forgot that aspect of the episode and prefer not to read about it. (In which case, see you in the next chapter.)

A Peaceful Start, Then Opening Conflict

We start, for a change, not with conflict but with a peaceful scene. A shot of the ocean. It is rolling. We see lovely waves, and there is calming music in the background.

Then we get our opening conflict. Xander, Willow, and Cordelia stand on the beach. We also see bonfires on the beach and lots of students around. Xander says what a stupid idea it is to have a party on the beach when it's this cold. He also says the swim team is not a "real" team. But Cordelia says it's about time school excelled at something.

Willow: You're forgetting our high mortality rate.

What A clear, quick opening conflict. Already we know it's a celebration for the swim team and that they are the first team to win anything at Sunnydale High in quite some time. Plus Willow quickly reminds us how many people die in Sunnydale.

Buffy And Cameron On The Beach

Buffy, however, is not with her friends. She is sitting on the beach looking out at the ocean. A swim team member (by the way, it's the boys swim team), Cameron, joins her. He says something about how beautiful the ocean is and how it's eternal.

And Buffy jokes that she was just thinking that it was big. He laughs, and she asks what he's going to do now that he's had this big win. He says he wants to spend some time hanging out with her.

Someone calls out for help from behind them. Jonathan is being dumped into a tub of water by another swim team member. Buffy runs over and pulls the swim team guy off of Jonathan somewhat violently. Cameron says his teammate had it coming.

At first, I sort of like Cameron. He clearly likes Buffy. He laughs at her jokes. While he's a little annoying with his profound comments about the ocean, he doesn't seem to approve of his teammate's bullying. So he seems like a reasonably okay guy.

Jonathan, though, is mad. He tells Buffy he could've handled this without her help. And he says, "Mind your own business" and stalks off.

Buffy (turns to Cameron): See, it's fun to hang out with me.

The Story Spark In Go Fish

An unnamed bully and another swimmer, Gage, walk on the beach. The bully complains about Buffy. He falls behind Gage. Gage notices that something smells terrible. He looks around. And at 4 minutes 35 seconds into the episode the camera pans to skin pieces on the beach. Skin and steaming flesh. Then there is a shot of a sea creature in what looks like a giant storm drain.

And we go to credits.

So that was our Story Spark or Inciting Incident, which typically happens about 10% into any story. Here, it is right on time at 4 minutes 35 seconds in. (It is about a 42-minute episode.) And it's a great hook, no pun intended. (Especially given all the fish puns we have right before the credits.)

Conflict Over What Winners Deserve

When we return, Willow is teaching the computer class. She walks through the room looking at the students' screens, telling them they are doing good pie charts. Until she gets to Gage.

Willow: Your pie chart is looking a lot like solitaire. With naked ladies on the cards.

Gage: What's your point?

The bell rings. Principal Snyder comes in as the class leaves. He tells Willow the board wants her to continue teaching the rest of the semester. They're having trouble finding a substitute to replace Miss Calendar.

(I mentioned in a previous chapter how only in Sunnydale would a student be asked to take over and teach a class. I have to wonder if some of that is that high death rate Willow mentioned. Perhaps substitutes are not too eager to come to Sunnydale.)

Willow, though, is excited. She says how much she likes teaching. And Snyder says he's glad she's a team player and he understands that there's a problem with Gage. Willow is relieved that he knows. She mentions behavior issues, and he doesn't do the work and his test scores – well, there aren't any test scores. Because he doesn't take the tests.

But Snyder's not interested in any of that. He's concerned that she's slapping a failing mark on a student on a winning team. That would disqualify Gage from swimming.

Willow says she's trying to be fair. Snyder points out the Gage is a champion, he's under a lot of pressure. Willow says, "You're asking me to change his grade?" Snyder claims he never said that. He just said that he thinks if she reviews her figures she'll find something more appropriate for Gage. In the area of a D.

In the hall later, Xander is appalled. He says that's a slap in the face to everyone who worked hard for their Ds. But Cordelia says winners deserve more, that's how the world works. Xander's mad that Buffy is not there to share his outrage about swim team perks because she's too busy being one of them.

We switch to Buffy and Cameron talking in his car in the

school parking lot. Or rather Cameron is talking. He waxes eloquent about swimming and philosophy. She interrupts and thanks him.

Buffy (with a little bit of sarcasm): I forgot how nice it is to just talk, or in my case listen, without any romantic pressure.

Cameron Attacks

Cameron assures her he's not about pressure. But then he turns on a dime and asks if she's wearing a bra. When she reacts badly he locks her car door.

Cameron: Relax, I'm not going to hurt you.

Buffy: Oh, it's not me I'm worried about.

He says, "You like it rough," and lunges for her. She grabs him and bangs his face into the steering wheel. He yells out that she broke his nose. All of this occurs as Principal Snyder passes the car. He stares through the windshield at both of them. Of course, he only saw the part where Buffy bangs Cameron's nose into the steering wheel.

Everyone Blames Buffy

About 10 minutes in, in the nurse's office, the nurse gives Cameron an ice pack. Buffy tells Snyder she wasn't the attacker, she was attacked. So at least Buffy points out that this was an attempted sexual assault. Though later she'll seem to be convinced – by the reaction of her friends no less – that it was really no big deal. Snyder says that's not how it looked to him. And Cameron claims that Buffy led him on and then went schizo.

Buffy: What do you mean I lead you on?

Cameron: Look at the way she dresses.

The coach comes in. He's relieved that Cameron's nose is not broken because he needs Cam to win the championship, especially with Dodd gone.

Nearing The One-Quarter Twist Of Go Fish

We're nearing the One-Quarter Twist, which should come, in well-structured story, from outside the protagonist and take the story in a new direction. Here, I am uncertain exactly where this happens or at what point. But right now, we are about 10 minutes 45 seconds into the episode. So timewise we are at the one-quarter point.

Buffy asks what happened to Dodd. Snyder tells her it's none of her concern. The coach tells Cameron to go take a steam, clear his nasal passages. And tells the nurse to take good care of him. He then turns.

Coach: And you. Try to dress more appropriately from now on. This isn't a dance club.

Blaming Girls

So on two levels this is awful. First and most important, it doesn't matter how Buffy dresses. It is not okay what Cameron did. Second, she doesn't look dressed for a dance club. She's pretty much wearing regular clothes anyone might wear to school.

The way Buffy is dressed suggests to me that the writers are trying to point out that this is awful, this blaming of girls for how boys act.

On the other hand, the way that she's dressed suggests maybe if she were dressed differently, it would be okay for the coach to say that. I don't think that is the writers' intent. I think that they are trying to show that the coach is a jerk, as he is. And that a girl should not be blamed.

I also have an issue with how this plays out in the next scene.

Side note: when I went to high school that is totally how that kind of thing would have been treated. It would definitely be blamed on the girl. Probably also true in the late 1990s when Buffy was made. I hope it's not true now.

Buffy's Friends Ignore The Attack

We switch to the library. Buffy is telling about what happened to Giles, Xander, Willow, and Cordelia. They have books all over the library table, clearly in the middle of researching something important. Buffy winds up by saying, "I'm treated like the baddie just because Cameron has a sprained wrist and bloody nose," and she doesn't have a scratch on her, which she admits does hurt her case a little. But he gets away with it just because he's on the swim team. And in case they haven't noticed, those guys get away with all kinds of things.

The others have no patience with her as they have noticed that. And she hasn't until now. At least that's the implication based on what we have heard before.

Buffy realizes that they are just staring at her in stony silence and says enough about her, what's happening with them?

Giles: Thank you for taking an interest.

Unintended Messages?

If the incident Buffy was complaining about were something else (I don't know what that would be, but not sexual assault), and she was going on and on about how unfair it was the way the team got away with things, the way the group reacted would work for me. They've been researching and working hard, they all noticed the perks for the swim team, and Buffy missed it or ignored it because she was dating one of them.

But the incident was an attempted sexual assault.

You could argue that Buffy was never in any real danger because she's so much stronger than Cameron, so that's why they ignore that aspect of it. Also, she was in far more danger in Season One, when Xander tried to assault her. At the time, he was possessed by the hyena and had superstrength.

I feel like that was different, though. At that point everyone was starting to suspect there was something wrong with Xander, that he'd been possessed. So it put that fight between Buffy and Xander more into the realm of the supernatural, which is what Buffy deals with all the time. Demons and vampires trying to attack her and assault her one way or another.

Here, we're talking about an experience with a boy she was dating and whom none of them has any reason (yet) to believe is possessed or demonic. So I am disappointed that the writers wrote this such that the characters seem to be saying, "Well, Buffy, you're so self-absorbed, going on and on about being assaulted, when we're upset that things like better grades are handed out to the swim team."

I don't think the writers intended that. I feel like it's a result of the time in which it was written and how such things were treated then. But it is a good example of why it's important to step back and consider the subtext of what you write to see if you've woven in messages you don't want to be there.

Human Remains And Puns

At about 11 minutes 40 seconds in the others tell Buffy that human remains were found on the beach and they were Dodd's. But it was not a vampire attack because he was eviscerated.

Xander: In other words, this was no boating accident.

That's a line from *Jaws* the movie. And it harkens back to Killed By Death where we also had the movie references, also from Xander. So he seems to be the one who spends a lot of time watching old movies. The group talks about how they are looking for a demon that eats a human whole except for the skin.

Buffy: That doesn't make sense.

Xander: Yeah, the skin's the best part.

Buffy: Any demons with high cholesterol?

Giles gives her a look.

Buffy: You're going to think about that later, Mister, and you're gonna laugh.

The One-Quarter Twist

I see the part about finding Dodd's remains on the beach as

the One-Quarter Twist here. That twist is what takes the story in new direction, even though, as audience members, we already knew all of this. We knew it was Dodd on the beach and that only his skin and some flesh was left. And that there was some kind of monster that was not a vampire.

However, Buffy didn't know this. So this does change her direction, setting her and her friends off to find out what's happening.

The next scene is in the locker room. Cameron sits in the steam room. And like all Sunnydale locker rooms, everything is dim and in shadows. We see an ominous shadow approach the steam room. But it's just the coach coming in to tell Cameron he's had enough and he should hit the shower.

Xander is heading to the vending machine for soda. Cameron exits the locker room and bumps into him. He yells at Xander for getting in his way.

Xander: Oh forgive me Your Swimteamlyness.

He then taunts Cameron about Buffy almost breaking his nose. Cameron ignores him. He's heading to the cafeteria because he's hungry.

Xander: Oh, too bad. The cafeteria is closed.

Cameron: Not for me.

Plot Turn Questions

In the lunch room, Cameron sniffs and says, "What is that?" Then, from the hallway, Xander hears Cameron screaming. Xander runs in and sees overturned tables and then clothes and skin on the floor. He turns away, about to vomit, and sees one of these sea monsters. This is at 15 minutes 15 seconds in.

So it's pretty soon after that one-quarter major plot turn. Yet it feels like it should be either that first major turn – because we find out, okay, it's a sea monster – or the last major plot turn that explains things so that we know it's a sea monster that is after swim team members. But, instead, this happens between our one-quarter and halfway points. This is part of what feels a bit uneven to me about the plot here.

Revenge Killings

In the library, Xander describes the monster and Cordelia tries to draw it. She produces a pretty good likeness. (Which makes me wonder is everyone in Sunnydale good at drawing? We saw Angel is a pretty good artist. Of course, he's had hundreds of years to practice.)

Buffy comes in. Willow says Buffy was right, Dodd and Cameron were the first and second best swimmers on the team. Buffy says that makes Gage next because he's the third best swimmer.

Cordelia: This is so sad. We're never going to win the state championship.

Giles thinks these may be revenge killings against the swim team. And they talk about who hates the team members. Willow reminds them the team bullied Jonathan. Buffy tells her to go question him. Willow's really excited about taking that interrogator role.

Giles tells Buffy that Gage might benefit from her protection. She should discreetly watch him.

So now we're getting to what I find to be one of the most fun parts of the episode – Buffy trying and failing miserably to be surreptitious. In the student lounge area, she watches Gage. He's sitting about ten feet from her reading. He looks over at her and she is so obviously watching him. She jerks her head back to her magazine.

The Friends At Work

In a classroom that's otherwise empty Willow shines a light in Jonathan's face. She's standing, he's sitting. She acts like a detective in an old-fashioned movie. She questions him about the team. He says he couldn't be on it because he's asthmatic. Willow interrogates him until he admits that bothered him, and he hated the way the team members pushed him around.

Willow: So you wanted revenge, didn't you? Didn't you? Jonathan finally says yes.

Willow: So you delved into the black arts and conjured hell beasts from the ocean's depth to wreak your vengeance. Didn't you?

Jonathan: No. I snuck in yesterday and peed in the pool.

We switch to the coach and Principal Snyder talking about the team. The coach says the rest of the team members will figure out what's happening. Snyder reassures the coach that he feels their pain.

Snyder: I don't know finer boys than Cameron and – that other one.

Snyder's sure those boys would want the team to carry on competing and win the championship. But the coach says they can't even compete unless they get another swimmer by today's tryouts. Snyder thinks that's no big deal. All the person has to do is wear a bathing suit. Xander, who was sitting at a nearby table with his back to the audience, turns around.

Buffy Tries Stealth

19 minutes in we get more Buffy and Gage. They're at the Bronze. Gage is playing pool by himself. Buffy watches him from the bar and then attempts to casually saunter closer. Gage walks over and stands right in front of her. He tells her the "me and my shadow" act is getting old. What does she want? Buffy claims to be a swim team groupie. Gage is skeptical.

Buffy: Oh, yeah, you know there's just something about the smell of chlorine on a guy. Oh baby.

Gage rolls his eyes and walks away and Buffy runs after him.

The Midpoint Commitment In Go Fish

We are now very close to the Midpoint where usually we see a commitment by the protagonist to the quest, a reversal, or both. Here, first we get a commitment. It's not quite as extreme as we sometimes see in the show, but Buffy does to some extent throw caution to the wind and go all in. She tells Gage what's going on. And I see it as a commitment because usually Buffy is trying to maintain something of her secret identity. She doesn't tell people, hey, there's a vampire after you. She's just protects them.

Buffy: Okay, okay, obviously my sex appeal's on the fritz today. So I'll just give it to you straight.

She then tells him something is out there killing people and she thinks that he's next. But he tells her she's twisted.

Gage: Cam told me about your games.

Midpoint Reversal With A Twist

Gage leaves. As he walks out of the Bronze, he mutters under his breath about "that bitch." Angel emerges from the shadows and and says, "You gotta be talking about Buffy." Gage asks how he knows, and Angel says he sort of had a thing with her for a while.

Gage: My condolences, Dude.

Angel pretends to commiserate with Gage. He says Buffy needs someone to knock her down. Gage says that would be sweet and does he have anyone in mind? Angel goes into vamp face.

Angel: You're in luck my friend. It just so happens I'm recruiting.

So now we get what looks like a Midpoint Reversal. It happens right at 21 minutes, 10 seconds in. (This episode is just over 42 minutes, so we are almost exactly at that Midpoint.) Angel attacks Gage. It looks like he's going to die. And that will be this major reversal for Buffy, who was there specifically to protect Gage.

But we get a twist.

I really enjoyed this because it's a surprise. Buffy hears Gage screaming for her and runs to him. But Angel has already backed off, and he is spitting out Gage's blood.

We then get a fun moment. Buffy has her hair up. She pulls

out a giant hairpin and threatens Angel with it. Her hair falls beautifully all around her shoulders. And Angel parodies one of those moments in the old movies where suddenly this woman who was supposedly dowdy (because she wore glasses and had her hair up), lets her hair down and the hero just realizes how beautiful she is.

Angel: Why Miss Summers, you're beautiful.

He grabs Gage again, throws him aside, and stalks off. I enjoyed this fake out with the reversal. I think that it makes that otherwise not super strong Midpoint work.

Gage Is Convinced And Xander Swims

Gage asks Buffy if that was the thing that killed Cameron. And she says no, it was something else. And unfortunately they have a lot of something elses in this town. She starts to leave but Gage asks her to walk him home.

Buffy attends swim practice the next day with Cordelia and Willow so she can keep an eye on Gage. All the swimmers wear yellow caps and goggles. It's hard to tell them apart. But Gage pauses in the middle of his lap to stop and wave to Buffy.

The three girls talk about Angel's spitting out the blood and speculate that he didn't like something in it. Maybe steroids. But Cordelia is distracted by a swimmer who walks in.

Cordelia: Oh, oh my. Now that girls is my kind of –

The camera shows the new swimmer, starting with his feet and panning up his very well-muscled legs.

Willow: Xander!

Cordelia: Xander?

She goes over to him and yells at him that he has to leave because he doesn't belong there. They're gonna throw him out. But he says he's undercover.

Buffy (smirking): Not under much.

He tells them he tried out last night and made the team so he can keep an eye on Gage when Buffy can't.

Willow (eagerly): When you're nude? (Buffy nudges her from behind.) I meant when you're changing.

The coach calls Xander over to the rest of the team.

Cordelia: I'm dating a swimmer from the Sunnydale High Swim Team.

Buffy asks Willow about Jonathan and whether he was involved.

Willow: Oh no, he just sort of peed in the pool.

Buffy: Oh. (Xander dives into the pool.) Oh. (Buffy winces.)

The Steam Room

At almost 25 minutes in, Xander is in the steam room asking the other guys why they like the steam so much. In the locker room, a grate over a large vent starts to move.

Buffy paces outside the locker room. Xander comes out. He says Gage is right behind him putting on his sneakers. But they're not the Velcro kind, so give him a couple extra minutes. And then he says to Buffy, "Tag, you're it."

In the dim locker room Gage is in fact tying his shoes. He sniffs as if he smells something bad. Then he smells both his armpits, then walks around the lockers, apparently looking for the source of the smell.

From out in the hall, Buffy hears him screaming her name. She runs in and a sea monster is confronting Gage. Before the monster touches him, though, Gage falls on the floor in terrible pain. Then his skin splits open and he emerges as a sea monster himself.

And we cut to the commercial.

Major Plot Turns In Unusual Places

That happened about 26 minutes 48 seconds in. It's another example of a really major shift in the story. Now we know it is not some monster coming after the swimmers – they are turning into monsters. That feels like it should be a major plot turn.

In most well-structured stories, the major turns are roughly at the one-quarter, halfway, and three-quarter marks. And this is kind of in between the halfway and the three-quarter. And it's not that you can't have other major turns. That can be a really interesting thing in the story. Also, you want various turns throughout to keep ratcheting up the tension.

But when you have such significant turns at these kinds of odd places, it can rob the one-quarter, halfway, and three-quarter points of their power and make the narrative feel a little uneven. I didn't know before I rewatched this episode for the podcast that this was how the major turns played out. But now I think it might be part of why this episode is never a fan favorite. And why it's always one that I think, "okay, Go Fish, I'll watch it but I don't feel super excited about it."

The Coach Is Not Surprised

Buffy fights off both sea monsters. They dive in through the grate, which apparently leads somehow into those giant tunnels below Sunnydale that are filled with water. (Throughout the episode it will be unclear why the school has these big grates. And later a trap door in the school that leads directly to these storm drain tunnels or whatever they are.)

In the nurse's office, the nurse bandages Buffy's arm. Giles tells the coach that the good news is, none of his team actually died. Buffy tells him the bad news is they're monsters.

While not much in this episode contributes to the season or series arc, there's a slight development here in that we see that in Sunnydale people no longer seem surprised about monsters. Or these Hellmouthy kinds of things happening. They may not know about the Hellmouth, but they know Sunnydale is a strange town. Giles and Buffy don't have to do anything special to make the case to the coach that his players have turned into monsters.

The Sea Monster Within Reveal

The coach claims, looking sad, that he doesn't know how this happened. He worked so hard. He hoped he was inspiring the team to greatness and maybe he was afraid to ask if they might be taking anything to help them along. Buffy looks suspicious of the coach claiming innocence.

In the next scene Willow looks at school records on the computer. She says that members of the team had fractures, depression, and other issues linked to steroid abuse. And Xander asks if steroid abuse is usually linked to turning into a fish. Willow agrees there must be something else involved along with the steroids.

Buffy suspects the nurse has something to do with this because she treated everyone on the team. She tells Xander to try to find out what the team is taking and how they're taking it.

This scene is about 29 minutes and 30 seconds in. And it adds to my feeling that the sea monster from within reveal should have been a major plot turn. Because it does send them in a totally new direction in that they are looking for some kind of steroid or other substance the team is taking that is turning them into monsters. So, yes, they were already speculating about steroids because of Angel spitting up blood, but now they know there is something altering these guys' DNA.

A Quick (And Unnecessary?) Scene

Buffy and Giles go into those watery tunnels with the tranquilizer gun to try to find the sea monsters. A sea monster follows them. They don't notice. And that's all that happens with that scene. There's no follow up with them later hunting or shooting any of the monsters.

This quick, short scene shows our heroes following up on a lead, doing something that we would expect them to do, though it doesn't result in any answers for them. And sometimes in a mystery or thriller your protagonist is going to follow leads that don't go anywhere. You need that to happen, or it would be too obvious what leads really mattered and there would be no suspense.

So I like that the scene does that quickly, and it's a good

example of how to do it in your story. On the other hand, this episode doesn't feel that much like a whodunit, and the scene doesn't go anywhere. So I'm not sure that it adds anything here.

Xander's Surprise In Go Fish

At about 30 minutes, 30 seconds in, Xander is back in the steam room. He hints around about ways to improve performance, saying he drank carrot juice. He's hoping someone will volunteer something. Finally, though, he just outright asks when do they get their next dose and who's carrying? The other guys laugh about aromatherapy and tell him it's in the steam.

We switch to the nurse. She's arguing with the coach in an area near the swimming pool. She wants to stop whatever they're doing. He calls her a quitter and says they just need to perfect the formula.

But she says they already lost three team members. The coach tells her they are not lost, and he throws her through a trap door into the water below. It's about waist deep.

This is what I meant about it being unclear why is there a trap door somewhere near the swim room that leads down into this water under the school. I know Go Fish isn't meant to be a serious episode, so maybe it doesn't matter, but I do think it adds to why this episode feels muddled.

The coach looks down at the nurse through the trapdoor and tells her he's still looking after his boys. They're still the team, and the team's gotta eat. He watches from above as the sea monsters attack the nurse.

And we cut to a commercial.

The Three-Quarter Turn?

The attack on the nurse happened at 32 minutes 45 seconds in. Timewise, it's the three-quarter mark in the episode. Which is part of why I say there isn't a lot of momentum with the Three-Quarter Turn.

Throwing the nurse to the team is a pretty major thing to do – and if you're the nurse it's horrible. It also reveals to the audience that the two of them were in on what was happening with the team, and that the coach has no problem killing the nurse. But it doesn't really spin the story. Also, the Three-Quarter Turn should grow out of the Midpoint in addition to turning the story in another new direction. And here it really doesn't do that.

Buffy doesn't find out about the nurse until much later, too late to affect the plot.

In contrast, Xander learning about the steam does arise out of Buffy's action at the Midpoint. That's when she told Gage the truth, which led him to ask for her protection after Angel attacked him. And that is part of what leads Xander to joining the team. Plus learning about the steam does propel the plot in a different direction.

So while it's a bit indirect, I think that quieter moment of Xander learning about the steam is actually the Three-Quarter Turn.

More Fish Puns

Xander is in a panic. Buffy tries to reassure him.

Buffy: I wouldn't break out the tartar sauce yet, you were only exposed once. Twice?

Xander: Three times a fish guy.

This is a play on the song Three Times A Lady. Xander continues to panic, saying what is he going to do.

Cordelia: You you you. What about me?

And she says it's one thing to date a loser and another to date the creature from the blue lagoon. Xander, really irritated, tells her that's Brooke Shields. Another movie reference. And that she means the creature from the Black Lagoon.

Buffy says they better lock up the rest of the swim team before they get in touch with their inner halibut.

Buffy Confronts The Coach

She then goes to the coach to find out what's going on. And she gets right to the point and asks what's in the steam?

The coach is surprisingly open about it. He tells her that after the Soviet Union fell documents became available showing that the reason their swimmers had won so many championships was that they were taking a combination of steroids, shark fins, and other ingredients. But no one could figure out the exact formula. Now he has almost cracked it.

He is shocked when Buffy asks why he would do that. He says for the win. She tells him there isn't going to be a win because there isn't going to be a team. And doesn't he care what happens to the team members?

Coach: Boy, when they were handing out school spirit, you didn't even stand in line, did you?

Buffy: No, I was in the line for shred of sanity.

The coach pulls a gun on her.

Buffy: Which you obviously skipped.

Now it's clear why he didn't mind telling her what he was doing. He tells her to jump into that open trap door where he threw the nurse. Buffy jumps down into the water. He tells her his boys count on him. She sees the nurse's bitten up body.

Buffy: So you're going to feed me to them?

And now we are coming to the second example of the episode treating the threat of sexual assault lightly.

Coach: They've already eaten. But boys have other needs.

A Sea Monster Mix Up

Cordelia and Xander are walking near the pool. Xander keeps feeling his neck and asking if it looks scaly. Cordelia tells him of course it does because he keeps rubbing it. Xander says he needs to go take a look in the mirror, and she should come into the locker room if he screams.

A moment later, Cordelia hears someone enter the pool area behind her. She jokes, "Any gills yet?" Whoever it is dives into the pool.

Cordelia turns around and sees a sea monster swimming underwater. As it goes across the pool she crouches at the edge talking to it. She says it's all her fault. She knows he joined the swim team just impress her. And she reassures Xander that she still cares about him. They can still date. Or not. She understands if he wants to see other fish. And she adds that she'll do everything she can to make his quality of life better, including bath toys.

Xander startles her by walking up behind her and saying, "That's not me."

Locking Up The Team

In the library, Giles herds the team into the book cage. He tries to reassure them, but runs out of things.

Giles: Either we'll find an antidote or...stay calm.

And he walks away. Xander and Cordelia come in as Willow is checking off the last of the team members' names. She says that Sean is missing. Cordelia and Xander say they found him.

Cordelia: He was in the pool skinless dipping.

The Climax

We switch to Buffy in the water. And she says another disturbing line.

Buffy: Great. This is just what my reputation needs – that I did it with the entire swim team.

At the climax at almost 40 minutes in, Xander comes to see the coach.

He asks what's up, trying to be casual, but he is looking for Buffy. He sees the coach's gun lying there. Below, Buffy fights the sea monsters under water. Above, Xander punches the coach.

Buffy is surrounded. Xander yells to her, reaches down, stretching his arm. Buffy goes into a crouch under water and shoots up out of the water. She grabs Xander's arm as she is kicking the creatures away from her. She climbs out with Xander's help.

The coach, though, has recovered. He lunges for both of them. They dodge and he flips over into the hole. Buffy grabs his arm and tries to hold him up out of the water, but he lets go. She yells down at him to grab her hand. The coach, though, is trying to talk to his team.

Coach: Boys, boys.

They close in on him and attack.

This resolution reminds me of The Witch. Amy's mom, a human being, was a serious threat both to Amy and to Buffy. Buffy stopped her, but she didn't kill her. She reflected the spell that Amy's mom had cast back on her. And it was poetic justice. Here, similarly, the coach meets the fate he meant for Buffy. So again, poetic justice.

Also, she tried to save him. His own hubris in believing he didn't need her help, and that he could control his team, is what killed him. Also, his attack on Buffy sent him over the edge and down into the water, not Buffy herself. So, as in The Witch, again we see that Buffy does not kill humans. In fact, even if they do evil things, we see here that she still tries to save them.

Falling Action In Go Fish

Now we're at our Falling Action, which is where we resolve the loose ends and tie up any subplots. First we get the last of our disturbing sexual assault jokes. It also makes clear what happens to the coach. Because Buffy and Xander are looking down through that trap door.

Buffy: Those boys really love their coach.

In the next scene, everyone sits in the student lounge area. Xander says he and the team are getting plasma transfusions. So we know they are going to be saved from turning into sea monsters. Cordelia tells Xander that he really proved himself to her. And she reassures him he doesn't have to join the new swim team. She'd be just as happy if he played football.

Giles says Animal Control just left. The creatures disappeared. Willow asks if they need to hunt them but Buffy says no. She thinks they won't bother anyone. Giles asks where she thinks they went, and she says, "Home."

In the last scene we see the sea creatures diving into the ocean. And that is the end of the episode.

A Self-Contained Episode With No Oz

Another thing to note about this episode is not only is Oz not in it, he isn't mentioned. This really was a self-contained one-off episode. It was meant to be watched in any order. You didn't need to know about Willow and Oz.

If you watched it before Halloween or before Phases, it wouldn't spoil anything. You wouldn't know that Willow had a boyfriend or that the boyfriend was a werewolf. I also think the writers wanted that little bit of sexual tension between Xander and Willow. As always, more on Willow's side. But I think the writers wanted to be free to throw that in without having to deal with Willow having a boyfriend now.

For that reason, it's a little inconsistent with the season arc. I'm willing to go with it, though, because I think Willow is written to always have that little bit of feeling for Xander no matter what else is going on, at least at this point in the show.

Spoilers and Foreshadowing

If Go Fish Were Written Today

In addition to thinking that we would not get those sexual assault jokes if the episode were written today, I also think today you would not see the coach pulling a gun on a student. You wouldn't see the gun at all. And as Buffy goes on, we'll see guns become less and less common. I'm pretty sure we've seen them more in Seasons One and Two than we will in the entire other five seasons.

Buffy Undercover

In the pilot of Season Three Buffy will recognize that she is just terrible at undercover. So she's not just having an off day, as she suggests here, when she's talking to Gage. She is just bad at it.

In that pilot she goes to a youth outreach center where she suspects terrible things are happening. At first, she tries to pretend she needs help. She says something like, "Oh, yeah, I'm all about the sin and the rock music...." And then she just gives up and says something like, "I suck at undercover," and busts into the place.

Jonathan Jonathan

Go Fish incudes major foreshadowing about Jonathan. Being bullied, getting mad at Buffy for helping him, and then this petty revenge he takes. All of which foreshadow a number of developments in the series.

In Season Three we'll see Earshot, where Jonathan has a rifle in a tower, and it is largely because he is always being bullied or ignored. His revenge hints at some of his actions in Season Six when he becomes one of the villains. I also wonder if Willow's comment about him going to the dark arts, summoning a hell beast, gives Jonathan some ideas. Because later in the series we will see him using dark magic. First in Superstar to make everyone think that he is amazing. And then in Season Six when he becomes one of the villains.

I like the interaction between Willow and Jonathan. That scene seems like a throwaway, but really could be sowing the seeds for Jonathan starting to think about how maybe there's a better way to get revenge than peeing in the pool.

Character Arcs

I think Jonathan's is one of the great character arcs in Buffy, and a terrific example of a character who at first just had a walk on role. But they wanted to bring the actor back, so they kept making him the victim.

Then you see the show take all of that and turn it into a

great back story for a character who does much more significant things. And almost all of that is hinted at here, though I don't think at this point they had a plan for Jonathan.

I do think there was a plan for the Willow, Cordelia, and Xander triangle. In this one-off episode we have that line from Cordelia where Xander walks into the swimming pool. (And we had to just go with the idea that none of them recognize him at first.) And Cordelia says something like, oh my that's my kind of – and Willow says, "Xander." She cuts off Cordelia. When Cordelia's still saying "my," Willow jumps in there.

This foreshadows that ongoing issue that Willow is still attracted to Xander.

Cordelia And Xander

There is also Cordelia foreshadowing because of two things. First, her soliloquy at the pool to who she thinks is sea monster Xander. It's silly and funny, but it also shows Cordelia has a depth of feeling for Xander. So when he betrays her, that is truly awful for her.

And in the Falling Action we see that despite that depth of feeling, and that she was willing to go against her friends and public opinion (and her own view of who she should be dating or who matches her status), she would really like it if Xander would join the swim team again. Or would play football. In short, do things to bring him closer to her social level.

All of that adds to her heartbreak in Season Three over him betraying her after she went against her friends and her ideas of social class. And while I don't necessarily think that's at the heart of her pain, it does make it worse for her. Because her friends do not let her forget that she lowered herself socially in their eyes to date Xander. They mock her mercilessly about it.

All of which leads to The Wish, where Cordelia makes a wish a vengeance demon grants, and we get one of my favorite Buffy episodes. I do think that, too, is intentionally foreshadowed here.

Questions For Your Writing

- Does your story open with conflict? Is it clear what it is?
- If your characters joke or use humor, are there any messages you don't intend in their lines? If so, are you happy with those messages? Do they fit the tone of the story?
- Can you include a twist in your story, taking what usually happens in your genre and revealing something unexpected instead? (Like Angel spitting out Gage's blood?)
- Where do your major plot turns occur? Do they keep the story moving forward?

Next: Becoming Part One

NEXT WE'LL TALK about Becoming Part One, where Kendra returns to Sunnydale and Buffy must face Angelus at last. The discussion includes crafting strong plot points and using flashbacks effectively to tell a story.

CHAPTER 9
BECOMING PART ONE (S2 E21)

THIS CHAPTER TALKS about Becoming Part One, Season Two Episode Twenty-One, where Buffy hopes Willow can return Angel's soul but remains ready to fight Angelus, and Kendra returns to help. Written and directed by Joss Whedon.

In particular, we'll look at:

- Flashbacks that tell a story of their own;
- Strong major plot points;
- Small moments that ratchet up the emotional stakes and make later character choices believable; and
- Sowing seeds of future unexpected plot twists.

Okay, let's dive into the Hellmouth.

OPENING Conflict - Voiceover

We start with a voice over by Whistler, a demon we'll meet later who seems to be on the side of good.

Whistler: Here's the thing. There's moments in your life that make you....Some are little or subtle and some are not.

A subtitle tells us we are in Galway 1763. Angel, when he's human, and a friend are being thrown out of a pub. The friend passes out in the street. Angel sees a woman. Her back is to him, and she walks down an alley. She looks a lot like the drawing of the woman in the fancy dress that Buffy saw in the Watcher diaries in Halloween.

Angel follows her and asks what a lady of her station is doing in an alley with a reputation like this one. Darla says maybe she's lonely. Angel offers himself as escort. He sounds like a bit of a smart ass and kind of smarmy. But she smiles and asks if he's up to the challenge. He says with the exception of an honest day's work there's no challenge he's not prepared to face.

As the two talk, Darla tells him she's from far away. From everywhere. Angel says he's never been anywhere himself. This is the first time he sounds genuine. There's a note of longing and almost wistfulness in his voice as he says he's always wanted to see the world.

Close Your Eyes

Darla's eyes light up, and she says she can show him things he's never seen. Frightening things.

Angel: I'm not afraid. Show me your world.

Darla: Close your eyes.

He does. She goes into vamp face, holds him, and bites him. Now his eyes open. As she is feeding on him, she lets go. Angel drops to his knees, and she draws her nail across her own skin above her breasts, drawing a line of blood. She brings his face to her, and he drinks.

This whole scene implies that Angel chose the vampire life to some extent despite that he didn't fully know what he was choosing. And maybe this is part of why the show blames Angel, or he blames himself, for his wrongdoing as a vampire.

Or at least it may be part of why he's so willing to take on that guilt.

We're at 2 minutes 52 seconds into the episode. This scene fades and shifts into Angelus in the present day. He is watching Buffy.

Angelus Watches Buffy Fight

Buffy fights a vampire in the cemetery. She knocks the vamp down and tells him to get the message to Angel that she's done fighting.

Buffy: I'm taking the fight to him.

But the vamp keeps fighting, and Buffy has to stake him. She walks behind a tombstone and helps Xander up. He says he's fine, and what is that, five vampires? Buffy says yes, in two nights, but no Angel. Xander asks if she's really that anxious to come up against Angel. And she says she wants it over with and then that they better go, she hasn't even started studying for finals get. Xander says something like, oh, finals, why didn't you let me die?

Buffy: Look on the bright side. It'll all be over soon.

The Story Spark Of The First Half?

We're at 4 minutes 19 seconds in. Angel, in the shadows, says to himself, "Yes, my love, it will."

And we go to credits.

This is about 10% through the episode. Usually at that point in any story we see the Story Spark or Inciting Incident that gets the story rolling. But Becoming is a two-part story told in two episodes, so 10% in would be more like 8-10 minutes in.

I think this comment, though, is that hint of conflict we need to keep our attention and keep the audience engaged. And the scene after the credits shows us what really got the story rolling, though we don't know exactly when it happened.

At 5 minutes 19 seconds in, two men in a museum work on a large rectangular rock. It stands about give 5 feet taller than the two men. It's a few feet deep and maybe five feet wide, grey stone, craggy, with writing on it.

Giles walks into the room. The curator is happy to see him, saying he called the Washington Institute and they told him that the best authority in obscure relics was right here in Sunnydale. Giles smiles, but says this might be a bit exaggerated. This is a minor conflict to help the exposition come in. If you hadn't seen the show before you would now know something about Giles.

The curator says the construction workers dug up this rock outside of town and they don't know what it is.

Giles Doesn't Like Surprises

Giles looks over the rock. He uses a pick to scrape a sample into a jar and sees a seam. He says he assumes they haven't tried to open the rock. The curator hadn't realized it could be opened. And he's ready to go ahead right now, but Giles asks him to wait. He wants to translate the text on it first.

Curator: You don't want to be surprised?

Giles: As a rule, no.

This is our first call back to the episode Surprise. That episode was Part One of the two-part episode where Angel lost his soul. A pivotal point for the series and for Buffy and Angel, as this two-parter now is. And I can't help thinking Giles's dislike of surprises relates back to that moment.

A Fish Story

The next scene takes place in the cafeteria. Xander acts out Buffy's fight scene from the night before using fish sticks and a toothpick. Cordelia laughs.

Oz: I thought it was riveting. I was a little unclear about some of the themes.

Willow is sitting on Oz's lap. So we quickly learn that she has a boyfriend even if we missed previous episodes. (Or if we only saw Go Fish and weren't aware of Oz at all.)

Buffy says the theme of the story is that Angel is too much

of a coward to face her. Xander says the other thing was buy American but it got kind of buried. Willow asks if Buffy thinks she's ready to face Angel. Buffy says she wishes people would stop asking her. She's ready. She's also willing and able.

Buffy: It's the one test I'm likely to pass.

Willow tells her don't worry, she'll get Buffy through finals.

The Story Spark Of Becoming

At about 8 minutes 30 seconds in they agree to meet in Willow's classroom to go over chemistry after six o'clock. I see this as the Story Spark for the two-part story, though it's a little short of 10% through the double episode. While we don't know why it's so significant, this decision sets the story in motion from Buffy's perspective. After school in the classroom is where and when Buffy will find that lost plastic disk with Jenny's spell on it to restore Angel's soul.

It's not completely clear, though, what the single Story Spark is. Unlike other episodes where even one unclear point muddles the plot, however, this story still works well. And maybe it's because we already have so many plots in motion. We've got this flashback on Angel (we're going to learn more about that because of Whistler's voiceover), the finding of this rock or monolith, Buffy's tension over schoolwork, and this moment that will lead to finding the spell and trying to restore Angel's soul.

Cafeteria Conflict

Back to the cafeteria. Cordelia expresses admiration for Willow. She says Willow really has the teaching bug. She's taking over the computer class, tutoring, and it's great because that way when she goes out and fails in the real world she'll be falling forward into something instead of falling back.

Xander says that was about 65% actual compliment and was that a personal best? This is more nice use of low-level conflict to get in more exposition, this time about Willow taking over Miss Calendar's class. Cordelia laughs and squeals as she and

Xander joke around. And she tells him to get his fish hands off of her. A nice double reference to the fish sticks and the last episode, Go Fish.

Principal Snyder, though, is not amused. He walks in and tells them that's enough. And he turns to Willow and says, "And you. Is there a chair shortage?"

Willow says she didn't read about one and then, "Oh I get it," and slides into a chair.

Snyder: This isn't an orgy, people. It's a classroom.

Buffy: Yeah, where they teach lunch.

Snyder: Just give me a reason to kick you out, Summers. Just give me a reason.

This echoes early in the season when Snyder told Giles something like, "I smell an expulsion coming." And throughout the season he's been pinpointing Buffy as what he sees as the source of a lot of the trouble in the school.

London Flashback

Now we're about 9 minutes 40 seconds in, and we switch to London in 1860. We see church grounds. There is a spire and chanting or singing in the background. A woman in a veil kneels and crosses herself in church. It's Drusilla. She goes into a confessional.

If you haven't been in one of these, there are three booths. The priest sits in the center and on either side a person can come in and wait to confess their sins to the priest. The booths were for the most part soundproof. You couldn't hear what was going on in the other side until the priest slid open a window. But there was a net or grate over that window so neither side could really see each other. And the idea was that the priest wouldn't know who was making their confession.

As the audience, we see that Angelus is in the confessional and has just killed the priest.

Drusilla is unaware. She says it's two days since her last confession. Angel plays the role of the priest. At first it seems like he's doing it just to avoid detection. But then he becomes intrigued by her.

So we are seeing the first time he meets Drusilla. And he is hidden from her in the same way that later in the episode he will be hidden when he first sees Buffy.

Drusilla sounds as lucid as we've ever heard her. And I love this glimpse into her life as a human. She tells Angel she's been "seeing again." That yesterday something came over her. She saw a horrible crash in the mine. Her mother told her it meant nothing. But then today there was a cave-in and two men died. Her mother told Drusilla she's cursed. An affront to God.

Drusilla says she doesn't mean to do it, to see things. She's so upset. She tells Angel that she tries to be pure. She cries.

Angel Manipulates Dru

Drusilla: I don't want to be an evil thing.

Angel tells her to hush.

Angel: The Lord has a plan for all his creatures. Even a devil child like you. All the Hail Marys in the world won't help that.

She begs him. She wants to be pure. Please help her.

And he says finally, "Say ten Our Fathers and an Act of Contrition. How does that sound?" She thanks him. And he tells her God is watching her.

From previous episodes we know that after this, he tormented her. Killed all her family and tortured her until she went into a convent. Then he turned her into a vampire. That part is not included here.

The Episode One-Quarter Twist

But we do see what ultimately happens to Drusilla because the scene switches to her drifting into the courtyard in the dark. She says the moon started whispering to her. Something terrible is coming it at the museum. A tomb with a surprise inside. That's our second mention of a surprise. And it cues us that this will affect Buffy and Angel in some cataclysmic way.

We're at almost 13 minutes 30 seconds in. I see this as a One-

Quarter Twist for the episode. That's the major plot turn that generally comes from outside the protagonist and spins the story in a new way. While we are in a two-episode story arc, and we're not a quarter way through the full story, having a major turn at the one-quarter mark of the first episode keeps its momentum going.

And this scene, where Dru, Angel, and Spike learn about the museum find, does turn the story, though not without a little bit of sparring between Angel and Spike.

Angel (to Drusilla): You can see all that in your head?

Spike: No, you ninny. She read it in the morning paper.

He hands Angel the paper with a front-page article about an obelisk being found.

Angel: Soon it'll stop whispering. Soon it'll scream.

Buffy Finds The Disk

The scene switches to Buffy and Willow in Willow's classroom.

Buffy: Waa, this doesn't make any sense.

Willow: Sure it does. (She takes Buffy's paper.) Oh, no, this doesn't make any sense.

Buffy says it senseless. She's frustrated and feels stupid. But Willow says at least she knows that, so she's learning. Buffy, feeling more encouraged, is about to look at her paper again. But her pencil slips out of her fingers rolls across the desk. It falls into the space between the desk and the file cabinet.

There we see a small plastic disk back from the episode Passion where Jenny was killed. She saved the spell to restore Angel's soul on this disc. And it fell between the desk and file cabinet and nobody knew about it.

Buffy doesn't see it now when she retrieves her pencil. She sits up again.

Buffy: Okay, I'm Learn Girl.

But then Buffy says, "Déjà vu." And says she has a perfect memory of the pencil rolling. She sets it rolling again. It drops again into that space. And this time Buffy notices the disk when she retrieves the pencil.

She hands it to Willow, who says it's not hers. It must be Miss Calendar's. She pops it into the disk drive. Buffy says it seems kind of morbid to look at Miss Calendar's files. And Willow says she's been through most of them. Buffy asks if that makes Willow more or less morbid, and Willow says she had to do it to teach the class.

Handling Backstory Without Spoiling Past Installments

So we have more conflict, somewhat minor, but it helps us get in that exposition. Why Willow is teaching, that she looked at Jenny's files, and that Jenny is dead.

The file decrypts. Buffy looks at it.

Buffy: Does that say restoration?

Willow, though, is not looking at the screen. She's looking at Buffy.

Willow: Oh, it's probably one of Miss Calendar's spells. Even though she wasn't a practicing witch....

So we get a little more exposition. And it fits because Buffy might not know all of what Willow has been finding on the computer or much about Miss Calendar's spells. And there is tension because Buffy is tense. She's staring at the screen, seeing something that Willow has missed.

Buffy: Willow.

Willow (looks at screen): Oh boy, oh boy. Oh boy.

And we cut.

That scene worked whether you knew the back story or not. So it's a great example of how to handle that. If you are writing any sort of installment series – a movie, a novel – sometimes you need to quickly catch your readers up on past events. And this is a good way to do it. Weave in enough, along with some conflict, to put the current scene in context for the new reader or viewer. But avoid having so much detail that it bores the audience that already knows what happened.

The Best Use Of Flashbacks

Our next scene, another flashback, shows the original spell to restore Angel's soul. It's in the point of view of someone running and breathing hard. We switch between that and a gray-haired woman chanting with candles lit. Then we see it's Angel running. He falls to the ground. The glass by the old woman glows. Angel's eyes glow. He is disoriented. He asks where he is.

A man has come to meet him, and he tells Angel that everything he's done he'll remember it all in a moment. The face of everyone he's killed. It will all haunt him and he will know true suffering.

Angel: Killed. I don't, I don't – (it all hits him) no no no.
He sobs.

This episode includes the best use of flashbacks that we've seen so far in *Buffy*. Because these flashbacks, if we put them all together, tell their own story. The story of Angel becoming a vampire, getting a soul, and later wanting to end the world, as well as some of what happens in between.

They also carry the theme of Becoming. Angel becoming a vampire. Drusilla becoming a vampire. And, a little bit later, Buffy becoming the Slayer.

The Curse

Nearly 18 minutes in we are at the library. Buffy and Willow tell the others that Miss Calendar was trying to replicate the curse to restore Angel's soul.

Cordelia: This is good, right? I mean, we can curse him again.

Giles says it points the way, but it requires more black arts knowledge than he has. Willow, though, says she's been researching the black arts for fun – educational fun –and she may be able to do the spell. Giles warns her that channeling such potent magics through herself could open a door she can't close. Buffy doesn't want Willow putting herself in danger.

Willow also says she doesn't want danger. Big No to danger. But she might be the best person to do this.

Xander: Hi. For those of you who have just tuned in, everyone here is a crazy person.

He goes on to say that so the spell might restore Angel's humanity. Who cares? Angel's a killer. He stands as he's talking.

Buffy tells him it's not that simple. They argue. Cordelia stands behind Xander and says he has a point. He gets angry and says for once he wishes she'd support him and then he realizes she did, and now he's embarrassed so he'll just go back to his point. Angel needs to die.

Giles says cursing Angel again seems to have been Jenny's last wish.

Xander: Yeah, well, Jenny's dead.

I think this may be the only time that Xander calls her Jenny rather than Miss Calendar.

Giles (steps toward Xander): Don't you ever –

They're all yelling and Buffy yells at them to stop it.

Buffy and Willow face each other. The camera does a close up on them. And Willow asks Buffy what she wants. As always, the great friend. Buffy doesn't know what she wants, but she says what happened to Angel wasn't his fault.

Xander: Yeah, but what happened to Miss Calendar is.

He goes on to say that Buffy can paint it anyway she wants, but the way he sees it, "you want to forget all about Miss Calendar's murder so you can get your boyfriend back." Buffy walks out.

Episode Midpoint Reversals All Around

We're a little past 20 minutes in, so we are nearing the Midpoint of the episode and the one-quarter point of the two-episode arc. At a story's Midpoint, we usually see a major reversal for the protagonist or a major commitment to the quest or both. So we will see one of those at the end of this episode, which is the Midpoint of the two-episode arc here.

But we do see a bit of a reversal here, nearly at the episode Midpoint, for Buffy. She is so discouraged that her friends – at least Xander and Cordelia – are not supporting her. And Giles is warning of the danger of doing this thing.

The next scene also includes something of a reversal for Buffy. Drusilla, Angel, and other vampires go to the museum and kill the curator. Angel looks at that giant stone.

Angel: I'll take one of these to go.

At 20 minutes 50 seconds in, Buffy is on the phone to Willow. She's gathering supplies for patrolling.

Buffy: Xander was pretty much being – Willow! Where did you learn that word?

This is nice. We don't technically need this moment. But I like that the show acknowledges that Xander was being awful. As Buffy gathers supplies, she sees the ring that Angel gave her. She is holding it and looking at it as she tells Willow she doesn't know what she wants to do. The Buffy and Angel theme music plays in the background.

A Surprise Visit

In the next scene Buffy is out patrolling and Kendra, the other Vampire Slayer surprises her.

Buffy: You know, polite people call before they jump out of bushes to attack you.

She guesses the reason Kendra is there is that Kendra's watcher told her a dark power is about to rise in Sunnydale. Kendra says that's pretty much it.

Buffy: Any idea what it is?

And here we get one of my favorite cuts in *Buffy* ever because we switch to Spike, Angel, and Drusilla. Buffy's just said, "Any idea what it is?"

Spike: It's a big rock. I can't wait to tell my friends. They don't have a rock this big.

Spike's in his wheelchair at one end of a long hallway along with Angel and Drusilla and the rock stands at the other end of the hall. Angel responds to Spike, and he is scornful. He says Spike never learned history.

Spike: Let's have a lesson then.

Angel says the demon Acathla was meant to swallow the world. But he was killed by a virtuous knight who pierced his heart, and Acathla turned to stone. He was buried, "where neither man nor demon would want to look. Unless, of course, they're putting up low-rent housing."

The other vampires open the stone box. Inside is Acathla, made of stone but with a sword piercing into his chest. Angel says that when someone worthy pulls out the sword, Acathla will awaken and swallow the world whole.

One-Quarter Twist Of Becoming

Angel approaches Acathla.

Angel: My friends, we're about to make history.

And this is the One-Quarter Twist in our two-episode arc. At about one quarter through a well-structured story we should see something come from outside the protagonist and spin the story in a new direction. And we get that here because now our story will focus on Angel trying to bring Acathla awake to swallow the world. And Buffy trying to stop him.

Acathla looks a little bit like The Judge from Surprise and Innocence. So it is another call back to that pivotal Buffy and Angel two-part story. And I don't think it's an accident that Spike and Dru through The Judge essentially wanted to end the world by ridding the earth of the plague of humanity. And here, Angel wants to have the world sucked into hell.

We cut to a commercial.

Giles Warns Of The Stakes

Then we are back in the library. Giles gets off the phone. He tells the others that the artifact (meaning that rock) is missing, and the curator is dead.

Buffy: And we're sure it was the tomb of Alfalfa?

She will mangle the name throughout the episode. Giles

corrects her, and Willow asks what sucking into hell means exactly. Giles says the demon dimension is different from ours. With one breath, Acathla sucks the world into it and all non-demon life will suffer horrible eternal torment.

Buffy: So that would be the literal sucked into hell. Neat.

Buffy tells Willow she should try the curse. Kendra disagrees, but in a much more kind way than Xander.

Kendra: I tend to side with your friend Xander. Angel should be killed.

And Buffy says she'll fight Angel, she'll kill him if she has to, but if she loses Willow might be their only hope.

Willow: I don't want to be the only hope. I crumble under pressure. Let's have another hope.

Kendra pulls out a sword from a case that she brought with her. And she says they have another hope. A sword blessed by the knight who originally slew Acathla. If all else fails, it might stop him.

Spells And Rituals In Becoming Part One

Willow needs another day to figure out the spell. And she needs an Orb of Thesulah, whatever that is. Giles says it's a spirit vault for rituals of the undead.

Giles: I've got one. I've been using it as a paperweight.

This is a nice call back to the episode, Passion, the one where Jenny was killed. She went to the Magic Shop to get an Orb of Thesulah. And the shopkeeper scoffed at the people who buy them as New Age paperweights.

Giles says Angel has a ritual of his own to complete before he can remove the sword and hopefully it will take some time. This at the moment seems like a bit of a throwaway line, or a way to explain why we don't immediately have the ritual go forward. But it turns out that this is key to a development at the very end of the episode.

Spike, Angel, And Drusilla

We switch to Drusilla. Spike is in another room alone and

is out of his wheelchair. She calls to him and he hops into it just before she comes into the room. She says it's time to begin.

In the long hallway a man is on his knees. His shirt is off. He's tied up. And Angel recites words for the ritual ending with: "Bear witness as I ascend. As I become."

Spike looks bored. Angel vamps out. He bites the guy and there is blood on Angel's hand.

Angel: Everything I am has led me here.

We switch to Manhattan 1996. Angel is again in an alley. So we have the repetition of that image from when he became a vampire. He looks very grubby. He chases a rat and misses and falls into bags of garbage.

A man a bit shorter and slighter than Angel who's wearing a bowler hat observes this.

Whistler: You're so sad. A vampire with a soul.

He takes Angel for a walk, introduces himself as Whistler, says he's technically a demon, but they're not all bad. And he buys Angel a hot dog and tells him that butchers are throwing out blood every day. But Angel is here living on rats. He needs to live in the world a little.

He also tells Angel he can go either way from here. Become a more vile rodent than he already is. Or he can become someone. Whistler wants to show him something – or rather someone – and Angel can decide.

Angel Sees Buffy For The First Time

The next scene visually contrasts to the alley. It is bright and sunny and open. Buffy walks out of a high school with three friends. (This is still a flashback.) She has very long hair and holds a lollipop

Angel is parked a little distance away in a black car with blacked out windows. He rolls down one a little and peers through – an echo of that confessional scene with Drusilla where he was hidden from her by that screen.

Buffy, very bubbly, is telling her friends how her dad wants her to wear a dress to the dance that she already wore before.

Buffy: And I'm like, Dad, why do you hate me?

One of her friends asks if Tyler is taking her to the dance.

Buffy: Where were you when I got over Tyler?

She says he'd have to crawl on his hands and knees to get her to go to the dance with him. Which he's scheduled to do after class, so she's going to wait. As her friends leave, she says, "Call me. Call me! Call me." So she seems very much like Cordelia, although a bit nicer. (Perhaps I'm just reading that in because I want to. But I do think that is the feel of the scene.)

Buffy Is Called

Buffy sits on the steps after her friends leave. A man comes up to her. He is balding and has kind of a big mustache. He wears a suit that looks like a cheaper version of what Giles wears.

Watcher: Buffy Summers?

Buffy: Yeah. Hi. What?

She asks if he's from the department store because she was going to pay for that lipstick, really. He tells her that her destiny awaits. She says she's destiny free and he says she alone can stop the vampires.

About 32 minutes in, it's night, and Buffy fights a vampire in a park. She's struggling and stumbling. But she finally gets it on the ground. She stakes the vampire but misses the heart. Tries again and hits it. And she leaps, or tumbles, back in shock when the vampire dusts.

Watcher: You see? You see your power.

Angel watches from a distance. We continue in his point of view, looking into Buffy's house. Joyce is yelling at her about being late and not even calling. Buffy says she was with Tyler and lost track of time. Joyce is still upset, but says she was just worried.

Buffy goes into another room, but she overhears Hank and

Joyce arguing. Hank is angry at Joyce. He says she won't discipline Buffy, and he always has to be the ogre. This is a call back to Season One, Nightmares, where one of Buffy's biggest fears was that she caused the divorce. She was the reason her father left.

Why The Flashbacks Work

At about 33 minutes in we switch back to Whistler and Angel. And Whistler says the Slayer will have it tough. She's just a kid. Angel says he wants to help her. He wants to become someone.

So we have seen Buffy and how she becomes the Slayer, something that we didn't get to see in the series before this. And it seems very fitting to have it here. And I think that flashback works because it is part of Angel's story, which is told through these flashbacks.

Unlike in some episodes, these flashbacks don't slow or stop the story. They're part of the story.

Whistler tells Angel. It won't be easy. The more he is in the world, the more he'll see how apart he is from it.

The Ritual Fails

We switch to present day. In the long hallway Angel is continuing the ritual.

Angel: I have strayed. I have been lost.

He approaches Acathla, grabs the sword, we get bright flashing lights, and we cut to a commercial.

We return to the same scene. The lights are flashing. Angel yanks the sword, but he can't pull it out. He's thrown back, a sort of echo of that scene of Buffy falling back the first time she dusted the vampire.

Spike: Someone wasn't worthy.

Angel is angry. Spike is amused. Drusilla is disappointed and says what will they do?

Angel: What we always do. Turn to an old friend.

He assures them they'll have their Armageddon.

The first time I watched this I did not think about Giles or what Giles was explaining to the others about Angel having a ritual to complete. So I didn't realize the old friend Angel referred to is Giles. I love that because it sets up the surprise – at least most audience members I think were surprised – when it turns out they're after Giles. And yet it fits so well. When you rewatch, you see how that was foreshadowed. The writers surprised the audience but played fair and didn't blindside them.

A Vampire Invite

At school Buffy is taking an exam. A vampire shrouded in a blanket walks in. Sunlight floods the classroom. As the vampire talks her whole body begins to smoke. She says that tonight, sundown, at the graveyard, "you will come or more will die."

And then she burst into flames. Raising the question, which I've asked before in the series, why are vampires willing to do these things? What's the payoff for them? But it is very dramatic. And it fits that moment in the beginning when Buffy was going to send a message to Angel through a vampire.

In the library, our friends talk about what to do next. Buffy says she has to go meet Angel tonight. The vampire said otherwise more will die. Kendra wants to go with her, but Buffy says no. Kendra should stay to protect the others. She reasons that as long as Angel's fighting her he can't do the ritual to end the world.

Buffy asks Willow if she's ready with the spell. Willow says she needs about half an hour once they get everything set up. And Giles tells Buffy she just needs to hold Angel off for that long. And we see that after that conflict, the friends are now united in supporting Buffy. Because Cordelia says, why not wait here? See if Angel calls her, and she'll know the spell worked.

But Buffy says she can't risk him killing any more people.

Dealing With Audience Objections

Cordelia asked a question many audience members might

be asking. Why doesn't Buffy just stay there and stay safe? This is a good way to deal with objections your audience might have. Or questions about the choices your characters make. Have another character articulate them. Then your protagonist, or whoever is making the choice, can answer it.

As Buffy is leaving Xander says, "Be careful." He sounds supportive. I'm sure he still disagrees with all of this, but he has calmed down and is offering support. Kendra gives Buffy Mr. Pointy, her lucky stake, showing solidarity with Buffy.

Buffy: You named your stake? Remind me to get you a stuffed animal.

This shows vulnerability for Kendra and the bond between them. Making what happens in the climax more heartbreaking.

Moving Toward The Episode Climax

And we are moving toward the climax of the episode, which will be our Midpoint of the two-episode story arc. At the graveyard:

Angel: Hello, Lover. I wasn't sure you'd come.

Buffy: After your immolation-o-gram? I had to show.

But she asks, shouldn't he be out destroying the world, pulling the sword out of Al Franken or whatever it is? He says time enough for that. She's the one thing in the world that he will miss. They fight. We're at 38 minutes in.

Willow starts the ritual. She is sitting at the library table, and Giles reads Latin. She reads English. Cordelia walks in a circle around them with incense. Xander stands on that second level where all the bookshelves are, and Kendra is near the main library double doors that lead to the school.

The Climax Of Becoming Part One

Now we reach the climax of the episode. Vampires attack from behind Xander and grab him. More come in the library doors. Giles yells at Cordelia and Willow to run. He and Kendra fight the vampires as Cordelia and Willow run up the stairs. A vampire pushes a bookcase over on Willow. It pins her.

We switch to Buffy and Angel fighting.

Angel: Is it me or is your heart not in this?

Buffy: Let's finish this. You and me.

Angel (laughs): You never learn, do you? This wasn't about you. This was never about you.

Buffy turns away and starts running. He calls after her.

Angel: And you fall for it every single time.

Buffy runs through the Sunnydale streets.

Drusilla walks into the library, claps her hands, and says, "Enough."

Giles has been subdued. Drusilla fights Kendra. First, physically. But then she gets Kendra by the throat and, looking right into her eyes. Drusilla moves her two fingers with her long red fingernails in front of Kendra's face.

Drusilla: Be in my eyes. Be in me.

Kendra sways along with Drusilla.

And we cut between Buffy running through the streets of Sunnydale and Kendra swaying in rhythm with Drusilla. Then Drusilla slashes Kendra's throat with her fingernail and draws a line of blood across it. Like what we saw Darla do to herself with Angel.

Escalating The Midpoint Reversal

We are at the two-part episode Midpoint. So we see a major reversal. And what is fascinating to me is that the Reversal itself escalates. Because Kendra dies. Drusilla drops her on the floor, and it seems like that's all. It's a major reversal. But –

Drusilla: Let's get what we came for.

And the vampires drag Giles away. This ups the stakes for the reversal because it is not just killing Kendra, it is taking Giles. The person that Buffy needs and relies on. Remember in Passion she told Giles, "I can't do this without you."

Now we hear Whistler again in voiceover.

Whistler: The bottom line is, even if you see them coming,

you're not ready for the big moments. No one asks for their life to change. Not really. But it does.

He speaks as Buffy runs into the school. Through the hallways. Now in slow motion. And the Buffy and Angel theme music plays. As Whistler finishes saying, "but it does," Buffy reaches the library. She stops. Stares at Kendra and in slow motion runs to Kendra, drops to the floor, and bends over Kendra's body.

Whistler: So what are we? Helpless puppets? No. The big moments are going to come. You can't help it. It's what you do afterwards that counts. That's when you find out who you are.

We're seeing Buffy with the camera angle from behind. She is holding Kendra's hand. A gun comes into the frame, and a cop's voice says, "Freeze."

So we get even higher stakes, because now Buffy is found over this dead body. And the police – who have been so absent in Sunnydale – are right there.

To Be Continued flashes on the screen.

Whistler: You'll see what I mean.

Spoilers and Foreshadowing

THE WORLD SUCKED Into Hell

Giles explains about the literal being sucked into hell, which foreshadows or sets up the horrible choice Buffy will face at the end of Becoming Part Two. When Acathla starts to awaken, but Angel has come back to being himself, she knows (and so do we) that if she doesn't kill Angel, the entire world will be sucked into hell. Giles made that so clear.

On first watch, we don't know what that is setting up. It just seems like Giles is telling everyone the stakes are really high here. The whole world is hanging in the balance. But we have no idea that Buffy will need to make this awful choice.

Close Your Eyes

Before rewatching for the podcast I forgot that moment where Darla says, "Close your eyes," before biting Angel and starting to turn him into a vampire. I didn't remember that she said those exact words, the same words Buffy will say to Angel before she kills him: "Close your eyes."

If you listen to the podcast Still Pretty, cohost Lani Diane Rich says that phrase and the theme music always make her cry. And I'm right there with her. It is just heartbreaking.

Foreshadowing What Angel Won't Know

Part of the flashbacks also add to the heartbreak of that scene. We saw when Angel was cursed the first time ad his soul was restored that he was confused. He doesn't remember what he did as a vampire, and he says, "Killed? I don't, I don't –" And then we see it hit him. So we have established that Angel, when his soul is restored, at first won't remember what he did before it happened.

So when Willow's spell works in the next episode, Angel is just as confused. He only knows he's with Buffy. Whom he loves. It would be easier for her if he were racked with guilt. If he remembered being Angelus and all the things he did. But he doesn't, and she has to kill him anyway.

That is another way that these flashbacks are used to such great effect. They tell their own story. And, though we don't know it yet, they set up this moment so that it's the most intense moment of the show.

Willow's Arc

There is also a lot of foreshadowing for Willow's entire story arc about magic. I forgot how early it started. Giles says the spell requires knowledge of the black arts, and that Willow might open a door she can't close. And, of course, we will see that happening in Season Six. Willow goes on to do another spell more dangerous than this one to bring Buffy back from the dead. She has to get the Urn of Osiris on the black market. And we see what that spell does to her, even as she casts it.

Then throughout the season we see more repercussions. Willow becomes darker and darker. Even her saying here, " I researched the black arts for fun – educational fun," hints that Willow's desire for knowledge may trip her up. She can learn so much and so fast. And she wants to. It's fun. But less and less often will she distinguish between filling her mind with things that are dark, things that can lead to evil, and those that help. She's not differentiating. It's all educational fun.

We see the seeds of all of that here when Willow is so innocent and really just wanting to learn and help. Later she'll transition to yes, wanting to help, but also using magic for convenience. To make her life easier. Then to try to change other people. To alter them, as she does with Tara, to make her relationships smoother. To get what she wants.

I would really love to know how much the writers knew when they wrote this episode about where Willow's character was going with magic.

Another Slayer

Kendra's death sets up Faith's arrival in Season Three. Earlier in the season we established that Buffy dying only for a minute called a new Slayer. Yet in Season Three, it seems no one really thinks about whether Kendra's death will call a new Slayer until Faith arrives. When she does, everyone puts it together pretty quickly and is like, "Oh, new Slayer."

Maybe they don't sort it out earlier because Buffy disappears at the end of the season. They're so concerned with where she is, finding her, that they don't really think about, hey, isn't there another Slayer?

The Slayer Line

All of this raises issues about the whole Slayer line. Because when Buffy dies a second time at the end of Season Five, no new Slayer is called. It seems as if Buffy died the first time, calling Kendra. Then the line of Slayers switched to Kendra. Kendra dies and we get Faith. Because Faith is still alive, we don't get another Slayer when Buffy dies.

Then in Season Seven the show deals in some ways with these questions by saying that the First Evil is empowered because of Buffy. Not so much her death, but because she was returned to life in the beginning of Season Six. And it throws off the Slayer line and the balance of good and evil.

And I think that's an example of an inconsistency in the lore of the show. Or you can see it as a question that was set up where the writers wrote themselves into a bit of a corner. And what they did was take that and make that the premise for Season Seven.

Though Season Seven doesn't completely answer what happened. If bringing Buffy back created all this dissonance that gave The First power, why didn't that happen the first time she died and Xander brought her back to life? While I could head cannon some reasons why, I don't think the show ever explicitly gives us any.

Recurring Images

The rock that hides Acathla looks a little like the monoliths we see in Agents of Shield, another show Joss Whedon had input into. Which shows that, like all artists, Whedon has recurring themes and imagery that come back into his stories.

I've noticed this in many writers' work, including my own. And I always feel like I need to be a little cautious about repeating those themes. On the other hand, it clearly is part of what drives each of us to create. And audience members are often drawn to those same visions and images.

Snyder, Point Of View, and Shoplifting

A last few quick foreshadowings.

Snyder says to Buffy, "Give me a reason to kick you out," and at the end of the season he will do exactly that.

We will see a point of view again where we are in the head of someone who is running through grass and breathing hard. That's in Season Three, Beauty and the Beasts, where Angel comes back. We don't know at first who is running through the grass. Is it Oz as a werewolf? Is it another student who has been making himself into a sort of beast? Or is it Angel?

I like that we will see that imagery again. I don't know if it was purposeful. But it seems like it fits.

And, finally, in a flashback Buffy says to the Watcher, who she thinks might be from the department store, that she was going to pay for that lipstick, really. In Season Six we will find out that Dawn has been shoplifting all over the place. I don't think there's an implication that Buffy makes a habit of shoplifting. But it's fun that one of the ways that Dawn deals with all the stress of Season Six is by shoplifting.

Questions For Your Writing

- Do your flashbacks tell their own story and shed light on the current plot?
- Study the plot turns in the first half of your story. Does each intensify the previous conflict or event?
- Can you include small moments that build toward plot twists so that your audience won't feel blindsided?
- If a character will later do something unexpected, do you include a line of dialogue or an action early on to hint at the upcoming shift without giving it away?
- Can you raise the emotional stakes of your climax by making the protagonist's choices harder, the potential loss greater, or giving your protagonist

what they want most, then taking it away (or threatening to take it away)?

Next: Becoming Part Two

NEXT WE'LL TALK about Becoming Part Two, where Buffy strives to stop Angelus from ending the world. The chapter discusses pacing, plot turns, and a pyrrhic victory.

CHAPTER 10

BECOMING PART TWO (S2 E22)

THIS CHAPTER TALKS about Becoming Part Two, Season Two Episode Twenty-Two, where Buffy learns that Angelus plans to open a vortex to Hell, Spike offers to help stop him, and Buffy and Angel have their final confrontation. Written and directed by Joss Whedon.

In particular, we'll look at:

- Creating genuine conflict among allies;
- Character choices and actions that show the high stakes;
- Dramatic irony that increases tension and emotion;
- A Pyrrhic victory; and
- Season Two themes and foreshadowing.

Okay, let's dive into the Hellmouth.

OPENING **Conflict Of Becoming Part Two**
We start right where we left off in Part One. It's a fantastic

opening conflict for the episode. Kendra's dead body lies on the library floor. One cop says, "Freeze," as Buffy leans over Kendra.

Two police officers pull Buffy away. One determines that Kendra is dead. The other says, "What about up there?"

For the first time Buffy looks up and sees Xander lying in front of the bookshelves. She tries to get to him. But the police officer drags her out. She protests that she didn't do anything as Snyder strides in with more police.

Snyder: Why do I find that so hard to believe?

He tells the cops that if there's trouble, Buffy is behind it. When Buffy tries to tell the male cop that she just wants to see if her friends are okay, he says that's enough and tries to cuff her. She punches him and runs.

The female cop comes out of the library and fires her gun at Buffy as Buffy flees. The woman cop radios in that a fugitive, a homicide suspect, is on the run and very dangerous. We are only 1 minute 13 seconds in, and we go to credits.

We come back at the hospital. Buffy wears a black knit cap. Her hair is still long and hanging down. But she is dressed unlike herself in this somewhat oversized dark coat that is not stylish at all. All the same, the cops' radio description included that she had long blond hair. So when two cops come in later and don't notice her, it cements the idea that the cops in Sunnydale are a bit slow. (Something Principal Snyder will explicitly say later on.)

Xander Is Serious - Willow Is Injured

Buffy sees Xander. They hug. She asks about Willow as the two cops come in. Xander pulls her closer. He lets go after the cops are gone.

Buffy: Okay, that was about equal parts protecting me and copping a feel, right?

Xander gives her this serious look and doesn't say anything. Buffy says, "What is it?"

We've established over these two seasons that Xander

always has the joke, the sarcasm. Or an observation that's often somewhat inappropriate and at inappropriate times. So when he says nothing and just looks at Buffy we already know something terrible happened to Willow.

The scene shifts to Willow in a hospital bed unconscious. There's a bandage on her head. At 3 minutes 21 seconds in, Xander tells Buffy the doctor said it's head trauma. Willow can wake up any time, but the longer that she is under the worse it is. Buffy says she should never have let Willow try the curse. That Angel must have known.

Dramatic Irony About Angel

So we have dramatic irony here – where we as the audience know something the characters don't. We know the attack wasn't about stopping Willow from doing the curse. It was about taking Giles away.

So there are two things that our characters don't know: (1) Angel's purpose, which is to figure out how to do the ritual with Acathala, and (2) that he sees Giles as the key to that.

Dealing With The Parents

Xander says he called Willow's parents. They're in Arizona with relatives. We don't expect to see her parents because we pretty much don't see anyone's parents other than Joyce. But for the sake of reality, someone needs to explain where they are. Otherwise, it would stand out so much the audience would be distracted by wondering why Willow's parents aren't there.

Buffy also asks about Oz. And Xander says he forgot. He'll call him.

Cordelia comes in. And just the way she and Xander hug we know it's the first time they've seen each other. She tells them that she ran. And she probably got through three counties before she realized no one was chasing her.

Cordelia (looks at the floor): Not too brave.

But Buffy tells her she did the right thing.

Story Spark For Becoming Part Two

We are now at 4 minutes 37 seconds in. In a self-contained episode this is where we would see the Story Spark or Inciting Incident that gets the main plot rolling. It typically comes 10% through. Now we're in a two-episode arc, so we're long past getting the story started.

But there is a Story Spark for this episode. Because Xander asks if Giles kept up with Cordelia. And she says she didn't see him. Xander tells Buffy he's not in the hospital. And this is the moment when Buffy realizes that Giles is gone.

Angel Tortures Giles

The scene switches to Giles, who is face down on the floor. Angel also lies on the floor on his stomach, head propped on his arms. He studies Giles until he wakes up. Angel says he wants to torture Giles. It's been a long time since he tortured anyone. They didn't even have chainsaws back then. But he walks over to the stone statue of Acathla.

Angel: Oh, yeah, Acathla. He's an even harder guy to wake up than you.

And Angel tells Giles that he has said the words. He's tried the ritual. He had blood on his hands and nothing. And he thinks that because Giles knows so much he'll be able to tell Angel what he's doing wrong.

Angel: But, honestly, I sort of hope you don't. Because I really want to torture you.

This is the darkest that we've seen Angel, and David Boreanaz really sells it. There's no joking, no sarcasm, no mocking. It is another time when we have built this character to be a certain way and to now see him so serious, without that mocking and joking, underscores that he means it. He wants his answer about Acathla. Yet in that moment, I completely believe that he would rather torture Giles.

The Police Question Joyce

We switch to the Summers's house where detectives question Joyce. One is that balding, thin detective who questioned

Buffy in the episode Ted. (Where Joyce's boyfriend turned out to be a robot, and Buffy thought that she killed him.) We will see this detective again. I really love that he keeps returning and we have that continuity.

Joyce says she doesn't know where Buffy is. She thinks she stayed over at her friend Willow's.

Detective 1: Willow Rosenberg?

Detective 2: Second victim.

Detective 1: Your daughter has a history of violence.

He gives Joyce his card and says to call if Buffy "decides" to stop by. Clearly implying that Joyce is a bad mom.

Buffy Meets Whistler

Buffy goes to Giles' apartment and finds Whistler. He's the demon we saw in flashbacks in the last episode. He set Angel on the path and showed him Buffy. And Angel made the choice to try to become someone in the world and do something positive.

Buffy asks what Whistler is doing there. He jokes that he's looking for a date for the prom. Buffy has no patience with this. She shoves him up against the wall. She says if he has information, she'll be grateful for it.

Buffy: If you're gonna crack jokes, I'm gonna pull out your rib cage and wear it as a hat.

This, too, shows Buffy acting differently than usual. Normally she is quipping. Even when she was fighting Angel in the last episode she was quipping and kind of jeering at him. Here she is so serious.

Whistler marvels at her use of imagery. But then he tells her it was not supposed to go down this way. He figured this would be Angel's big day. But he thought Angel would be here to stop Acathla, not bring him forth.

Whistler: Then you two made with the smoochies and now he's a creep again.

A great line of understatement and exposition combined.

Being somewhat cryptic, Whistler questions Buffy:

Whistler: What are you gonna do? What you prepared to do? What are you prepared to give up?

Buffy says he obviously doesn't have anything useful to tell her and goes on:

Buffy: What are you – just some immortal demon sent down to even the score between good and evil?

Whistler: Wow. Good guess.

Buffy: Well, why don't you try getting off your immortal ass and fighting evil? Because I'm sick and tired of doing it myself.

Whistler: In the end, you're always by yourself. You're all you've got. That's the point.

Conflict Through Personalities And Circumstances

This scene is a good example of how to use contrasting personalities and circumstances to create real conflict between allies. The last episode established that Whistler likes to draw on what he probably sees as a kind of wry humor or wise guy persona. He also doesn't want to say things outright. He led Angel to where he wanted him to go, or hoped Angel would go, by showing him Buffy. And by parceling out a little bit at a time so Angel could reach his own conclusions.

He's adopting the same strategy here. While he feels some urgency, he doesn't have the same investment as Buffy. He's an immortal demon. It isn't as vital to him as to her. So you have conflict. She wants answers. Now. He wants to trail out the breadcrumbs. I like that contrast. And it raises the tension in a scene where all that's really happening is Buffy is getting information. Or trying to.

She becomes disgusted and leaves. As she heads out the door, Whistler calls after her that the sword isn't enough, she has to know how to use it.

And now I will walk back a little of what I said about this being a nice example. Because while in some ways it is, it also feels a bit artificial to me that Whistler parcels out this information. Especially because Buffy will come back later and he will just be there waiting for her. So it feels like the writers just didn't want Buffy to get all the information at once. But it helps that we've established that this is how Whistler does things.

Also, I did not realize until I watched for the podcast that Whistler actually has given her something really valuable that we don't recognize. Because it sounds like he's just being cryptic. That's how it is, you're all you've got. Blah blah blah. But it turns out that advice is key.

Spike Wants To Save The World?

Buffy is now walking in the park, and a cop car pulls up behind her. So this cop, despite Buffy's ingenious disguise of a knit cap on her head, recognized Buffy. He gets out and pulls a gun on her, but someone from offscreen kicks and punches the cop and knocks him out. The cop is lying on the hood and Spike enters the frame.

Spike: Hello, cutie.

Buffy's eyes widen and we cut to a commercial. This is a great hook because of course we want to know why Spike's there and why he intervened.

Also, this is another small amount of dramatic irony. As the audience, we know that Spike got out of the wheelchair and has been hiding that from Drusilla and Angel. But Buffy doesn't know that.

She punches Spike. He tries to hold her off without really fighting her, saying that he's waving a white flag. But Buffy pulls a stake and says they're mortal enemies. They don't get Time Outs.

Spike: You want a go-around, pet, I'll have a gay old time of it. You want to stop Angel, we'll have to play things a bit differently.

Buffy asks what he's talking about.

Spike: I'm talking about your ex, pet. I'm talking about putting him in the bloody ground.

Buffy is skeptical. She's still holding the stake. But as they talk, she gradually lowers it while saying she can't believe they think she'll fall for this trick.

Spike: He's got your Watcher.

Spike adds that Angel is probably torturing Giles. And that's what convinces her. We know from previous episodes that Giles is the one person Buffy cannot get through this without. And, of course, she knows Giles has disappeared, which adds to the idea that Spike might be telling the truth.

Spike (with a slight smile): I want to stop Angel. I want to save the world.

Then he tells her vampires like to talk big, ending the world, it's "just tough guy talk." As he's explaining he grabs a cigarette from the cop who's still passed out, lights it, and continues on. About how he loves the world. It's got dog racing, and Manchester United, and billions of people walking around like Happy Meals with legs. And then someone comes along with a vision, a real passion for destruction. And he says Angel could really pull it off.

I feel like Spike's use of the word Passion is not accidental, given that Passion was the name of the episode where Angel killed Jenny Calendar. Buffy is still skeptical. She ask why would he ever come to her? Spike looks at the ground and says he wants Drusilla back. The way she acts with Angel, he can't stand it.

Buffy says he's pathetic.

Spike: I can't fight them alone and neither can you.

After punching him again, Buffy says she hates him.

Spike: I'm all you've got.

I love this scene between the two of them. They are both being honest with each other. And it takes Spike a while to convince Buffy. As it should. If she just went along with him, despite that we know he is telling the truth, she would seem far too gullible to be our hero.

Then we get a great ending. Buffy finally tells Spike to talk. But the cop starts groaning and Spike starts turns toward him.

Spike: Just let me kill this guy. (Buffy clears her throat.) Oh, right.

They walk off and leave the cop on the hood.

Becoming Part Two – Episode One-Quarter Twist

We're now about one quarter through the episode at 10 minutes 47 seconds in. That moment of Spike and Buffy agreeing to work together is a great One-Quarter Twist for this episode. Usually at that point in a story we see a major turn that comes from outside the protagonist and spins the story in a new direction. It also often raises the stakes. All of that is exactly what we have here.

We're well past the Midpoint in the story as a whole. So for the two-part story arc we don't really have to have a specific one-quarter major plot turn here. And yet we do, and that is what helps keep this episode moving along.

Also, notice that overall so much is happening in the present-day story, which contrasts Becoming Part One. That part still had a strong plot structure and moved along, but half of it involved telling the story of the past. Now all the scenes take place in the present day. The episode is moving forward and paying off all that we learned in the flashbacks.

Xander At Willow's Side

In the hospital, Xander holds Willow's hand. She's still unconscious. And he talks to her, telling her to wake up. He needs her. How else will he pass Trig, and who will he call each night to talk about all the things they did all day?

Xander: You're my best friend. You always – I love you.

There is some controversy in the fandom about these lines. Is Xander saying, "I love you," in a romantic way? I have always read him as saying from his heart how much he loves her, his best friend, and she has always been there. But part of the strength of the episode is that character choices can be read more than one way, and each way works for the story.

Willow starts to wake up.

Willow: Oz?

Oz (walks in as Willow speaks) I'm here.

Xander quickly moves out of the way and says he'll go get the doctor. The way he does that is part of why I see Xander's declaration of his deep love as being for his best friend without romantic overtones. Nothing in his actions suggests he was disappointed when Willow said, "Oz."

Joyce Meets Spike

Spike and Buffy are walking together to Buffy's house. When they reach the front walk, Joyce pulls up in her SUV and leaps out, she's been looking for Buffy. She's really worried.

Joyce: Who is this man? What's going on?

Spike: What, your mum doesn't know?

Buffy shoots him a look and tries to cover. She tells her mom she's in a rock band with Spike. Spike says that Buffy plays the triangle, but Buffy, at the same time, says she plays the drums. They are both awkward.

Joyce is skeptical. She looks at Spike.

Joyce: And what do you do?

Spike; Well, I sing.

Which is funny because James Marsters really is a good singer.

Buffy keeps trying to get Joyce to go inside, but Joyce wants answers. Then a vampire attacks. Buffy and Spike without a word fight him together. And Buffy dusts him. It's the first time they act as a team. And it happens so seamlessly. Spike says it was one of Angel's boys.

Spike: He won't get a chance to tattle on us now.

Joyce is really confused and shocked. And finally Buffy tells her the truth.

Buffy: Mom, I'm a Vampire Slayer.

This line also underscores Buffy and Spike becoming a team. Buffy told her mom this monumental thing that until now she's been hiding and covering up. And she did it in front of Spike. In a way, with Spike's support.

And we cut to a commercial. So another great hook. Because how is Joyce going to take this? But the writers delay the answer to that.

Body Language Signals Emotion

Buffy, in the kitchen, is on the phone with Willow. Willow says she's okay. The doctors don't think her brain got mushed. She's sorry she didn't get to turn Angel back. But Buffy says that's okay. It makes it easier because now she knows she'll never get Angel back.

In the living room, more great use of body language to convey feeling. Joyce sits on the couch in front of the coffee table clutching a drink with both hands. Her feet turn awkwardly inward on the floor, with her toes pointing at each other. Spike sits in a chair. His hands are folded in his lap, and he's angled slightly away from Joyce. It conveys his awkwardness so well because normally we see Spike in motion. Even in the wheelchair, his body language and his face are always expressive. He gestures with his arms.

But here he just sits still, looking awkwardly away from Joyce.

Now Buffy talks to Xander on the phone. (This is before everyone had cell phones. They existed, but mostly people talked on landlines, which is why Buffy is in the kitchen talking, leaving Joyce in the other room.)

Buffy tells Xander Angel is holed up with the others at a mansion on the edge of town. It's the one she and Xander noticed once before, so this is a really quick way to establish why Xander later in the episode will know where to find Buffy. She tells Xander she's hitting the mansion at daybreak. But she doesn't need backup. She's got it covered.

In the living room, Joyce and Spike talk.

Joyce: Have we met?

Spike: You hit me with an axe one time.

He mimes holding up an axe from that scene in School Hard where Spike was introduced, and Joyce intervened to help Buffy.

Spike: Remember? "Get the hell away from my daughter."

Joyce (nods, takes a breath): Do you live here in town?

And I love Joyce trying to make conversation with Spike even though she is in shock over all of this. Fortunately for both of them, Buffy comes back. She reassures Joyce that Willow is fine and then speaks directly to Spike. He walks over to her.

Cutting A Deal

Spike and Buffy stand face-to-face. He wants her to let him and Drusilla leave town. In exchange, he'll help her kill Angel.

Joyce: Angel your boyfriend?

Buffy (ignoring Joyce): No deal. Dru killed Kendra.

Spike: Dru bagged a Slayer? She didn't tell me. Ickle for her. Though not from your perspective I suppose.

As the scene continues, Buffy and Spike continue making their deal and Joyce keeps interrupting. Sometimes Buffy gives her a quick answer; other times she ignores her. One of the things Joyce asks is whether Kendra exploded. Buffy says no, that Kendra's a Slayer.

Joyce: Honey, are you sure you're a Vampire Slayer?

And a few lines later she says:

Joyce: Have you tried not being a Slayer?

In between, Spike makes the case for letting him and Drusilla go. He says they'll leave the country and Buffy will never hear from them again he bloody well hopes. Buffy finally agrees, but:

Buffy: If Giles dies, she dies.

This is probably the hardest thing for Joyce to see and hear – concluding the deal by saying she will kill Drusilla. Maybe

Joyce grasps that Drusilla is a vampire. She probably does. But there's so much she has to take in here.

Joyce And Buffy Argue

Spike leaves. Joyce and Buffy argue. Joyce is saying things like, "It's because you didn't have a strong father figure isn't it?" And Buffy tells her it's fate, accept it. But Joyce is in denial. She wants to call the police. Buffy says it'll only get the police killed. It's a great example of, again, two people who should be allies, who really care about each other, but who are in genuine conflict.

We saw Buffy in Season One struggle with rejecting her destiny as the Slayer. And she continues to fight it, always saying she wants a normal life. But she has had this time to figure it out. Joyce, though, has been in denial the whole time. Now that she's forced to the face the truth her initial reaction, and it is awful, is to question Buffy's life.

Which is where the metaphor is so strong as well to the Coming Out story. Buffy has told her mother this thing about herself that she kept hidden. And her mom reacts in the way that Buffy probably always feared. Yes, she didn't tell her mother because it was a secret identity and she needed to keep everyone safe. But on some level, Buffy probably feared Joyce would reject her. And initially that's what Joyce does. She refuses to believe Buffy, despite what she saw.

Buffy tells her to wake up. Joyce has washed blood out of her clothes how many times? But Joyce wants to maintain her denial. And then ultimately she will almost throw Buffy out of the house.

Episode Midpoint Commitment

When Buffy tells her how hard it is to be the Slayer, Joyce doesn't listen.

Joyce: Well, it stops now.

Buffy: No, it doesn't stop. It never stops. Do you think I

chose this? Do you have any idea how hard it is? How lonely? But I have to save the world. Again.

Joyce: This is insane. Buffy, you need help.

Buffy: I'm not crazy.

Joyce tries to keep her from leaving. Buffy pushes her aside.

Joyce: You walk out of this house don't even think about coming back.

Buffy leaves, but she doesn't shut the door behind her. Very symbolic, and it also conveys her emotions. Joyce's face kind of crumbles. She sags onto the counter and puts her head in her hands. And we know that she already regrets how she handled this.

I see that scene where Buffy tells her mom the truth as the episode Midpoint Commitment. Buffy has thrown caution to the wind by telling her mother the truth about herself. And a major commitment is one of the things that we see at a strong Midpoint.

The Three-Quarter Turn In Becoming

As far as the two-episode arc, we are at or nearing the Three-Quarter Turn. As it should, the Three-Quarter Turn here arises from the Midpoint – that reversal Buffy suffered where Kendra was killed and Willow's spell was interrupted.

Now we're in the hospital. Willow will make her own sort of "throw caution to the wind" commitment, which also will spin the story. Cordelia comments on Buffy's showdown tomorrow morning. And she says she wishes they could help – "you know, without dying." Willow wants to try the curse again. She never got to finish the spell. Xander doesn't like the idea. It's powerful magic, and Willow is weak. (A very quick reminder and call back to Giles talking about the dangers of doing this spell.)

Willow insists she's okay. We get some humor because Xander says she doesn't look it. And she does still look weak. She still has his bandage on her head. And he says to Cordelia to tell her.

Cordelia: You should listen to him. The hair, it's so flat. And the lips....

Willow insists she can do it.

Willow: Do you see my Resolve Face? You've seen it before. You know what it means.

And she points out if the curse works it'll stop Angel from awakening Acathla. Oz has been sitting in a chair off screen. And he says something like, "Wow, I sure missed a lot. Because this is all making a kind of sense that's not."

This is such a quick scene, but it includes so much conflict and a major plot turn. Plus it fills in some information for viewers who missed Becoming Part One. That is a lot. So again, the pace in this episode is very quick in contrast to Becoming Part One.

Willow tells Oz to go with Cordelia to the library to get supplies. Then she tells Xander to go to Buffy and tell her that Willow is trying the spell. Maybe Buffy can stall Angel.

Spike Under Cover

Back to Giles and Angel. Giles looks exhausted, as if he's been through so much. Angel tells him he's been brave but it's enough, Angel can make the pain stop. Anthony Stuart Head does a great job of acting like he is ready to give up. He haltingly tells Angel that to be worthy and wake Acathla he must perform the ritual – in a tutu.

Angel: All right, someone get the chainsaw.

Spike: Now, now don't let's lose our temper.

Angel: Stay out of it, Sit and Spin.

But Spike says Angel will never get answers if he kills Giles. Angel is suspicious of this and asks when Spike got so levelheaded.

Spike: Right about the time you became so pigheaded.

Angel buys it. And I love that Spike is so much better at undercover then Buffy. Which we knew because he's been hiding from Drusilla and Angel that he can walk. Now Spike tells Angel there is another way. He calls to Drusilla and asks if she wants to play a game. So we also see that Spike is clever. And throughout he will devise ways to put things off, and keep Giles alive, without it looking like that's his motive.

Buffy Crosses Principal Snyder

Buffy goes to the library to get that sword that we saw last episode (that Kendra brought). She's just unzipped its case when Principal Snyder walks in. He tells her this is a crime scene, but then she's a criminal. Buffy argues that the police will figure it out, realize she didn't do it.

Snyder: In case you haven't noticed, the police in Sunnydale are deeply stupid.

Also, Snyder says it doesn't matter, Buffy has proved to be too much of a liability for the school. He pauses and says that this is the type of moment you have to savor.

Snyder: You're expelled.

Buffy doesn't answer. She just pulls out the sword. Snyder looks nervous. She studies the blade.

Buffy: You never ever got a single date in high school did you?

Snyder: Your point being?

This exchange doubles down on some of the High School is Hell metaphor. This idea that some teachers and others in authority take out their frustrations from their high school experience on their students.

Buffy points the sword toward Snyder but doesn't touch him with it. She walks around him and out.

Stripping Everything Away

In the interview on the DVD, Joss Whedon says his point in Becoming Part One and Two was to strip away everything from Buffy. She has now lost her family. Joyce tells her don't come back because of who Buffy is, because of her duties as the Slayer. Now she has also lost school. So gradually she's losing all the things that to this point have helped her survive. Until now, not letting herself be defined down solely to her role as the Slayer has kept her alive. But these things are being taken away.

Story Questions

Snyder dials his cell phone.

Snyder: It's Snyder. Tell the mayor I have good news.

We'll never find out in this episode why he called the mayor. This is a great example of the type of story question that you can weave in and leave open for a while and that the audience wants answered. Usually, you want to answer the questions by the end of your novel, and readers will often keep reading to find those answers. If you write an installment series, you probably want one or two small questions you don't answer for some time, perhaps not until the last installment. That keeps the reader going into the next installment, the next book, or the next episode or film.

So here, this is a little question that makes us wonder: What is the role of the mayor? How is Snyder connected to him?

You do have to be a little careful. Too many open questions at the end of the current installment and readers will get angry. Because they have read this whole book, and they have not gotten answers. But here, the mayor's role in Sunnydale doesn't affect this story. So it is okay leaving it hanging there. And it makes us curious. Also, I like that we don't know what the good news is. Is the good news that he expelled Buffy? That Buffy has the sword and maybe can stop Acathla? We don't know.

Drusilla Tricks Giles

Back to Giles. Drusilla stands behind him.

Drusilla: Let's see what's inside. Of course.

And she moves in front of him. Her face right in front of his face. Her words are very similar to what she said to Kendra in Becoming Part One.

Drusilla: Look at me. Be in me. See with your heart.

She covers his eyes with her hand, takes her hand away, and

now she is Jenny Calendar. Giles is near tears for the first time that we have seen while he's being tortured.

Giles: I thought I lost you.

Jenny says she'll never leave him. And plays this out as if she's worried. Asks did he tell Angel about the ritual and how can she help. And gradually she gets it out of him.

Drusilla (as Jenny): Tell me what to do.

She says he knows she'll help, they'll be together, and have "all the things we never had." Eventually, Giles says to keep Angel away from Acathla. And finally that Angel's blood is the key. Drusilla, still as Jenny, kisses Giles. Angel and Spike are watching. And Angel says of course it has to be his blood. His life.

And then he says to Drusilla, "Kill him." But Spike says what if he's lying? So again, Spike saves Giles's life. And Angel says, "Right, don't kill him." And then that he kind of likes having Spike watch his back. It's like old times. They both turn and really see that Dru is still kissing Giles.

Spike: Drusilla.

Angel: Honey.

Drusilla: Sorry, I was in the moment.

And we see Giles' face as it hits him that it was not really Jenny.

Whistler Again

At 28 minutes 53 seconds in Buffy's gone back to Giles' apartment to talk to Whistler. She asks what did he mean – the sword is not enough? After making another joke he tells her. Angel is the key. The blood opens the vortex, and Acathla will open his mouth to swallow the world. We knew that, but now we learn that only Angel's blood will close it. With one blow, Buffy has to send them both to hell and close Acathla.

But he warns her she should get there before Acathla opens his mouth, because the sooner she kills Angel, the easier it'll be for her. She says don't worry about her. She has nothing left to lose.

Whistler (as Buffy leaves): Wrong, kid. You got one more thing.

This last line, it's a hook or a question that is meant to keep the audience coming back. You want to have that with a scene or chapter ending. Usually, I think *Buffy* is fantastic at this. This one, though, feels a little artificial to me.

I guess you could say its purpose is also its foreshadowing. It's preparing us. But to me it feels purposely put there, and it distracts me from the story, though it's a tiny thing to say.

Upping The Stakes In Becoming Part Two

We are almost at 30 minutes, and that means we have about 12 or 13 minutes left. Yet it feels like the whole thing from here on is the climax. The end of the episode uses a technique similar to what we saw in Becoming Part One. There, Buffy suffered a major reversal with Kendra's death, and we thought that was it. That was the Midpoint. Instead, Part One upped the stakes to a greater reversal and then another.

In the same way, we'll see more than one moment, each worse than the last, that could serve as the culmination or the climax. But instead, the tension escalates.

The sun rises over the trees. Buffy walks toward the mansion with the sword. Xander jumps out and says the cavalry's here.

Xander: The cavalry's a frightened guy with a rock, but it's here.

Buffy gives him a stake and tells him to get Giles out. She'll be too busy fighting and killing to protect Xander. He admires the sword. She says it's a present for Angel.

Xander: Willow. She told me to tell you –

They both stop and look at each other. And you can almost see Xander making this decision.

Xander: Kick his ass.

Buffy just walks on.

Xander's Motives

This is another area of questioning and controversy, among the legions of fans, podcasters, and commenters. What are Xander's motives? A lot of people read his choice as coming out of pettiness and jealousy about Angel. He doesn't want Buffy to have her boyfriend back, or he resents that she still loves Angel.

I always read it as Xander fearing that telling Buffy that Willow is trying the curse again might undermine her. Make her fight less hard against Angel and stall for time instead, which could get her killed. Buffy even told Willow it makes it easier knowing she won't get Angel back. So I read Xander as trying to choose what will help Buffy the most.

Even that can be problematic because he is making a decision for her about the information. He thinks she is better off if he withholds it. Also, doing so goes against Willow's instructions to tell Buffy. Which is very significant because throughout the show Willow is the one consistently on Buffy's side. Even when she is worried for Buffy or disagrees with Buffy, she supports her friend. Xander is ignoring that. He is contradicting it. And worse, he makes it sound like Willow callously said, "Kick his ass," knowing how hard it is for Buffy.

I love the moment because there is so much going on there. So much for the audience to consider and think about.

The Rituals Start

Angel, inside, chants in Latin before Acathla.

In the hospital, lit candles sit on a tray. Cordelia has the incense. Willow tells Oz he doesn't have to understand the Latin. She hopes. Just say the words.

We cut back to Angel. He's cut his hand so he has his own blood on it. Buffy, from nowhere, kills a vampire.

Buffy: Hello, Lover.

Her words echo what he said to her before they started to fight in Becoming Part One. Angel is annoyed.

Angel: I don't have time for you....Do you really think you can take us all?

Buffy: No, I don't.

Behind Angel – this is such a quick moment—Spike stands, and he clocks Angel. I don't know if he has a pipe or a cane. But he knocks him to the ground. Spike wails on Angel as Buffy fights the other vampires. Drusilla runs at Spike. Xander comes in and punches one vampire.

At the hospital, Oz reads Latin aloud. Willow speaks the spell in English.

Willow: Not dead, not of the living.

Back to Xander, who gets Giles untied. Giles doesn't cooperate because he doesn't think Xander's real.

Giles: They get in my head. Show me things I want to see.

Xander (looking at Giles): Then why would they make you see me?

Giles: You're right. Let's go.

Spike and Drusilla are still fighting. Buffy is fighting with all the other vampires. And Angel gets up off the floor.

Angel Draws The Sword

We're at 33 minutes 30 seconds in. Angel grabs the sword and draws it out of Acathla. Lights flashes everywhere. In the hospital, Willow falters. Her words slow down. Buffy and Angel sword fight. Angel tells Buffy Acathla is about to wake up and she's going to hell.

Buffy: Save me a seat.

In the hospital again, Willow breathes hard. Suddenly, her head jerks up. She's staring at the ceiling, and then her head jerks back down. She's looking down, but she's not reading. She switches to Latin. And she's speaking very fast.

Oz: Is this a good thing?

Cordelia: Hey, speak English.

At the mansion, Angel, winning the fight, drives Buffy out into the courtyard, which is mostly in shadows. Inside, Spike finally overpowers Drusilla. He gets her in a choke hold, cutting off her air, and she goes unconscious.

Which is inconsistent with the show's vampire lore. Remember how Angel couldn't give Buffy CPR in Prophecy Girl because vampires have no breath? This bothers me. Why can Spike choke Dru into unconsciousness? All the same, the first time I watched – probably the first couple times – I didn't care about the inconsistency because the story is so good. The emotion is so strong.

And the important thing is Spike overpowers Drusilla. (I suspect the writers wanted to do it in a way that was not overly violent. Spike wants to get her out. He does not want to hurt her.)

The Climax Begins
Angel fights Buffy into a corner. As Spike leaves, he sees them and looks worried.

Spike: God, he's going to kill her.

Then he tilts his head, arches one eyebrow, gives a little shrug, and walks out carrying Drusilla.

Buffy is crouching in a corner against a wall. There is a slant of sunlight over her face. Angel stands over her, pointing the sword at her face.

Angel: That's everything. No weapons, no friends, no hope. (Buffy shuts her eyes.) Take all that away and what's left?

He thrusts his sword for the kill. But Buffy raises both hands, though her eyes are still shut, and claps them together around the sword. Stops it dead.

Buffy: Me.

She shoves the sword back at him.

This moment calls back to when Whistler said, "You're always alone. You're all you've got." So he did say something that mattered. Though I like to think Buffy would have gotten here anyway. She would have said this anyway.

It is powerful, and the whole momentum of the fight changes.

Another Metaphor

This instant also is a nice inversion of what Spike said in School Hard. He got so disgusted because he was trying to kill Buffy and Joyce appeared and helped Buffy. And Spike said something like, "A Slayer with family and friends – who ever heard of that?" It's clear her connections give Buffy her strength, help her win fights and survive.

But here we see the opposite. And I feel like this is another metaphor, not for high school, but for life. The need for balance. Between having a centered, developed self and this strong feeling of who you are inside, and needing family and friends and outside aspects of your life you love and enjoy. Then you're balanced. And throughout the season Buffy has drawn on both. In the Season Two pilot she tries to push everyone away and go it alone. And that doesn't work. That is very dangerous.

But now, here, she finds if she has to, she has the strength she needs inside herself. So I think the message of this season is that Buffy as the Slayer needs both. As we all do.

Weaker Possible Climaxes

So now we are at the Climax.

In a weaker story, we could've had a climax where Spike knocks out Angel, there's this fight, then Buffy fights Angel and prevails. Without that moment with Buffy saying, "Me," and pushing back.

That could work in the sense that Buffy as the protagonist would still prevail. And it would be because she made that alliance with Spike, which was her choice to enter into. But there wouldn't be the deep emotion we get, the moment where all is lost and she looks like she's going to die, but then she gets through it by calling on her inner strength.

Or the writers could have written a much, much weaker

climax. Where Angel and Buffy fight, but Willow's spell works, Angel's back to himself, and all is good. That would be weaker because then Willow, not Buffy, really prevails. And in a strong story, the protagonist needs to save they day. Or lose, but out of their own efforts, not someone else's. Ideally, the protagonist, win or lose, should pull out all the stops. Having someone else come in from outside and save the day is a problem I see in plot outlines I review. Or the conflict resolves through luck – Angel slips and falls on a stake. As writers, we don't always know quite how to have the protagonist use all their strength and skill and cunning and yet still have it be a dramatic fight. Sometimes we don't want to torture our protagonist. We like that protagonist so much we don't want to make it hard for them. But you really need that in a climax.

The Climax Sets Up A Last Twist

We get an amazing Climax here. It would've been a big enough moment for Buffy to say, "Me," turn the tide and win the fight. But instead it becomes so much harder for her, so much more painful, and takes so much more emotional strength for her to prevail.

The first time I watched, with all that happened, I'm pretty sure I forgot that Angel had pulled the sword out and that Acathla was still going to open. The plot construction here is genius. We've seen Drusilla and Spike fighting, Willow casting the spell with strong hints of danger to her, the sword fight (amazing in itself), and that moment with Buffy and Angel in the courtyard. If Angel ran to Acathla now and pulled out the sword, viewers might grasp right away that hell was about to open. As it's written, though, we're focused on Buffy's triumph as she fights Angel back into the manor.

Next we see Spike driving Drusilla out of town in a car with all the windows blacked out. Very much a reflection both of Angel, when he first saw Buffy and was looking out of that blacked out car, and of the moment Spike first drove into town in School Hard.

I'm betting most audience members didn't realize that the vortex was already in play as we switch to Willow in the hospital. The tray table with the candles on it rocks. Willow grips it and keeps chanting. The orb glows, and Willow blinks. Her body slumps, and we see she is back to herself.

Buffy drives Angel into the manor. He falls on his knees, much like we saw in that flashback in Becoming Part One when he first was cursed with his soul. Also like the moment Darla made him into a vampire. He was on his knees in front of her.

His eyes glow – just as they did in the flashback. There, he was confused and asked what's happening. So we needed that story from Becoming Part One to know that, yes, when Angel gets his soul back he won't remember everything right away. He won't remember what happened. There is lag time. Because Part One established that, we don't expect him to just snap back to himself.

Buffy keeps her sword raised, uncertain.

Angel: Buffy. What's happening?

She very gradually lowers her sword, much like she gradually lowered that stake in the conversation with Spike. Finally, she is convinced. Angel stands. They hold each other.

Buffy (whispering): Angel.

He says he feels like he hasn't seen her in months. They're standing in front of Acathla. Angel's back is to the stone demon and the camera. We see Buffy's face as they hold each other. She's so grateful he's back, yet you can see all the pain that she's been through. The Buffy/Angel theme music. Then Buffy opens her eyes.

Close Your Eyes

Buffy is facing Acathla. Her eyes widen, and we see that the demon's mouth is starting to open.

Angel asks what's happening. She tells him to hush, don't

worry about it, as the vortex opens behind them. It swirls, gradually getting larger.

Buffy: I love you.

Angel: I love you.

Buffy: Close your eyes.

Just what Darla said to him.

Buffy kisses Angel one last time. The vortex has become giant. It swirls behind them as they kiss. Buffy steps back. Angel still has his eyes closed. And with one blow of the sword she strikes right below Angel's heart. The vortex pulls him in. Slowly, so we see him being dragged backwards into this vortex, one hand outstretched toward Buffy, the sword is sticking out of his chest.

Angel: Buffy.

Angel is gone, Acathla's vortex closes. And Buffy's face just breaks.

The Pyrrhic Victory

Buffy won, but this is a pyrrhic victory. That's where the protagonist achieves a victory or goal at too great a cost. And that Climax is the perfect example of it.

So at the climax of any story the protagonist wins, loses, or wins but at a great, almost unbearable cost.

Falling Action In Becoming Part Two

We are now in the Falling Action at 48 minutes 11 seconds in. Acathla is turned back to stone. Dormant. Buffy stares at it. And we hear a sad Sarah McLachlan song (Full of Grace) about winter and not seeing the sun for weeks. It is also about love.

Buffy walks to her house. She looks at it from outside. We switch to inside. That song keeps playing throughout. Joyce goes up the stairs, looking exhausted.

Joyce: Buffy?

But when she goes into Buffy's room we see empty hangers in the closet, a few clothes on the bed, and a note. Joyce sinks down on the bed and reads it. The note tells us something about their relationship. Buffy didn't just disappear. She did leave a note.

We switch to school. It's bright and sunny. Oz wheels Willow in a wheelchair. Cordelia stands with them. Xander and Giles meet them. No one has seen Buffy.

Oz: But we know the world didn't end because – check it out. (He gestures to the sun to everything around them.)

Giles tells them he went to the manor. Acathla is dormant. And they speculate on what happened. Maybe Buffy had to kill Angel, and she needs to be alone. Willow hopes the spell worked and Buffy and Angel are off being alone together. They all agree that there is still school so Buffy will have to come around soon. They don't know that Snyder expelled her. Willow is the most hopeful that Buffy will be back in a while. They all walk into the school.

Clothes And Actions Show Buffy's Feelings

Buffy watches them from across the street, then turns and walks away. She wears a baggy sweatshirt and baggy overalls, much like we saw her in Ted after she thought she killed him (and that he was a human being). She carries a large shoulder bag.

Buffy's clothing tells us how Buffy is feeling. So does the fact that she stays apart from her friends, watches them, and doesn't go to talk to them. Doesn't let them know that she's okay. At least she left a note for Joyce. But no hint for her friends, which I didn't think about before breaking down the episode for the podcast. Maybe this is because of the message she thinks Willow sent her –"kick his ass." That seems so cold to her, or she feels that they will not understand. So she just walks away from them as well.

Also, and this is what I thought when I first watched it, Buffy is simply overwhelmed. She cannot handle all this anymore, so she's going to leave.

The scene switches to a bus window. We see Buffy's face, and then a long shot of the bus driving down the road, passing a sign that says You Are Now Leaving Sunnydale.

And that is the end of the episode.

The Monster Needs A Hug

On a more fun note, I saw something when I watched for the podcast that I'm almost certain I never noticed before. You have to watch all the way to the end of the credits where the little monster goes across the screen. It usually says, "Grr. Argh." This time he goes across the screen and he says, "Oh I need a hug."

In the DVD interview, Joss Whedon commented that the biggest challenge of the show overall was keeping the tone of mixing horror, comedy, and soap opera. He also said that he always aims for the audience never knowing what to expect. And that is definitely the case in this episode. I am sure the first time around it never occurred to me that Buffy would get Angel back, but only when it was too late and she would have to kill him.

Angel, Dru, And Spike

Whedon said that they deliberately left the relationship between Spike, Drusilla and Angel unclear. Is Angel really still that attracted to Drusilla? Or does he just act like it to drive Spike crazy? I think the ambiguity works because either way it motivates Spike's alliance with Buffy and we believe it.

Spoilers and Foreshadowing

A Start For Spike

The moment when Spike is about to kill the cop, he's so casual. "Let me just kill this guy." But Buffy just clears her throat, and he stops. That moment is the first time we see Spike alter his behavior, or his essential nature because he's allying himself with Buffy. He is willing to do things her way. Or, more realistically, he knows he has to or she won't work with him. This is such a great start for what we will see in Season Four, when Spike gets that behavior modification chip and cannot behave like he normally would. I feel like that journey begins here with this small choice to alter his behavior.

In contrast, you cannot picture Angelus ever doing that. But Spike genuinely can recognize oh, right, this is Buffy's perspective. Even about Kendra, Spike has enough empathy to realize that Buffy sees it differently: "Oh, Dru bagged a Slayer. Ickle for her. Though not from your perspective I suppose." He doesn't need to add that last comment, as Buffy probably was going to work with him regardless. But he does.

Which foreshadows Spike's entire arc. While the chip takes him quite far in that arc, there is also the part of him that makes choices. And, unlike Angel, whose soul is thrust upon him, Spike will later choose to get a soul back.

Obviously, these scenes also start setting up Spike and Buffy. That at some point they will have a deep relationship. Though it's clear Spike has not totally altered his behavior. His moment of empathy for Buffy doesn't change him being willing to walk out and let her get killed. He's done his part of the deal. He helped Buffy put one over on Angel and get the upper hand, at least for a while. And he got Drusilla out. He does not feel obligated to stay and see it all the way through. Spike doesn't care that Buffy, he believes, is going to get killed.

Or does he?

Now I'm going to flip sides because in Season Three, Lovers Walk, Spike returns. And we find out that Drusilla ultimately broke it off with him. And yes, it was because he turned against her and Angel. But she says later that she saw the Slayer all around him. So Drusilla early on sees something greater in Spike's choice to align himself with Buffy.

Foreshadowing The Psychiatric Ward

Another hint or foreshadowing occurs when Joyce says to Buffy that this is insane and she needs help. Buffy responds: I'm not crazy.

In Season Six, Normal Again, under the influence of a drug her enemies inject her with, Buffy thinks that she is in a mental institution. That all of her life as the Slayer is a delusion. Then, in a lucid moment, she tells Willow that when she first told her parents about vampires and being a Slayer, they put her in a psych ward.

That felt retconned to me. But at that point Dawn was added into the world. So I thought, well, maybe that's something that came in when the monks changed everyone's memories. Maybe that was part of the altered landscape. But rewatching this episode, I wonder if the writers had an idea that a psychiatric ward could be part of Buffy's back story. (That idea is also supported by the episode Ted, where Ted threatens to expose Buffy's diary writing about vampire slaying and believes it'll put her in a mental institution.)

On the other hand, it's not that strange that Joyce might say that. Sure, she knew Buffy got in fights and in trouble (and she washed blood out of Buffy's clothes). But most of us wouldn't think based on that evidence, oh, well, my daughter must be fighting vampires.

Damaging The Buffy/Willow Friendship

Xander's "Kick his ass" lie reverberates through the series, though it's only mentioned once. Buffy never finds out that was not Willow's message. The closest we will get is in the Season Seven episode Selfless where Anya has returned to her vengeance demon ways. She slaughters fraternity boys. When Buffy sets out to kill Anya, Xander argues with Buffy, accusing her of protecting Spike but not Anya because she has feelings for Spike.

And Buffy says, "I killed Angel. Did you forget that?" She

adds something like, "Oh, and your message." She looks at Willow. "Kick his ass?"

Willow looks so taken aback. She can't process the comment quickly enough to say she never said that. And so much else happens so fast that it's never revisited. And it really makes me wonder how much damage did Xander's lie do to Buffy's and Willow's relationship. Perhaps that's part of why Buffy withdraws from her friends after Season Two.

It's always felt a little weird to me how often Buffy pulls away. It feels like something the writers force on her to give her inner conflict and vulnerability. I'm often sure Buffy would share with her friends, not hide from them. But now I wonder, is this episode part of it?

Buffy feels like at that moment when she so needed to feel her friends' support – not to fight, but so she didn't feel so alone – they abandoned her emotionally. From her viewpoint, Willow not only passively didn't support her, but actively said something so hurtful to Buffy. And Xander passed it on. Buffy already knew she had to kill Angel. She'd already told Willow that. So there is in her mind no excuse for Willow to send that message to Buffy.

Specifically, it may inform why when Buffy is back in Season Three, it takes her so long to tell her friends that Angel changed back to himself before she had to kill him anyway.

Joyce And Spike

Finally, one of my favorite parts of the show is foreshadowed in this episode – the relationship between Joyce and Spike. Joyce will always treat him like a person. She will try to be polite to him. Even here when her mind is reeling as she tries to take all this in, Joyce makes conversation. She's polite and tries to make things seem normal. She treats him like any other guest in her house. Especially one who is there to help her daughter.

After Joyce dies, Spike will say this. He tells Xander Joyce is the only one who treated him with respect. And he says something like, "She always had a cuppa for me." And she does. More than once Spike confides how he's feeling to Joyce and she really tries to listen.

Often he is also doing something nefarious. This also sows the seeds for some fantastic confusion in Season Three for Joyce. Because Angel comes back. It's a tough road but he is good again. Joyce, though, doesn't know that. And Spike weasels his way into her kitchen because he still has an invite to come in. She's getting him hot cocoa (with the little marshmallows in it). Angel comes to the door and can't get in though he fears Spike will try to kill Joyce. But so far as Joyce knows, Angel is evil and Buffy had to try to kill him. Based on Becoming Parts One and Two, it's perfectly reasonable that Joyce thinks Spike is the good guy and Angel is the bad guy.

Questions For Your Writing

- Do your allies come into conflict with one another? Is that conflict genuine, arising out of their different character traits or goals?
- What are the stakes for your protagonist?
- For your antagonist?
- Do their choices and actions show how much they have to gain or lose?
- Can you add body language, clothing, or setting details that convey your characters' emotions?
- Have you used dramatic irony in your story?
- What is a Pyrrhic victory?
- Would you ever consider that type of victory for your protagonist? Why or why not?

CHAPTER 11
RESOURCES

I HOPE you found the breakdowns of the *Buffy* episodes and the related topics and questions fun and helpful. I've learned so much from watching, rewatching, and now podcasting about *Buffy the Vampire Slayer,* and I love sharing that with listeners.

If you're a writer or storyteller, in addition to the free story structure template (also known as worksheets, but you don't want to think of writing as work, do you?) at WritingAsASecondCareer.com/Story, you may find the rest of my Writing As A Second Career series useful.

Those books include *Super Simple Story Structure: A Quick Guide To Plotting And Writing Your Novel*; *Creating Compelling Characters From The Inside Out*; and *The One-Year Novelist: A Week-By-Week Guide To Writing Your Novel In One Year*. If you're struggling to get a novel or story started, or to finish once you've begun, you may want to look at *Write On: How To Overcome Writer's Block So You Can Write Your Novel*.

You can find a full list of my books for writers, which include the other *Buffy and the Art of Story* books, in the Also By section at the end of this book.

I also coach authors, particularly those juggling writing with other full-time jobs or responsibilities. If that sounds like you, or you want to check out my soon-to-be-released courses for writers, you can find out more at:

WritingAsASecondCareer.com/WritingHelp

Thanks so much for taking this journey deeper into *Buffy* with me. Best of luck with your writing!

―――――

DID you enjoy this book and find it helpful? Please write a review to help other writers find it, too. Even a sentence or a few words can make a difference.

ALSO BY L. M. LILLY

The One-Year Novelist: A Week-By-Week Guide To Writing Your Novel In One Year

Happiness, Anxiety, and Writing: Using Your Creativity To Live A Calmer, Happier Life

Super Simple Story Structure: A Quick Guide to Plotting and Writing Your Novel

Creating Compelling Characters From The Inside Out

How To Write A Novel, Grades 6-8

Write On: How To Overcome Writer's Block So You Can Write Your Novel

Buffy And The Art Of Story Season One: Writing Better Fiction By Watching Buffy

Buffy And The Art Of Story Season Two Part 1: Threats, Lies, and Surprises in Episodes 1-11

Buffy And The Art Of Story Season Two Part 2: Writing About Love, Loss, and Betrayal in Episodes 12-22

As Lisa M. Lilly:

The Awakening (Book 1 in The Awakening Series)

The Unbelievers (Book 2 in The Awakening Series)

The Conflagration (Book 3 in The Awakening Series)

The Illumination (Book 4 in The Awakening Series)

The Awakening Supernatural Thriller Series Complete Omnibus/Box Set

When Darkness Falls (a standalone supernatural suspense novel)

The Tower Formerly Known As Sears And Two Other Tales Of Urban Horror

The Worried Man (Q.C. Davis Mystery 1)

The Charming Man (Q.C. Davis Mystery 2)

The Fractured Man (Q.C. Davis Mystery 3)

No Good Plays (A Q.C. Davis Mystery Novella)

The Troubled Man (Q.C. Davis Mystery 4)

The Hidden Man (Q.C. Davis Mystery 5)

Q.C. Davis Mysteries 1-3 (The Worried Man, The Charming Man, and The Fractured Man) Box Set

ABOUT THE AUTHOR

An author, lawyer, and adjunct professor of law, L. M. Lilly's non-fiction includes **Happiness, Anxiety, and Writing: Using Your Creativity To Live A Calmer, Happier Life; Super Simple Story Structure: A Quick Guide to Plotting & Writing Your Novel; Buffy And The Art Of Story Season One: Writing Better Fiction By Watching Buffy**; and **Creating Compelling Characters From The Inside Out**.

Writing as Lisa M. Lilly, she is the author of the best selling **Awakening supernatural thriller series** about Tara Spencer, a young woman who becomes the focus of a powerful religious cult when she inexplicably finds herself pregnant, and of the **Q.C. Davis mystery series**. She is currently working on the latest book in that series.

A member of the Horror Writers Association, Lilly also is the author of **When Darkness Falls**, a gothic horror novel set in Chicago's South Loop, and the short-story collection **The Tower Formerly Known as Sears and Two Other Tales of Urban Horror**, the title story of which was made into the short film Willis Tower.

Lilly is a resident of Chicago and a member and past officer of the Alliance Against Intoxicated Motorists. She joined AAIM after an intoxicated driver caused the deaths of her parents in 2007. Her book of essays, **Standing in Traffic**, is available on AAIM's website.

www.ingramcontent.com/pod-product-compliance
Lightning Source LLC
Chambersburg PA
CBHW050313120526
44592CB00014B/1892